POETRY

The Best of Charles Mwewa
2d Ed.

CHARLES MWEWA

2023

POETRY

The Best of Charles Mwewa, 2d Ed.

In text: Author, 2023

In published edition: Africa in Canada Press, 2023.

First edition published in 2020;
Second edition published in 2023 by:

AFRICA IN CANADA PRESS
Ottawa, Ontario
Canada

All rights reserved. No part of this may be reproduced, stored in a retrieval system of transmitted, in any form or by any means, electronic, mechanical, photocopying or otherwise, without the prior written permission of the publisher.

© In text: Charles Mwewa

Author: Charles Mwewa, www.charlesmwewa.com
Typesetting and design by Charles Mwewa
Cover design by Niranjan Mohammed, Diamond Books, India, USA and Canada
Printed in Canada, USA and Zambia

ISBN (Canada): 978-1-998788-00-2

DEDICATION

For

Chola Kulu,

R.I.P.

CONTENTS

DEDICATION iii
CONTENTS v
INTRODUCTION: xxv
Charsian Poetry xxv

BOOK I LOVE SUPREMACY

1. My Love, I 1
2. My Love, II 2
3. Tenderly 3
4. Fondest Memories, I 4
5. Fondest Memories, II 5
6. Fondest Memories, III 6
7. Fondest Memories, IV 7
8. Fondest Memories, V 8
9. Fondest Memories, VI 9
10. Fondest Memories, VII 10
11. Veronice 11
12. Chara 12
13. My Face 13
14. Till I Have You 14
15. Jenevive 15
16. Stronger Than Death 16
17. Till the Bells 17
18. Look at Her 18
19. Gold 19
20. My Darling 20
21. Tenderly, Sweetly, Saucily 21
22. Write Me a Poem 22
23. Does Love Hurt 23
24. Sweet Fountains 24
25. Thai Gold 25

26. Slow Dance 26
27. Bites of Love 27
28. Ode to Loves 28
29. Love's Jealous 31
30. Love Tonight 32
31. Smile, My Love 33
32. Bleeds of Love 34
33. Just Black, O Juliana 35
34. Eye of Beholder 36
35. Like a Sunset, O Angelian 37
36. Ka-Reign 38
37. Woman, a Wife I 39
38. Woman, a Wife II 40
39. Woman, a Wife III 41
40. Woman, a Wife IV 42
41. Woman, a Wife V 43
42. Woman, a Wife VI 44
43. Woman, a Wife VII 45
44. Woman, a Wife VIII 46
45. Daughters 47
46. Graceful White 48
47. Tu es beau Kassandra 49
48. Marry at 30 50
49. Love You So Much 51
50. Yours is Chubby 52
51. At the Lips 53
52. Love Songs 54
53. Beside Me 55
54. No Capacity 56
55. Claria I 57
56. Claria II 58
57. Claria III 59
58. Claria IV 60
59. Claria V 61
60. Claria VI 62
61. Cuteravive 63
62. Miracles of Love 64

63. Love to Remember 65
64. Daughter for Loves.. 66
65. How Lovely... 67
66. Love Can Build a Bridge 68
67. Tashany's Song.. 69
68. A Mother's Love 70
69. Mended Heart... 71
70. Awanda 72
71. Suzy Sisess 73
72. Jamaican Girl... 74
73. Stolen Hearts... 75
74. Conquered Heart... 76
75. Stagnet... 77
76. Why Love 78
77. Love's Absence.. 79
78. Love and Death 80
79. Love is Like 81
80. Be My Valentine 82
81. Hips... 83
82. More for Nothing.. 84
83. Sonnet to Buttocks.. 85
84. Women Buttocks... 86
85. Ms. Taco 87
86. Love Star... 88
87. Recover, My Love 89
88. Song for Loves... 90
89. Simple Love... 91
90. One Step Too Beautiful 92
91. Shine Baby Shine 93
92. Beautiful People I.. 94
93. Beautiful People II 95
94. Beautiful People III... 96
95. Who You Marry.. 97
96. If I Were a Girl 98
97. Recover, My Baby 100
98. Juicy Hone-y... 101
99. Deep Passion 102

100. Love Like Before 103
101. Zimba 104
102. I Die 105
103. I Live 106
104. Love I Know 107
105. She 108
106. Angels without Wings 109
107. Little Loves 110
108. Like Heaven 111
109. Wife 112
110. Exception Has a Name 113
111. Black Beauty 114
112. Marriage Myth 115
113. Thank the Bra 116
114. Flesh and Bones 117
115. Lovely the Dance 118
116. Diminished Beauty 119
117. Sex Aren't Love 120
118. Musonda 121
119. Poetry of Sex 122
120. Painful Thought 124
121. Women 125
122. So Lucky, So Jackie 126
123. How Lovely 127
124. Ten Out of Ten 128
125. From Canada with Love 129
126. Pain of Our Departure 130
127. Friends Forever 131
128. Love 132
129. Sunshine 133
130. Charsian Song, I 134
131. Charsian Song, II 135
132. Charsian Song, III 136
133. Charsian Song, IV 137
134. Charsian Song, V 138
135. Charsian Song, VI 139
136. Never Left 140

137. Kristin 141
138. 100 Reasons 142
139. Glorious in Beauty 147
140. Love's Instrument 148
141. Like a Breath 149
142. Sweet as Sky is Skype 150
143. Like Two Ways 151
144. Lovely to Have 152
145. Write for You 153
146. Ode to Aushi Women 154

BOOK II NATURE'S EXCELLENCE

147. Nature's Love 161
148. Nature Says It 162
149. When Death Be Sweeter 163
150. The Heart 164
151. Saying Sorry 165
152. Fruitless Lullaby 166
153. Each Face 167
154. Thank God I'm Black 168
155. Moody Toronto Whether 170
156. Heartcry 171
157. The Mighty Fall 172
158. Aren't Just a Number 173
159. Someone Help 174
160. Fits Any Size 175
161. Summer Dammar 176
162. Sounds 177
163. Diapers 178
164. Oh, My God 179
165. Newspapers 181
166. Bemba Tales 182
167. Music in Zambia 184
168. Free Soil 185
169. No Sorry Life 186
170. Nests of Newmarket 187

171. The Way You Are 188
172. Healing Poesy 189
173. Canadian Spring.................................... 190
174. Down Recession Street 191
175. Highways 192
176. Money 193
177. Four + 1 Messengers 194
178. No Author of Tragedy 195
179. Didn't Feel Like Writing 196
180. Shakespeare Unedited.......................... 197
181. Filibusting... 198
182. Tear of God 199
183. Move On 200
184. Rise and Go.. 201
185. Sleep On 202
186. Morning Joy 203
187. Gain in Pain 204
188. Investment Principle............................ 205
189. Mulock Drive....................................... 206
190. The Transit.. 207
191. The City 208
192. City of Livingstone.............................. 209
193. Father's Day 211
194. Dying While Black 212
195. Experience of Songs 213
196. More than Toys 214
197. Be Happy.. 215
198. Stormy August 21 216
199. Arms of Death..................................... 217
200. Death Shall Not................................... 218
201. Change or the Same 219
202. Why Not Me 220
203. Change with Change 222
204. No Fundamentalist 223
205. Fear Nothing.. 224
206. Come What May................................. 225
207. End Shall Last...................................... 226

x

208. Smells of Coffee 227
209. Insulted in America 228
210. Ashen Pebbles 229
211. Words of the Departed 230
212. Do Not Cry 231
213. Dirge of My People 232
214. Friends Gone 233
215. Goodbye to Sara 234
216. The Grip 236
217. Elegy to Kenya 237
218. Destiny Killers 238
219. Life in Circles 239
220. Secure 240
221. Mad 241
222. Unfaithfulness 242
223. Cry We Cry 243
224. Journey 244
225. Never to Forget 245
226. Only Child 246
227. Presidential Challenge 247
228. Among Warriors 248
229. Dreams at Lusaka 249
230. Our Name 250
231. Lost Feelings 251
232. Lights at Christmas 252
233. Music in the Sky 253
234. Bodies 254
235. Be Mine 255
236. So Lovely 256
237. IndyGenius 257
238. Beauty Pillar 258
239. Native Excellence 259
240. I Have a Witness 260
241. Dancing Aura 261
242. Impossible Love 262
243. Bringer of Joy 263
244. After We Met 264

245. Love Me One More Time 265
246. Love Till Death 266
247. Swallow Me 267
248. Overflowing 268
249. Among Millions 269
250. Weekend of Love 270
251. In New Light 271
252. First Voice 272

BOOK III PATRONAGE ULTIMATUM

253. Struggle of My People 275
254. My Zambia, I Cry 276
255. Dreams of Poverty 277
256. Dreams of Africa 278
257. O Africa 282
258. Apolitical Theory 284
259. Hillsboro 285
260. Mibenge 286
261. Bye-Bye Bishop 287
262. Eagle`s Feathers 288
263. Mother Zambia 289
264. South Africa 2010 290
265. Africa I Love Despite 291
266. The Stairs of Kabwata 292
267. Canada 293
268. Black Africa 294
269. I Am a Proud African 295
270. Hawaii, I 297
271. Hawaii, II 298
272. Los Angeles 300
273. Over the Seas 301
274. Christian Nation 302
275. My Canada 303
276. Heroes of Freedom 304
277. Heathrow 305
278. Over Paris 306

279. Joe Biden 307
280. Mr. Thairu 308
281. Kingdom Within 309
282. Perfect Full-Stop 311
283. Congo 313
284. Idyll Phonoriah 314
285. Chitambo 315
286. Mr. Conductor 316
287. Banguanaland 317
288. War Sonnet 319
289. Nuclear Dysfunction 320
290. Rwanda 321
291. *Worst Antilife* Report 323
292. Colovery 325
293. Adventures 329
294. Schipol 330
295. Bernados 331
296. Brutus 332
297. Canada, O Country 333
298. First Black 334
299. Democracy 335
300. Tip of Africa 336
301. Epidemics 337
302. Inside a Genocide 338
303. Kilimanjaro, the Mound of Gods 339
304. No Longer an Alien 340

BOOK IV ALIEN EXTRAORDINAIRE

305. Sweet Name 343
306. Broken Lullaby 344
307. Subway 345
308. Love-Marriage Mystery 346
309. Goma Lakes 347
310. Sun 348
311. Mantras 349
312. Wealth 350

313. Chaisa 351
314. Northern Hemisphere 352
315. Feeble Rights 353
316. Weird Thinking 354
317. Industrial Towns 355
318. Free Existence 356
319. Dreams of an Alien 357
320. Schizophrenic 358
321. Hope 359
322. Rich People 360
323. Critical Thinker 361
324. Race of Women 362
325. Idle Mind 363
326. Time 364
327. Good and Evil 365
328. Rules of the Game 366
329. Rundlehorn Drive 367
330. Fall from Purity 368
331. Super Problems 369
332. Emmerance 370
333. Clientele 371
334. Preachers and Politicians 372
335. Love Theorem 373
336. Money and Politics 374
337. Boiling Soul 375
338. Payday 376
339. Woman's Side 377
340. Bed Chamber 378
341. Rulers 379
342. Ignorance 380
343. Roundness of the Globe 381
344. Epiloguia 382

BOOK V DIVINE SUPERIORITY

345. Sonate to Plenty 385
346. Words Fail Me 386

347. Indescribable YOU 387
348. Ultimate Prayer 388
349. Good Grace 390
350. In Your Mercy, I Trust 391
351. Essence of Presence 392
352. When I Pray 393
353. Jesus Christ 399
354. Works of Charity 400
355. Cheerful Giver 401
356. Mercy and Grace 402
357. God and Wine, I 403
358. God and Wine, II 404
359. Under Attack 411
360. He Answers Prayers 412
361. Religion 413
362. Human Love 415
363. Favored 417
364. The Church 418
365. Tithe 419
366. God's Glory 420
367. Incomparable Jesus 423
368. In the Land of My Enemy 424
369. Falling though Not Down 425
370. Windsor 426
371. Fail, Well 427
372. Eli, Eli lama Sabachthani 428
373. Ancient of Days 429
374. 2018, a Prayer 430
375. No Shame 433
376. My All is Thee 434
377. Again, Again and Again 435
378. His Mercies 436
379. A Wonderful God 437
380. Sweet Story 438
381. Wow Pleasure 439
382. Lindsay 440
383. Injustice into Victory 441

384. Wisdom of Christ 443
385. It's Finished 444
386. A Christian Life 445
387. Holier, Lowlier 446
388. Insult to Mercy 447
389. Heart of Prayer 448
390. Burden of Nations 449
391. Cantata to Sounds 450
392. Mulungu, God of Africa 451
393. Bisrat and Ojo 455
394. Peter Stehouwer 456
395. It's Wichtig 457
396. Praise in Every Genre 458
397. Earth You've Colored 459
398. Dear My Rarest 460
399. Afghanistan to Tajikistan 461
400. Akrotiri to Laos 462
401. Ethiopia to East-Timor 463
402. West Bank to Western Sahara 464
403. Andorra to Angola 465
404. Argentina to Bosnia-Herzegovina 466
405. Armenia to Estonia 467
406. Barbados to Comoros 468
407. Antigua and Barbuda to Bermuda 469
408. Burma to Panama 470
409. Canada to Grenada 471
410. Colombia to Zambia 472
411. Congo to Congo 473
412. From Island to Island 474
413. From Land to Islands 475
414. From Islands to Lands 476
415. From Monarchs to Republics 477
416. Bahrain to Spain 478
417. Greece to The Holy See 479
418. Indonesia via Malaysia 480
419. Italy to Mali 481
420. Belgium to Vietnam 482

421. UK to US 483
422. Paraguay to Uruguay 484

BOOK VI POETRY OF COVID-19

423. Down Corona Lane 487
424. Los Angeles 488
425. I Can't Breathe 489
426. America 490
427. Pandemic of Racism, I 491
428. Pandemic of Racism, II 492
429. Pandemic of Racism, III 493
430. They Count 495
431. Courage to Say "No" 498
432. It'd Be Well, I 499
433. It'd Be Well, II 500
434. Canceled 501
435. Politicians as Leaders 502
436. Easter Poem 503
437. Covid War 507
438. The World in Mourning, First Wave 508
439. Second Wave, I 510
440. Second Wave, II 511
441. Second Wave, III 512
442. Second Wave, IV 513
443. Dr. Fauci 514
444. They Gather 515
445. Western Virus 516
446. To Lock or Not to Lock 517
447. Lamebration 518
448. Delta Variant 519
449. Omicron Variant 520
450. Vaccine Inequalities 521
451. Poorland 522
452. March 2024 523

BOOK VII OTTAWA SPECTACULAR

453. By the Meadows of the Rideau River 527
454. 312 528
455. A Hug 529
456. Air 530
457. At Your Wall, O Jerusalem 531
458. Balcony Etc. 532
459. Barrhaven 533
460. Bridge by St. Lawrence 534
461. Burning Earth 535
462. By the Quebec Border 536
463. Client 537
464. Cobourg Traffic Jam 538
465. CTV Morning Ottawa 539
466. Daly 540
467. Death of a Monarchy 541
468. Double Deckers 542
469. Down Stewart 1 Street 543
470. Dream Ruins 544
471. Drive Me Crazy 545
472. First Nations 546
473. Food Cheer 548
474. From Kitchener with Love 549
475. Full Moon 550
476. Ganja 551
477. Hard Knocks 552
478. Hell's Angels 553
479. High Commission 554
480. Hunt Club Road 555
481. I Don't Feel Like Writing 556
482. If Not with You 557
483. Inside the Convoy 558
484. Bye-bye Kitchener 559
485. Jungles of Thought 560
486. Kenneth Kaunda 561
487. Kingston Ontario 563

488. Looking for Grace 564
489. Married to Two Women 565
490. Near 1000 Islands 566
491. Ngalula 567
492. Northumberland 568
493. Factions 569
494. O 570
495. Open and Wide 572
496. Glouster 573
497. Silhouettes of Metcalf 574
498. Open for Heaven 575
499. Ottario Lawyer 576
500. Ottawa Mission 577
501. Ottawa 578
502. Pizza Friday 579
503. Red and White 580
504. Satisfaction Guaranteed 581
505. Shandalara 582
506. Sherbrook by Belgrave 583
507. Skin Tight 584
508. Churches of Ottawa 585
509. The Finest 586
510. The Half Moon 587
511. The Smell of Rains 588
512. The Supreme Court 589
513. To African Music We Danced 590
514. Tomorrow Land 592
515. Traffic at 6 593
516. Tyendinanga 594
517. Convenience Store 595
518. Many Sides of Manotick 596
519. Big Mother 597
520. Double Bic Mac 598
521. 417 599
522. All So Near 600

BOOK VIII VALLEY OF ROSES

523. Valley of Roses 603
524. City Called Beautiful 603
525. Victories after Victory 604
526. Beauty for Ashes 604
527. A Feast for the Faithful 605
528. Like Dew in the Morning 605
529. Flower Every Hour 606
530. Unapproachable Glory 606
531. Ancient in All, Present for All 607
532. Halleluiah, You Always Hear Me 607
533. White Flowers 608
534. Even Time Bows to You 609
535. Only One God 610
536. Intelligence Supreme 611
537. Glad in My Sleep 612
538. Standing at Two Confluences 612
539. Fountain of Knowledge 613
540. Beaming with Delight 613
541. Sings Eternal 614
542. I am Loved 614
543. Constitution of the Anatomy 615
544. Worthless Scale 616
545. Pedestals of Renown 617
546. Warrior of Warriors 617
547. Trust in His Mercy 618
548. Sweet Name 618
549. My Genius 619
550. Only the Lord 619
551. Smirked by God 620
552. Daddy's Horsy 620
553. Lovely Like a Rose 621
554. Gargantuan Legs 621
555. Wiser than Magicians 622
556. Praise Him Early 622
557. Reclining at His Pavilion 623

558. Blessed Generation 623
559. Science of Worship 624
560. Law's Magnificence 625
561. Your Excellences 626
562. Blissful Feeling 627
563. Happiest Pain 628
564. My Soul's Show-Stopper 629
565. Free Freedom 630
566. Joyous Peace 631
567. Darling Savior 632
568. Praise Time is Good Time 633
569. Church's Glorious 633
570. Desserts in the Desert 634
571. Mortally Live 634
572. Breeze of Victory 635
573. Ten Thousand Halleluiahs 636
574. Beautiful Word 637
575. Spacious Places 638
576. The Perfect I AM 639
577. Good Sharing 640
578. God of Everything 641
579. Master 643
580. Battle's Won 644
581. More Desirable 645
582. Life's Fountain 646
583. Sweet Meandering 647
584. Power's Hour 648
585. O Immanuel 649
586. Calmly Flowers 650
587. Sun of Sweetness 651
588. Shadow of Sweetness 651
589. Sea of Sunsets 652
590. Moon of Mercy 652
591. Seasons of Sunrise 653
592. Center of the Sun 654
593. Palm of Pleasure 655
594. Fountain of Floras 656

595. Garden of Glory 656
596. Garden of Gold 657
597. Garden of Goodness 657
598. Cradle of Flowers 658
599. Brilliance's Boulevard 658
600. Tower of Power 659
601. Garden in Eden 659
602. God Spring 660
603. Little Munks Praise 661
604. Sunbelt of His Presence 661
605. Fall into Fondness 662
606. Step into Splendor 662
607. Ultimate Trapper 663
608. Wonderful Grace 664
609. Music to My Ears 665
610. Villa in the Valley 665
611. Morning for Mourning 666
612. Star of Siavonga 667
613. Glint in the Darkness 667
614. Suspended on Nothing 668
615. Heavens Declare 668
616. Mwansabanga 669
617. Valley of the Doll 669
618. Darling Father 670
619. Flowers of Beauty 671
620. Good Morning, Lord 671
621. Power House 672
622. Aroma of Rome 672
623. Be More in Me 673
624. Chief Judge 673
625. Kwacha, Good Morning 674
626. Waterfall of Blessings 674
627. Fairest Furthest 675
628. Holy Thy Holi 675
629. Birds of Glory 676
630. Bird of Beauty 676
631. City of Kindness 677

632. Maple Tower 677
633. Sun's Supreme 678
634. Valley of Visions 678
635. Awe of the Owl 679
636. Worship at Wonderland 679
637. Elephant's Wit 680
638. Hippopotamus from Heaven 680
639. Grace Like Giraffe 681
640. Gaze of a Gazelle 681
641. Happy Village 682
642. Graceful Mountainside 682
643. Sounds of Silence 683
644. Fairest Strides 683
645. Love the Church 684
646. Saving Shelter 684
647. Whether the Weather 685
648. Whisper of Loves 685
649. Darling God 686
650. Glorious Snow 686
651. Apple of My Eye 687
652. Lovely These Places 687
653. Last Day Bliss 688
654. Living Bread 688
655. Begotten Son 689
656. Mighty Creator 689
657. Dearest Deer 690
658. Genius Father 690
659. Creative Father 691
660. Soul Watcher 691
661. Lion of Love 692
662. Fairest in Justice 692
663. Invictus Victus 693
664. Permanent Inheritance 693
665. Beautiful Things 694
666. Ultimate Purpose 694
667. Hallowed Be 695
668. Wonderful Works 695

669. O, Adonai, O Elshaddai............................ 696
670. Praise Him... 696
671. Depth of His Riches 697
672. Hosanna... 697
673. The Only Wise.. 698
674. Worthy Lamb.. 698
675. Meadow of His Ville 699
676. Majestic Silence...................................... 699
677. Praise in Every Genre............................. 700
678. Earth You've Colored 700
679. Dear My Rarest....................................... 701
680. No Fear in Death 701
681. All Things to All..................................... 702
682. Everlasting... 702
683. A Wonderful God 703
684. How Excellent 705
685. Original Spirit... 706
686. Multiplier Effect..................................... 706
687. Masterful... 707
688. Picturesque of Elegant Supernova.......... 707
689. Rose of Rhapsody 708
690. Kingdom First 708
691. Love You, Bible...................................... 709
692. Condemned to Praise 709
693. Honest Answer....................................... 710
694. Beautiful Thought 710
695. Pure Grace.. 711
696. All You Made I Love.............................. 712
697. All of a Kind 713
698. Only In-Christ....................................... 714
699. All My Favorites 715
700. The Doxology... 716
ABOUT THE AUTHOR 725
AUTHOR'S CONTACT 727
INDEX 729

INTRODUCTION:
Charsian Poetry

Charles Mwewa has been writing poetry since he first knew how to string words and senses together. All of his first poems, beginning in 1983, were lost because, "Mwewa wrote them on his thighs using sticks as pen." The first attempt to collect his poems happened to be just for fun in the early 1990s. By 1997, Mwewa had largely collected his poems for future publications. During the 1990s, then as a student of literature at the University of Zambia (UNZA), Mwewa, in the company of other poem-lovers, helped to collect an anthology of poems using the UNZA Poetry Club, which he had co-founded with Elliot Phiri. This anthology was lost and did not see the light of day. Between 1998 and 2000, Mwewa had produced numerous pamphlets on religious prayers and praises, which were mostly for internal use.

It was in 2007, inspired by his friend and former language professor, Charles Calder, that Mwewa first published some of his poems in a book called *Song of an Alien*. Mwewa had just immigrated to Canada, and saw the window and opportunity to put some of his love, personal growth and political poems into a book. Since then, Mwewa has gone on to publish *Sail without Ship* (republished in 2022 as *I Dream of Africa*), a collection of political poems celebrating Africa and Zambia's 50 years of independence; and *I Bow*, a collection of 350 prayers written purely in verse of iambic pentameters. By and large, Mwewa has written several poems on war, disease (Covid-19 poems), children (including his published small book for children), law, love, and so on.

This book, however, is unique and comprehensive. It covers a period of over 30 years of selected poems. Most of the published and unpublished works of Charles Mwewa are compiled into this one collection, earning the title, *The Best of Charles Mwewa*. Mwewa's style is *Charsian* – styled in a mixture of rhythmic verse and iambs, where desired, and "poetic prose" where needed, creating a mixture of sound and sense that captivates the mind/reason, engages the soul and records, corrects or makes history.

This is the second edition. The first edition published in 2020 was a limited edition produced mostly for the Zambian public and the learning institutions, and all the printed copies were readily sold. The book became such a popular book in Zambia and globally that copies could not be distributed fast enough to meet the demand. In this second expanded edition, two more sections (Books VII and VIII) have been added and that is nearly 140 additional poems, and this includes around 18 poems inserted into Book II, bringing the total count to 700 poems.

Books VII and VIII comprise poems uniquely written in Canada and for Canadians, respectively. The author celebrates and adores His God for the nearly 20 years of domicility in Canada in poems collectively known as "Valley of Roses," (Book VII) and he has immortalized Ottawa City in "Ottawa Spectacular" (Book VIII). *Poetry, The Best of Charles Mwewa* is a triumph, in that it moderates international and local motifs that span a period of close to 40 years, twenty of those years emerging from Africa and the other twenty, from America.

Charles Mwewa
Canada

BOOK I
LOVE SUPREMACY

1. My Love, I

My love warms me when I am cold,
She means to me more than pure gold
She knows the secrets of my soul
And with her I can't long for more

She will delight and fulfil me
My love is but the good I see
He is the soul within my soul;
In his arms I gladly give all

Be closer than breath, all my days
Be a friend I trust, in all ways
Put your arms around me, all night
And guard my nude heart, from all sight

Come to me, I die without you
Each day I wait for your true feel
Take out from my eyes all my tears
And rid my heart of pain and fears

2. My Love, II

My love hides me from the sun's heat
In her kind voice mind and soul beat
She thrills like the sun in the sky
And stills like moonlight lullaby

I feel bounds of raging tenses
And miss my love with five senses.
My soul does languish with plight,
Yet our hearts flourish with delight

In the depth of quiet reflections,
Rhythms of my roused recollections
Rhyme to the sound of his name
For to love and rescue me he came

In your soul my whole being belongs
My drained heart for you alone longs
Come to me, my love, come to me!
All you want, to you I will be.

3. Tenderly

She rises delicately with every caress,
The woman under the arms of tender play,
She is feeble like a sponge, stronger as grace,
And every curve is like angels when they pray.

She breathes deep with every kind word,
The woman in the presence of a caring man,
She is tenderly lost in this but her world,
And she dies slowly like one shot without a gun.

She dances rhythmically to every thrusting force
The woman who has been carefully tutored,
She is in control, and she is her own boss,
And skins him like flesh warily butchered.

She comes down speedily like a falling star
The woman who has been properly loved,
She is all smiles, her laughter reaches far,
She's safe like a doctor who's been gloved!

4. Fondest Memories, I

It was cool, calm, cold and clean
Down Keele to buy ice-cream
Hand in hand, we walked
With rare sacredness, we talked.

Love is a living thing, they say
Which no words can say,
No mind can understand,
And no soul can comprehend.

I love you, and I cannot explain it
Because loving you is pleasurable.
I love you, and I don't know why,
For loving you is easy, that's why.

You are everything that I want
More than the oil wells of Mid-East;
More than the diamonds of Africa
More than the gold of America!

5. Fondest Memories, II

Since we parted, it has been hard.
And partings cost us everything.
I admit, I am not strong,
And you cannot be too wrong

Lonely like an island
Absence breaks our hearts
Could I and you now just agree?
Our love is hurt by some degree?

I will follow you through the rains
Because my heart belongs to you,
Come; let us meet like two ways
And promise never to part ways!

6. Fondest Memories, III

My bride, my black lover:
To you this music I bring
From rhythms in my soul
I beat for you in cords of twos
And record for you a melody
Of a revolutionary orchestra

My bride, my youthful hart:
Dearly loved and treasured,
Your temperament is phlegmatic;
Cool, quiet and beautiful!

You are fair, my love, you are fair.
You have no flaw in you.
Your eyes are doves
And your lips drop honey.
For you, my heart beat in harmony.
Oh, catch for me my dear doe;
Let me rejoice all night long
And feel the warmth,
The power of two sweet loves.

7. Fondest Memories, IV

You are the wife of my dreams
A friend closer than a brother
Together we stick like a letter
And follow each other like shadows.

Like a hare trotting on the Drakensburg,
You came along
Lovely to behold, soothing to touch
And your eyes met mine,
And our hearts agreed,
That we belonged together.

Days go like flakes in the sky
And night comes rushing in
In your heart are red roses
Whence I spread a bed of our deep romance

My wife glitters like the sun;
In her bosom reason and emotions harmonize
And bring meaning to a life on its last legs.

8. Fondest Memories, V

Your eyes are a thoroughfare
Straight like a pine tree
Your face thoroughly shines,
As one who has been to the fellowship of angels

I wonder why all such beauties aren't at gun-point robbed!

Why were you made thus bonbon?
Why do I crave for you with psychotic lunacy?
Why does sleep leave me at the thought of you?
Why do I gaze at you like a newly born baby?

Your lips drip of vanilla
Your borders in chocolate drawn –
Your tongue of cinnamon brand,
Your heart, a sanctuary of gods!

9. Fondest Memories, VI

Your shape is a dream of knighted lords
Shaped through fragile contours
You are curved as a god in Aphrodisiac casing
With such a small waist on ivory-paired legs
I wonder why such tiny feet support such frail figures!

Your hand tender, soft as sponge
As splendid as taintless gold

The back of your yard
Couth and carefully cultivated
Arranged as twins of the same design.

10. Fondest Memories, VII

Thy gyrations doth move mine entrails
Thy neck long, soft and vivid…
Thy embrace in mine arms grips
How comfy and delightful!

Fools doth attest to thy beauty
The strong doth faint in thy presence
The wise in thy breath words deny
Bragging men and loafers, thou loath

Thy head with wit brims
Thy mind with brilliance rims
Thy faculties with reason drone
Thy hairs full, long and grown

Thy make-up, costly and lavish
Thy men's spirits thou break
Thy equals labor thou render null
And thine rivals cry foul.

11. Veronice

This heart has made a clever choice,
With these lips we utter a voice
Of our lovely Veronice,
A girl so sweet and very nice

She heals like a veronica
And cures like a Santonica;
She is a clear memoranda
Of issues on observanda

Hard to face as a facular
She glitters as a nebula.
Her flesh is all fresh synovia
In red roses of Monrovia

We composed her a fantasia
Imported from Eastern Asia
To be rubbed with spices of India
In charmed scents of Parafindia!

12. Chara

I knew it that very first time
When I looked at your smiling face
And reasoned you were in your prime,
Even so I thought I could chase.

Chara, I love you with my whole heart

And time came for being closer friends
I knew it was not a mistake
For it wasn't like we could be fiends
When there was so much at stake

Chara, my love for you is pure art.

13. My Face

I recall the first time I saw you.
Since then so many things have happened
And that early excitement has gone.

There comes in one's life a time and season,
When the first bunch of roses fades
And only dry memories remain.

On these scattered memories, my love
I have dutifully spread a bed
With a pillow top of dead rose leaves.

Many times, beauty is deceptive
And charm, a passing wave of the wind
And only inner chaste makes life sure

For always my face in yours I see
This I call faultless Epiphany
When in your beauty, mine I see, too.

14. Till I Have You

Not till I have you, will I rest,
Not till you become my sole quest,
Not till the drums beat at their best
Not till I rise to be the first
And riffraffs turn into champions,
Will I be your soul companion?

I'll not detour by matters of shame
Nor divert by flashes of fame
The sting of the rose may prickle
The rays of the sun may sparkle
You and I shall reach the summit
And there we shall glow very bright.

You dream of the team of the best
And not till you're mine, shall I rest!

15. Jenevive

She is only called Jenevive.

Her bosom is the King's armor.
She mixes the tastiest of soups,
Prepares the cleanest of chambers
And wears the widest of all smiles.

She possesses the grace of does
And struts with the pride of male lions.

Her womb bears the healthiest babies
And her man married the noblest.

She is only called Jenevive.

16. Stronger Than Death

She dies softly and slowly,
The lady in a song
Of pure love:

Her eyes small and dizzy
Her touch gentle and lazy
She gazes by the eye sides
With hidden black pupils.

When she is fully cuddled
She dies in the ramblings
Of the seventh heaven
And whispers in overtones of love.

When she feels the flow
Of living streams,
She grumbles meaningless promises,
And demands she be tightly held.

Then sense and reason
Doubly crash with a bung,
Bone and marrow mar the bounds
And hands and words
Become one!

There is no feeling greater
No orgasmic sensation better
No life sweeter
And a death so fair and swifter!

17. Till the Bells

Honey,
They are saying we are not strong
And they are all wrong.

Honey,
Because they don't know the truth
About the values we hold dear
That we have been through the fire
And have come out pure.

Honey,
But they may be right
Because it may happen after a fight
That their vows couples don't hold tight
And of their duty they may lose sight.

Honey,
Our love is like a rock,
In the middle of Lake Michigan;
Waters rise and on shores knock
Yet it never goes back where it began.

Honey,
Let them be talking
And let's keep walking!

18. Look at Her

She climbs down the stairways of Toronto
My woman who walks on ivory legs.

A sheer glance perturbs even the stronger
And the most alert of minds.

Her moves are a dance and her steps are tempos
Beaten by invisible skill.

The capture of her bosom, yields peace and fire
And her eyes sparkle with shining glory.

She gold-chains her neck and ring crafts her ankles
And garbs herself in red garments.

Look at the woman, I say
Look at her and afterwards pray.

19. Gold

I was not dreaming about gold
Nor hallucinating of gold
I swerved on my bed and saw gold
Before me were presents of gold,
My eyes ogled at pure gold
And she was admirable gold.

My words came out simple and clear
And I could hear them too clearly;
They sprung with brilliant clarity:

She is in her very own class
The best out of seven classes
And first in her beauty classroom.

And the all parade shouted: "gold"
Then the echo grew loud and bold
Passing in gaps of heat and cold
Bracing the memories of old,
Bringing out great pleasures untold
And treasures never to be sold.

20. My Darling

My darling is first with daughters
A gem washed with holy waters
She reads classics of ancient books
And only dates men with good looks

My darling is an example
Of a star reared in the tempo
Of superb divine conception
Where angels man her reception

Daughters of the brave and mighty
Gathered to placate Aphrodite
With their complicated hair-dos
And she beat them clearly in twos

Daughters of nations, far and near
Come and get her charm, true and dear
And she will teach and show them all
In Athena's decked palace mall.

21. Tenderly, Sweetly, Saucily

She is firm, her breasts to my feel
She responds surely, my begging to the heal
She is in perfect shape, she deserves the time
She looks gorgeous, a hare in her prime
These legs of hers, wrapped in chocolate seasoning
When she kisses, she perturbs all manly reasoning
I hear her heartbeat; I love the way she dies
No, she is the one killing me, with her sighs
Oh, this heavenly entrance, her V-power
Sumptuous to my taste, sweeter every hour
When she moves, every inch of her bottom
She cuts the nerves to the smallest atom
To the command of love, she waits patiently
Her heavenly excellence stiff, oh, very anciently
I am broken, beaten, stricken and shaken
Early I come, oh darling, am I forgiven?

22. Write Me a Poem

You ask me to write you a poem, O sweet tongue
How that this request is to me a longed-for fang
How should I write for you, for you're my poem
My heart knows, my soul renders it in deep solemn
For you, the words have no power to describe
And I wish a sage I was and not a Scribe
For I would have sung you a song of love
And express the details that my mother gave
So, from you, are stars flying across my soul
And about you, is a season that soothes all
O Julicia, that in your hands I find faultless care
O delicious, your embrace I crave for like a dare
Let me hold you, and die the same death twice
My cold heart you've turned warm this thrice.

23. Does Love Hurt

Do tell me, I am on my knees begging
And all my heart's veins all aching
Does love hurt like a sharpened sword
Or does it comfort like a right word
If so, tell me, and end my deep agony
For what you bring to me is pure harmony
And what I am learning about you
Is a privilege only available to a very few.
Sadly, you think of yourself very low
Happily, I know you are pretty and more
Oh, come out of the cocoon and smell me
For in my scent I say all the beauty I see
And in your tenderness, my heart melts
Hold me tight, with strengths of many belts.

24. Sweet Fountains

You're a fountain of three reservoirs
And at the third you open into heavens
The sky widens and the waters float
When the wind blows and stalls,
You bring a breeze, happy and fulfilling
For fountain's first, we drink of holy saliva
At the second, the summer bump, how intoxicating
And then we fall down to the edge of the golden goblet
And there, we drink of life-giving force
You're a dynamite ready to explode,
A volcano, ready to erupt
And a tower leading to the heavens
When you open those endless sources
Oh, how all that makes sense become null
And all we treasure become dull
Please let me be your champion,
Let your breath and heart capture mine
I live in your dying defences
I faint for your open fences,
I survive in your rising heartbeat
Surely, sweet also are your environs,
When I worshipped at your holy temple
When you looked with love in my dimple
And our souls met in the third heaven
To the brink of insanity, you got me driven
Then you shouted, "This man I most love!"
And "His machine I love to have."

25. Thai Gold

You looked directly into my eye
Surely, you shine like stars on high
Even for a second, I can't let you go by
For your love is better than all the gold of Thai

I saw the tattoo on your shoulder
And another just near your border
I asked, "Who was this bolder?"
That he touched with ink thy beauty`s splendor?

26. Slow Dance

Like two pieces of a jigsaw puzzle,
Flesh to flesh, skin to skin
Like the hard ground that the harmers muzzle
Flesh to flesh, skin to skin
The silence mixed with a soft dance
Flesh to flesh, skin to skin
Each gyration is tone of sweetness' ounce
Flesh to flesh, skin to skin
The way you break from side to side
Flesh to flesh, skin to skin
And induce the sanely feelings that hide
Flesh to flesh, skin to skin
Surely laughter and joy have been married
Flesh to flesh, skin to skin
And all the fear and worry have been buried
Flesh to flesh, shin to skin
Oh, this daughter was well-taught
Flesh to flesh, skin to skin
The best, the bright, she has caught
Flesh to flesh, skin to skin
Tenderly, sweetly, your love is truly divine
Flesh to flesh, skin to skin
Dance, again, dance, and all shall be just fine
Flesh to flesh, skin to skin!

27. Bites of Love

Bite me, again and again
Please bite me
For your bites be lovely
And your teases of the neck be calmly
But it is the naggings of the ears
That be beautiful
Oh, how I cry under your bite
And if a bite be this sweet and nice
Then bite me hard till I bleed!

28. Ode to Loves

This ode to you I sage,
O love of loves
Let me sing if a voice
I should borrow
For your bosom is gold
That you have
And like a sheep to a slaughter,
I follow
O love of loves,
How you beam with vigor,
O love of loves,
Why all shouldn't be like you?
Face it, none dances
With elegance and rigor
Brace it, no-one is better,
You compare to a few.
I have gone early,
Looking for little foxes
And I have set seven traps,
To catch the little doves.
My surging emotions
I hide in three boxes;
And all my regrets
I have laid down in caves.
In the silence of raging nerves,
I find reason
In the din of resounding glory,
There are flurries
Surely, by the sea-side,
I set my eyes to the horizon
My senses I deny,
For a moment my edge tarries.
I see with my mind,
And I hear beatings of love
Oh, come to me and hold me so tight,

Very close to my heart
Eat me alive and bury me,
Deep down in a trough
O loves, swallow me head first,
Legs are only dross
Do brush me perfectly;
Rub me so good so much
And let me swim freely,
In the waters of your deeper grave
Though I may stand,
I fall to the soft of your touch
Let me be a coward,
To love I aren't any brave
By your splendid brand,
I offer a quiet prayer -
In the noise of your groaning,
I feel the blooming roses
As you I unwrap completely,
Layer by layer,
O loves; my stamina gives way,
To your galloping horses;
I join the throng of singers,
Without a miming choir
For the rule is:
Don't provoke the resting doe,
For love unfulfilled,
Is as dangerous as fire.
A passion untamed,
Is meaner than a foe;
Those *areolas*,
When they choose to fight;
Those firm twins,
When they camp against fingers;
Oh, again hold me,
To your breast so tight,
And cure this thought of you,
Which lingers like a migraine.

I am damned, totally condemned,
To your flowing flood eruption;
But I brag of your desire,
To please my seventh sense.
And see, you`re pure,
You have no blame.
When you move inside,
Your frame dances;
As though dead,
I let the rhythm of life flow.
I feel the volts pass through me high;
I change, my pace speeds,
And my eyes glow;
Oh, how hilarious,
When you pull me up high,
Oh, how gorgeous,
When you let me draw nigh;
You have warmed my heart,
Like a currency of power
By the shore of your mouth,
I swim my tongue every hour.
I hear you call loudly,
With greater urgency.
As you do, I stay limp,
As one who hangs limp,
This love I`ve surely got,
This route is truly hot;
A goddess without fault,
Oh, love I`ll never forget!

29. Love's Jealous

Love's real test is a jealous heart
Show me a lover who ignores no flaw
 I show you a passion without art
For love without borders knows no law
And so, dear one, when you cry
Because I did something you hate
You know it was meant not to be by
Lean on me, together we cheat fate
For your love grows in size like cancers
Your dream becomes clear as it hatches
And everywhere you look, you see answers
For jealousy is a sure sign you love me
Even when it stings you deep like a bee!

30. Love Tonight

Today, not tomorrow
I want you today, tonight, and now
Your image never ceases to wow
And when I need to bow
You bring me alive to the real brow;
 Just the rare you, yet ordinary, you`re magician,
Upon embracing you, I touch angelic antenna
Like a Benz, you`re cute, and agile as a Ferrari
In you, sweetness combines on a romantic hill
And I`m inspired in the heart of your plateau
Now or never, tonight write a poem at Hotel Taj.

31. Smile, My Love

My love is not just a mind, she has a brain
When she presses for results, they all drain
Like a silent missile, she attacks and conquers
And like steady ship, she sails and anchors
Oh, bring me a woman as good as her
And I will show you they are very far
She wakes up early, she works herself fit
She stays at job late, and joins the night fleet
Yet, she cooks the most delicious meals
And when she gives advice, it all heals
This, is not your typical beauty, she's one
This, is the trophy once must be won
To love you, is a spring of calm waters
By your bosom, all salute, none falters
She rarely engages in energy dance
If she does, you wish for another chance
Labour, my love, work, we all thank you
Study and exile, those like you are few
And this husband loves you, with adoration
And your kids sing of your wise declaration
Oh, my love, I sing of your sound brilliance
Oh, my kids' mom, smiles are in your glance!

32. Bleeds of Love

Thy love moves, they be with great strength
How upon thee hast thou mastered this technique
Thou art romantic, thy teeth sharp as swords
How perfect thy high tactic
In thy mouth, thou hideth both pain and pleasure
Thou, indeed, art inventive and unique
Come to me, I beg, bite me with thy breath
Thy deep sting mine karma prick
And how these be more powerful than words
Oh, thou catchest me with thy trick
In mine blood thou oozest life like a treasure
Oh, if this love be,
Then cut me through as thou pleaseth
If love maketh one bleed,
Then mine ear bite hard as thou fixeth.

33. Just Black, O Juliana

Just black, this woman called Juliana
In a black dress or call it a skirt
Just black, she struts inside a temple goddess
Walking glidingly in divine heels of perfect sheds
Just black, with immaculate aura, she is a queen
In her face, hope and love mingle
Life and death marry
Just black and they give birth to soothing whisper:
"We die and live in thy presence
Oh, sweet Juliana; you're so adorable"
Just black, it is fair to be black
And fairer still to dress elegantly in a black tight.
Just black,
So cute, so pretty in black, O Juliana.

34. Eye of Beholder

She blindly teases his shape,
curatively
At first, it was just in her mind,
figuratively
Her eyes can't stop gazing,
emphatically
She closes her eyes, he shows up,
automatically
Oh, her eyes of dove,
are sickly in love
This feeling is haunting her,
down and above
He's just an ordinary guy,
but makes him a god
He can't be wrong, to everything he says,
she will nod
A second in his presence,
makes more sense
His absence,
burns her like fire, intense
She has fallen,
Her heart, stollen
Her mind, stricken
Her mood, sicken
Her doubts, trodden
Her pride, forgotten
She knows, she's in love
And she can't wait, him to hold and have.

35. Like a Sunset, O Angelian

Like a sunset when the weather is cool
Like the sunrise when the sun is white as wool
Your lips shower billions of nerves, sweet and kind
A diadem, a trophy I have by accident find
Even your name, Oh Angelian, O Angelian
Spells like July, the season of the summerian
How beautiful you're in every way
For others may be stricken by their say
But you, a black angel with a pink heart
Your love is perfect in shape, in form art
Come to me, run, and don't stop
Let me hold you till we drop
Oh, how lovely is your tender bosom
How I miss your true and real bottom.

36. Ka-Reign

You're beautiful, and so good to behold
You're exceptional, and out of this world
Your step, is like a goddess' crown
Your speech, is made from a princess' throne
How cute your smile,
Even when you mean not
Kings will desire to walk with you every mile,
Your eyes are gracious; you have no fault.

37. Woman, a Wife I

Who said that the woman is a small thing,
a weak vessel, an appendage of creation?
For that a one has never known
the vulnerability before a woman,
not just a woman, a wife
John Legend pens it even so well,
"Perfect imperfections…
When I lose, I am winning…
my worst distraction…my downfall…"
Oh, how appropriate, for this woman,
a wife,
is my most powerful friend,
and my worst enemy.

38. Woman, a Wife II

How can you say
she will bulge under pressure;
You have not known a woman?
She nags unendingly,
and makes lethal insistence,
and does not give up on issues
And yet without her
life is dull and even boring,
But with her,
and you know what I am saying,
she is a true pain,
a terrible teacher
and poor coach
What, then do you say –
leave her and be alone,
freedom, viva
and let us tonight find peace.

39. Woman, a Wife III

You're wrong,
for immediately she is away,
she is out,
war breaks out –
not a battle for territory
But a loneliness too thick
for smog to succumb,
and yet still you wish
she was gone forever
Nay, she is still here,
in your veins,
in your blood
and in your all life sources –
you miss her again.

40. Woman, a Wife IV

Oh women,
who shall deliver us
from their devilish stratagems,
their evil machinations and smug
And again pause, you're wrong,
the woman, a wife,
is the easiest critic,
you fall naked before her
 And yet she keeps all your children
under lock
and calls you
each time you spend time at the office
You think about it,
so, she cares,
but she behaves as though
she is your worst nightmare.

41. Woman, a Wife V

Women, a woman, a wife,
a weapon of mass destruction,
a love bullet, a poisonous chalice
She is all that,
and yet, you cannot live without her –
you wish she was not there; you cry
Is this what they call love
 – insanity –
yet we all have it,
and we know when it is not there.

42. Woman, a Wife VI

Women, a wife,
my greatest adversary,
and still we live together,
year after year after year
How possible,
why impossible not to be without her,
and what a league of extremities!

43. Woman, a Wife VII

A woman, a wife,
a knife that cuts deepest,
yet a sponge that soothes the nicest – yelp!
A woman, a wife,
a necessary inconvenience,
a silent missile,
a spirited competitor – oh help!
Yet, sweeter than honey,
braver than a lioness,
and steadfast as a strong warrior- she is!

44. Woman, a Wife VIII

A woman, a wife,
tender to behold and chubby to caress,
yet hard as a rock when she bugs
Tender as the shoots of the onions,
yet irritating as its leaves
out-flames its killing rhythms
I would rather, have one,
a woman, a wife,
than spend all my days
dodging the weapon of love!

45. Daughters

She is adorable, she is precious, she is my daughter
She comes to hug me without preconditions, only pure laughter
She holds my hand and whispers, "Daddy, I love you,"
She is not like any other, among the children of men, there are few,
I love her back, in fact, I have loved her even before birth
There is nothing I value more than her on this crowded-earth
Her life is intertwined with my own, I feel her joy, I hear her pain
When she is not well, a part of me simply stops to gain;
I don't need to place flowers in my chamber, she is my flower
Her scent fills my heart to the blink, hour after hour;
When she does wrong, even in my rebuke, I dance in affection,
My mind always yearns for her glory and passion;
I can't believe that I have more than three of them to behold,
I thank God that I hold in my care what is more precious than gold.

46. Graceful White

Sometimes poetry is a means of telling stories
Other times, it can be for lost glories
But for you, this poem I write with clarity
For you are most endeared in roses and charity
I saw your eyes the other day – gracious
I heard your lovely voice when you spoke –
precious
The gods that look on you are flashing your fame
The galaxies dance and chant your name
Surely, a deserved mother with wits you are
Your child has your perfect heart near her
Smile, and merry more, your destiny is all well
And hope and enjoy life, your dream will not fail
[Thank you for the ride today;
Much appreciated].

47. Tu es beau Kassandra

You're so pretty, so much so beautiful
You bring the sun to a snowy heart
And summer to a wintry season
Your smiles, so wide, so eventful
You brim with the grace of a hart
You're lovely, and more so for a good reason
And so, you may know, you're a goddess, too
Oh, strike a wand, I die in admiring you.
Tu es beau, O Kassandra.

48. Marry at 30

Most of them marry at 25
That's when things move, *mwana*.
Dreams now are all the same
And strength is overwhelming.

I tell you marry at 30
That's when reason fails,
Dreams have all ceased
And feelings do not overwhelm.

There is a struggle now, *mwana*.
With warm burning passions
And relief plays very far
Serve to just marry, *mwana*.

Do not add another year, *mwana*.
Two, three or more years
You will become insane
And lose the flavor of life.

At 30 marry your woman, *mwana*.

49. Love You So Much

Hello, darling, they are saying:
"He loves her like his sister"
But they also brag that you love me.
They say that we talk alike.
They shudder that we have passion.
They say that it flows so natural.
They compare us to the two elbows
And always demand for an answer.

They do not know the secret, darling.
Though eyes they have, they don't see.
They know not that love given
Is the love that one receives.
When I hold you closest to me,
Then natural grace points at you
And I praise your natural splendor.

50. Yours is Chubby

I will sing you this song
With no wit of poetry.
Because of your deep rift
And your chubbiness.

You have planted an orchard
In the form of a triangle
And in the middle of which
Is a living fountain
With a warmth of wet heat.

51. At the Lips

You plant sweetness
And in your mouth
Are watermelons
You have apples in your eyes
And garlands of ivory
In your legs.

But the middle and fundament
That guard of heightened sensors
That takes the brain of a child
And turns it into manhood
Is the prize of the well-bred.

52. Love Songs

My bride and my cherished love
From the rhythms of my heart
I create concertos in tunes
I beat dual codes
And for you
I record
Songs

My cute bride is my dear hart
She is kind and gorgeous
She is fair and dear
She takes my heart
And brings joy
With love
Songs

My mom once told me to hear
The words of my love's beat
And not to dare miss
The true meaning
Of love themes
Veiled in
Songs

My dad was not wrong at all
When he told me to learn
To hear and perceive
What is unsaid
By my dear
In love
Songs

53. Beside Me

I would have thought "Mary"
When besides me sat a figure
The aura on her head
And the precious visage
Were out of this world
Her labia dripped honey,
Pure from the honeycomb.

The space between her chest
Was narrow, lubricated scented fluid
And proudly comforted men.

The styles embedded hairs
Would have given expert saloons
Great difficulties in phathomation
In my subconscious I fainted
Till the one besides me left
Then I wondered how that
Beauty is no respecter of reason.

54. No Capacity

If looks could kill
My eyes would be long dead.
We see in part
But then the entire thing
And he who cannot perform
Is not fortunate.

The crow cries "No capacity"
When a guy fails to bring his lady to ice

The hare with curiosity asked:
"Foolish vultures, why kill
And fail to eat?"

The saint remarked:
"I married, not buried!"

So are the sounds of life
Soaring with vibes of life
Socking all the pains of life
Soaking all the juices in life.

55. Claria I

Claria your eyes are little doves
The brand even mighty Zeus loves;
They have been fashioned from above
And given to us all in love.

Claria your cute eyes are gracious
Certainly, full-size and precious
While clearly round and capacious
Yet brownish and very spacious.

Claria your eyes do shine brightly
With pupils well placed just rightly
To allow heat only slightly
And endow with sight delightly.

Claria is decked in color red
Sight very well tidy and bred
That the cowardly dash in dread
Yet her acumen is well spread.

56. Claria II

You're thirty-five,
I cannot believe
you have grown this far.
When I first met you,
on a sunny afternoon,
wearing a corduroy pant,
nay, a white long dress.
A shy, resolute darling doe
soothing in the end of relocation
I never thought a lad as innocuous
as you would someday be my wife.
You persisted;
I never resisted;
you showed you had the gats
to get into my way,
And I into yours.
Even Mike, couldn't stand,
Nor Patrick understand.
For what had been fated,
Could not be hated.

57. Claria III

At Patience's discernment,
I began to realize you carried a heart of gold
You displayed the strength of an ox
and the elegancy of a peacock
Oh, Africa, how I have loved you,
Oh, Congo, a nursery that birthed a princess.
And you, Zambia,
a flowerbed of beauties.
I longed to be your side's suitor,
your loving flower when the forest is burned
I found you,
I loved you
and the fear to love forever was healed.

58. Claria IV

Oh, Claria,
you hold a heart of champions,
you're surely the best of women
How can I not tell
how much I love you,
for love for you is just inadequate
But yet, I love you,
and will love you,
and continue to, till death
This vow have I once made,
this vow will I never make again
For you to me are like two roads
that meet and promise never to part
For you to me are more than just a wife;
you're more than a lover
I love you more than words can say,
more than I can show you
For you're more to me,
more than I can show or tell,
more than life.

59. Claria V

Oh, my Claria
For you're the gem that inspires me to live,
the aura than covers my fears
Oh, sweet Claria,
know that to me you're special,
more special than the sun's rays
And more valuable than the currency
when it performs, and even more
Because you're the nest
of all God's female creatures,
the ever lovely
And now I tell you,
never ever disbelieve my love for you,
please never
So that I may never repeat,
even when I make mistakes,
My love for you is forever.

60. Claria VI

Oh, Claria, forgiving Claria
I know you know
I have disappointed you sometimes,
and I agree I did
But never forget
that the lesson I have learned
is that no-one is like you
For when the many ladies that I have met
have been just good meat
You, however,
have been the real steak,
the best,
those like you
are only you.

61. Cuteravive

My Cuteravive, my sweet song
The nice thing to which I belong
I have longed for you for long
And now you are here, I am strong.

My Cuteravive, my source of Spring
From you, all nice things of life spring
In your soft voice, heaven rhythms ring
Your presence, many loves they bring.

My Cuteravive, my sweet play-doll
When we shop, I laugh and love all,
Your fashion taste is Summer and Fall,
You are adorable in person or in call.

My Cuteravive, super new clear brain
When you shop, more money you gain,
You lack nothing, in sunshine or rain,
You're love' genius, cute in the main.

62. Miracles of Love

Babies used to be miracles of love
When people in their simplicity
Did not use science and drugs
To stop the fusion of ripe cells.

Death used to be a stranger
When people in their simplicity
Did not use science and drugs
To stop the spread of infections.

A boy in the presence of love
Shall force the growing of beards.
Babies and more babies
And cessation of monthly cycle
Are all miracles of love.

Birth and marriage and death
Are all miracles of this life
Even when men conquer them
They are still miracles of love.

63. Love to Remember

I remember…
And skies testify.
My heart leaped.
I remember…
Your young long face
Of which poets are fond of-
Kin sister to morning star.
I know no beauty as yours.

I remember…
The feeling and the taste…
The view and pictures.

I remember …
A mind made up,
A fearless resolve
And the risky trips.

I remember…
Love greater than life
And your tender graces.

I remember…your love.

64. Daughter for Loves

Thou art a flower growing painlessly in the thorns
Thou escapeth all the pangs of ruthless brushes
How that thou be different, yet natural
That thou conducteth thyself with majesty
Thy tongue dripeth with honey,
Thy thighs are towers of power
 Oh, open, open the fountains of thy youth
And therein floweth beauty unspeakable.
Oh Julian, a daughter made for loves;
A girl unforgettable, beaming with doves!

Thou art a heart, but of thousand angels
Thou carrieth a beauty, of myriad goddesses
And thy tenderness, is of million darlings
As thou fervently groan, "So sweet,
For thou always sweepeth off my feet
With thy words full of the charm of poesy
And the tamarind with which they oozeth."

65. How Lovely

How lovely, the embraces of my lady
How darling her eyes when they bend
She covers herself in shy fur sturdy
She is all smiles to the very end
Who can argue, she is not gorgeous
Her face does tell it, her heart sings it
But closer, she is diamond for obvious
And in her perpetual bosom, all is fit
How lovely the sweet games of loving
How vital to life the rims of her carving.

66. Love Can Build a Bridge

Love can build a bridge
Between your heart and mine
Love can erect a passage
In the conflict of many interests.
Love can construct a canal
In the midst of witlessness.
Love can make the sky blue
In the place of gloom and dullness.
Love can dig a long tunnel
And reach to wonderful lands.
Love can build a bridge
Between your heart and mine.

67. Tashany's Song

Thank you, for my kids
Thank you, for the joy that they bring
Thank you, for dark nights
That they turn into mourning
And grey days they turn to white.

Thank you, for the privilege
Thank you, for life they lavish with purpose,
Hope they bring to shattered dreams,
And furious storms they calm with peace.

Thank you, for the miracle
Thank you, for the tender shoots
Thank you, for the innocent pulsing hearts
Sleeping silently in see-saw cribs
Surrounded by angels and perking wings.

Thank you, for second chances
For in them, loafing drives emerge
And frustrated opportunities surface again.
In them, mooching ideas emasculated
Rise to the test of hope
To bring forth attitude, kind and dear.

Thank you, for this love
That no mind can grasp
And no intellect can clasp.

68. A Mother's Love

Mother,
Because you have a mother's love
Other loves,
Do not match a mother's love.
Together,
Let us cherish a mother's love.
Hitherto,
Earth stands on a mother's love.
Either,
We choose war or a mother's love.
Rather than gold,
Trade with a mother's love.

69. Mended Heart

You break my heart, with every charm
You mend my soul, you mean no harm
You're in my dream, every daunting night
Forgetting you totally, is my regular fight
Never did I think you had composed me
Forgive me, I was blind I couldn't see;
Now, day and night, your voice is heard
Your sweet memory does not at all fed,
You infest me like an incurable disease
Only at thoughts of meeting I rest as ease.

70. Awanda

There is a place truer than nature
An abode fairer than paradise
In the inner chamber therein
All dearest memories
Of things said and unsaid
Do find boundless expressions.

There is a person known to us
More than we know our palm
Whose voice rings music to us,
And whose countenance strikes
A breath-taking enigma.

There is a love, deeper than bliss
A feeling soother than a kiss
A person more desirable than peace
And a name we'll never miss.

Like her sweet name, Awanda,
Oh, is it just a dream, I wonder.

71. Suzy Sisess

Sweet to my senses is Suzy Sisess
Sighing so sensually and so souly
Speaking in sassy sextet syllables
As she stands alongside the skydom

Silly, sexy, she swears in her silence
So snootily strong are her silky smiles
She sends sugary sounds in intense sleeps
Saying and singing in sweet small stanzas

See, soldiers stumble at his safe station
Sailors swim across these infested seas
Speakers stammer in Suzy's shy essence
As such stories are especially artless.

72. Jamaican Girl

Look and see, for Poshy is her name
Gaze and watch, luxury is what she loves
Out of factories, her desires untimely wonder
And her men, large and long she wants them

For signs of wealth, she looks
But only broken pebbles, she finds
In her house, there are three siblings
And each of them, has a different dad

An irregular visitor is the absent dad
"My babies' daddy" she calls him
But high and bright are all her shoes
And only in black and tinted cars, she hikes

Around her waist, are two cell-phones
One to money, another to race, she answers
Clearly at welfare offices, she's known
And men are only used, as economic chips.

73. Stolen Hearts

She refused to let her heart away
While her instigators she kept at bay
A man with many plans she would sway
While heroes never danced her way.

She would come early to Victoria bay
To grant hundred suitors their pay
And she counted months till May
When she would pick a suitable day.

In suits and breasted jackets they pray
Her heart strong, her soul as a shy prey
But she knew when men might spray
Their evil tactics of the matter of grey.

74. Conquered Heart

My heart, frail and empty
Any of my parts is yours
And you won my soul
When you held my hands.

O, my once strong heart
In hands strong and hard
In embraces gracious and bold
There, my peace lay.

My love my soul you've won
My love my defence you've broken
With your tender kiss and hug
My heart you have conquered.

75. Stagnet

My tears pour out like rain
Just inside my longing heart
For my strength you've taken
Just with your charm and love

Your love like nothing else
Your hands hesitantly given
Your body in shape unveiled
Oh, might you have broken

By my side you shyly lie
Your back to my front brought
As if your two diamond breasts
In my poverty soul surrenders

Softly my hands move yours
Where the two golden legs meet
And in your sweetly magnet
And the voice cries, Stagnet.

76. Why Love

Why do I love you so much
Why should I love you that much
In your presence
Like wax, I melt
In your absence
Like a tax, I pelt
Why am I captivated by you
Why do I dream only of you
To your name
Like music, I dance
To your fame
Like panic, I prance
Why are you made so perfect
Why on you all is just perfect
By your side
Like a pet, I cower
By your pride
Like a bet, I dower.

77. Love's Absence

You are my greatest love
And my strongest enemy
In your presence I live and dwell
And there's my danger as well

In your arms I comfortably rest
And in your hands I gently die
For you are the only one I know
Who crashes my weakly soul

In the middle of fervent summer
I still feel deathly cold
And whenever you leave me
I wilt like a plant, scorched and wee

With you I live a double life
For I am alive when I am in love
And I die when you leave for another
One I can't have without the other.

78. Love and Death

Love protects and kills
For in love,
There is healing
And death lurks, too
Love can charm hearts
And can break them, too
For love is a cure
And a poison, too

Love unites and divides
For in love
There is laughter
And great sadness, too
Love can create dreams
And can shutter them, too
For in love there is hope
And grave danger, to.

79. Love is Like

I
Love is like a fast-flowing river
It quickly forgets about faults
Love is like a heavily pouring rain
It quickly washes away worries.

II
Love is like a mother hen with chicks
It risks its own life for theirs
Love is like an old skin-shading snake
It changes to begin a new life.

III
Love is like a tough-going teacher
It holds the stick to clean blunders
Love is like an obedient slave
It lets off to serve its master.

IV
Love is an emotion with many faces:
In the morning it expresses joy;
In the afternoon it fosters care;
And in the evening, it closes the gates.

80. Be My Valentine

You are my ever-shining star
My all to you I surrender
This Valentine, take me away
And in your love, let me stay.

Bring me ever closer to you
For without you, I quickly faint
The sound of your name is fair
My heart leaps like a little hare.

So, to you I willingly come
Since in your embrace I belong
And your kind shinning eyes
Drives out my fears and lies.

81. Hips

It dangles lazily down
The square-shaped back-head,
Blondish, shinning in the shades
Of the elements' brilliance
Like a flock of newly-borns,
It dances to the gyrating hips,
And elegantly swings side to side
Along her darling skin,
Simple, slimy and sizzling
The bends within its concaves,
Reflecting the singing whispers
Of perfect affinity.
It leaves a gap –
And her dancing skirt frolics with
Enticing rhythms –
The hips shower down to
The knuckles, raising spasms of
Splendor and
The lips shyly branch to the
Dripping colors;
Hair so fair,
A face drawn with grace.

82. More for Nothing

He woke up in the heart of the night
"More of the same," he spoke to himself
He gazed from his left and his right
He was alone all by his self

He dressed in his old pairs of pajamas
Which spoke to him all night long
"See, you are still not famous
You wonder and ponder, for how long?"

He tried to shut up his voluminous soul
Closer to him than his own door
He realized he was his own foe;
All he chased was a dying shadow.

83. Sonnet to Buttocks

Let me be blunt, may the gods bear me witness
I have no known wit, only basic mental fitness
For the buttocks of a woman have pyrrhic lures
The damage to the brain a man surely endures
Buttocks – two friends beating from altered code
Buttocks – two enemies traveling the same road
Flesh bumps wiring the heart to its beautiful death
Dazzling knocks denying Nature its needed breath
Never looked at once, twice saints turn to sinners
Eyes do salivate, even losers become winners
Buttocks – lovely as morning dew, end to end
Buttocks – gracious to behold, intellect they bend
Oh, this adorable punishment, cold blood it boils
And the virile engine of men it gladly oils.

84. Women Buttocks

Oh, these fleshly, uniqueness
They come in all shapes, all fonts
In all sizes, all forms and all sheds;
Some are protruded, others flat
Some are oblong, others long,
Some are wide, others compact,
But whatever they are, they are.
Talk of juicy, crispy, chunky or fruity –
All are embroiled in their ambience.
Men turn more frequently, amazed,
They look back commandingly, dazed.
Oh, woman buttocks,
They're not your usual sitting pads,
They are more, they dance, and sing.
Oh, what a beauty, what a thing.
It's music to the senses, firm
And tender to behold, calm.
Oh, Gyrating Master, sweet pair
A few can say bad of you, fair.

85. Ms. Taco

You're called many names,
But you're known by all
You live by two pillars of pure gold
And have a sweet guard at the door
Your entrance drips with honey
Your taste, no money can buy
Your voice, is silently lovely,
Even when it is not talking.
You conquer all, swallow all
But you remain largely calm, hidden.
You fail no-one not in a hurry,
And disappoint none who cares.
You have a punch, life flows;
You generate electric current,
Not even earth can shunt it;
You're boisterous, callous, frantic,
But you're sweetly, even toxic.
The entire universe, worships you,
And you captain all wondering nerves;
You kill, and give life at the same time,
In one shot, you destroy the world,
And in the other, you rebuild it.
You have three cute angles, a triangle,
And an endeared soldier within,
And no matter who looks at you,
You cause hallucinations, tantrums.
All eyes gaze intently where you stay,
Absent-mindedly, they forget themselves;
You capture all senses: Feelings, sight
And even your smell is gorgeous.
Oh, lovely Conche, wise umpire,
Worthy opposites!

86. Love Star

My lucky star, bright, fine from afar
In blue night dress, bare and fresh
A beauty in human form, oh, Pure, my love
A gift from above, softly gracious a voice
Oh, how great a choice!

87. Recover, My Love

Recover my love, for thou art fair
Recover, for all that we share
Recover because I deeply care
Recover, for our love is ever dear.

88. Song for Loves

Let me sing for you my love
Let the song of love freely swell
For all on you is nothing but well
Your frame made from above!

You are a sample of divine creation
A picture of saintly phathomation;
Your curves speak of designer's craft
And your contours, of an artist's graft!

A trophy so sacred to the winner
For gods as men for you all stumble
Your beauty, outer and inner
Yet, so elegant and yet so humble!

89. Simple Love

I woke you up at midnight
Just to tell you I love you tight
I stroke through your bouncy hair
Just you can know I care
I spread the bed with followers
So, I can be with you for hours
I put the kids to sleep early
Just so I can stroke your belly
Fading Beauty.

Thou art strikingly beautiful
Myriads boys and men adore thee
Thy graces, divine
Thy looks, splendid.

Thou hast won angels hallowed hearts
Thy speech strikes with perfect codes
Thy struts like a peacock
Thy nature's aura, blissful.

Thou aren't gazed at only once
The greatest among men for thee vie
Thy thoughts, the wisest
Thy visage, brilliance sparks.

Thou art secretly called Ruxtovia
A name priceless to mention
Thy old self, enchanted
They present looks, fading.

90. One Step Too Beautiful

Lazily, out of Grand AM, she drops
A ring chains her ankle
A smile lines her face
And a short skirt barely hides
Her divine curves.

She is lean like a pine tree
Slender like a bamboo branch
Rare like golden diadems
And scarce like diamonds.

Like a goddess, stately she walks
Like rhythms of music, she talks
Eyes brimming, like starry skies
And her hair puffs like gazelles' flock.

She stands behind a counter
To order coffee brewed by lords
Hearts she blows whence she moves
Wherever she goes men's hearts
Sheeresly follow.

91. Shine Baby Shine

Shine baby shine
Show them you can dance
Strut baby strut
Shindig and jive to rock and roll.

There are many lovely people
There are few grumpy humans
Only you can know them
For they are real beauties.

Shine baby shine
Shake up your frail figure
Sing baby sing
Show off your fleshly giggledoms.

The world is full of beautiful people
The earth lacks no curved shapes
And your joy is complete
When you dance till you fall.

92. Beautiful People I

People are beautiful and helpful
You drop a coin and they pick it up
You get sick and they charge you a fee
And when in trouble they call for police

People are special and kind
They help you realize your dreams
They give their best for you
And pray that peace be on earth

People are gentle and nice
Even on a rainy and murky day
When the sun is on its head
They brave all to make you happy

People are good and sweet
They can be trusted for a short time
They tolerate only when they're not hurt
And do their utmost to laugh at failings

93. Beautiful People II

People are beautiful
They just don't know
When you help them out
They say thank you
When you share with them
They show their love
When you ask for more
They call you names.

94. Beautiful People III

People are beautiful
When they are dying
They are plain and truthful
And they speak without lying

People are beautiful
When they are buying
They are nice and fruitful
And they sell without spying

People are beautiful
When they are trying
They are focused and dutiful
And they work without sighing

People are beautiful
When they are flying
They are gentle and mindful
And they share without vying

95. Who You Marry

There is a thinking that is wrong
A perception, lofty and unattainable
But people will care who they marry
And will know when it is too late

Men, overwhelmed by impulses
Give their best strength to women
And women, deceived by words
Learn of a boy they hardly thought of

They marry only for the love of beauty
And they hate it when it fades off
Because in the flesh flows red blood
And for the sake of it, life drains away

Let charm and splendor pass you by
For such are forms in need of a spirit
Women are trophies only when prized;
Men are heroes when in the bed chamber

96. If I Were a Girl

If I were a girl
I would talk less
And listen more
I would humble myself
Even when I know
I am more intelligent
Than most boys

If I were a girl
I would balance
Between how I look
And I how I reason
I would not talk
About a boy I admire
Or repeat his name
Because I feel jealousy

If I were a girl
I would know boys better
Cook and dine early
Get kids to bed
And then tell me,
"I can make a good wife."

If I were a girl
I would not watch too much
Reality television
I will not question people
But I will let them know
That I have my own views
Of love

If I were a girl
I would occasionally be silly
Tell my hubby I needed him

Buy him little nothings
And make him his best dish

If I were a girl
I would not be intimidated
I would look in shape
And prepare my work well
I would listen to great speeches
And make my own notes.

97. Recover, My Baby

These tiny limbs in agony lay
In pain no language expresses
On your side I am here to stay
As your frame my soul depresses

I in goodwill spread my cards
For your well-being I offer a prayer
For your smile love it adds
More million reasons you must repair

There is no occasion as this
When my baby you say so little
And for dad, anguish is all his
To see you squeeze those hands

Oh, my little angel, recover again
And let Dad stroke and tickle you
For sickness shall not be your chain
Many gifts of laughter are yours, too.

98. Juicy Hone-y

Truth still lingers deep in my fainting soul
As words fail to come with sound verbal flow
Even where there is no evidence
In these chosen lines lies the essence:

"A goddess thou truly art
And of pure gold, is thine heart."

With peacocks' majesty, you barely walk
Like streams of quiet waters, is your fair talk
For your bosom is a legend's armour
That slays dead every aspiring charmer

Those who see your divine curves, die in awe
A little chat with you, is a big score
Many proudly court your grace and beauty
In wordless thoughts they sigh, "Oh, how pretty."

One word in vernacular rings true love
"Yes, sweet chaos, but your email I must have."
For your name is fondest blend of Juicy
And your heavenly lips drip pure Hone-y.

99. Deep Passion

Love that grows on strange paths
Love that bears in scotched deserts
Love that brings forth wild flowers
Love that is forsaken and stained

So shall your sex be great tonight
When your hearts shall fondly meet
In a night full of verbal silences
Where offence never brings a face

Your love which endures all elements
The rain that pours over you is harsh
The winds that blow past you is dirty
And snow buries your soul alive

Love will be made sweeter today
When two mute people shall talk
Without words, in passion's depth groans
Feelings so strong, and love so steep.

100. Love Like Before

Tell me your love is still good
Done every night in the hood
While days pass without food
Since you don't mind that mood

I was taught by my religion
To read only stories by the Gideon
To abscond from lessons in the legion
And fly away quickly like a pigeon

But the truth was later found
When I was on a trip west-bound
How many affairs end on mound?
And divorce rates highly astound

Silence we cannot keep any more
Hiding in our false beliefs and all
While beds only regrets, they store
When love can be good like before.

101. Zimba

Zimba was her last name
A girl so cute and famous
Boys would bate on her fame
A girl so sweet and gorgeous

Whatever she played, she won
Not by genius or sophistication
But by how she was just born
Full of nature and simplification

She always walked elegantly
In beauty, she had no rivalry
In looks, she needed no gallantry
In grace, she attracted chivalry

So simple was what she wore
That even simplicity had a brand
And simply by saying "no"
She simplified style without a wand.

102. I Die

I die in your love, my love
If death comes this gently
So, let me die a million deaths
Kill me with a billion kisses

You break my power, O love
Just with one squeeze of your touch

You scatter my lonely night
In the light of your presence
And you conquer my aching heart
Just at the point I feel your love
While the strength in me
Gives way to streams flowing
I feel the energy in you.

103. I Live

I live in the shadow of your love
I breathe under the rhythm
Of your gentle embraces
I surrender at the altar
Of unending kisses

Without you, I know not who I am
For only in your presence
Does my soul find joy
And my whole being
Find pure rest

Touch me and hold me closer to you
In your arms my soul belongs
Take me and save me
From the stain pains
Of a lost heart.

104. Love I Know

Love I know
When my night turns to day
Love me more
When my grey turns to blue
Love I know
When what I touch turns to gold
Love must make whole
When my fears turn to strength
Love I know
When I am special and just myself.

105. She

She dangles lazily
With lips painted in heavenly red;
She wears a smile
Fashioned on the artist's carving bed;
She lies yonder,
Like several angels gloriously made;
And I say again,
I love her, tenderly, sweetly dead.

106. Angels without Wings

These little tender shoots
In little beds tenderly sleep
For all in me for them fends
As I work tenderly for them

Angels with wings
And gods without a heaven
Who has known a queen
Without a crown and throne!

Sleep, soundly sleep, O angels
Close your pure and bleeping hearts
Within my soul I shed a tear
All I want is only your good

Sweetly and tenderly awake, O loves
Though my bones be in pains
And my strength all be gone
Yet your heaven will be done

107. Little Loves

Sleep joyfully, my young loves
Dream of angels and fairies
Reach to grand laying fields
And swing in heavenly colors

By your side I will stand
When in thoughts and deed
Your innocence loudly rings
And forever you are blessed

Never will I leave you, O loves
Never even when it rains
In snow or in strong winds
Shielding you I will for eternality

Forever, you will be mine
In my heart, you will always be
And when your wings grow
With you I will fly to azure places.

108. Like Heaven

Like the heavens be far and azure
So, your enemies be far and unsure
Like the grace that made your beauty
So, God put an angel for your duty
In this life you will know one thing
That my love, for you is everything
So gorgeous your beauty is to behold
And this I see and I was not told
May your God in truth bless you;
Beauties like yours are rare and few.

109. Wife

You are the flower of my exotic gardens
The light in the darkest part of my heart
The cheese on my tasteless cake
And the energy that makes my soul roar.

If I say I love you, and you don't believe
If I say you move my every being
And you're still uncertain
Then know that it doesn't make it any less true.

Girl, you are simply the best, the first and the most
Girl, you're to me everything I dream about
Girl, don't be too mad or too disturbed,
Girl, we differ to love each other better.

110. Exception Has a Name

You wear an aura of difference
A statement of distinction
An emblem of resourcefulness
And an element of exceptionality

You are a symphony of many sounds
Yet a ring of expensive perfumes
You glitter with a strong presence
Yet soft like the heavens be smiling

The girls all around the world marvel
They match not your charm of travel
They gossip in quitters mambo jumbo
Your genius, never shall ever stumble.

111. Black Beauty

It's not the brightness of color
Or the lack of it;
It's the proportions – ditto –
Same from ear to ear;
Pimples squeezed, melodiously
Into cheering eyebrows;
Cheeks squared, deliciously
Spacious, face ripe and
Just the right size;
Lips – of perfect congruency –
In shape and size, luscious
And proportionately accurate;
Of the entire countenance,
Value and shape meet together,
Strength and grace mellow
Into a framework tender and divine,
In dimples, a playing field of joy,
And all admix into Mona Lisa idyll;
Beauty – is not what you see,
Beauty – is what you feel.

112. Marriage Myth

One is as ten, as 20 is like 50
The open kingdom of duality
Is the most closed dons of secrets.
Those who marry young may be spared,
But not even many years of living together,
Entitles couples to truth.
It is like a radio
Which plays all your favorites,
And yet you know little of the singers.
Music is like a pain-killer,
And marriage is like a sharp-shooter.
It bothers that people be one,
Only in money problems, if lucky.
Though their hearts be far, their minds are closer.
For more they share, the more they care.

113. Thank the Bra

To men, it is a piece of silky cloth
Of two equal flaps and a string;
It may wangle in black or in white;
Floral replicas are not uncommon,
Yet, it is still a bra.

Secrets for decades it has carried
For cultures, and tastes in it meet
For sure order and shape it brings
And the chest of women it comforts.

Thank the bra when the babies grow
And their faces glow;
Thank the bra since a breast is more
Than just a blessed ball.

114. Flesh and Bones

They grow powerful,
And they are still humans;
Flesh and bones
Elegantly avoid each other
Like the shores of
The same sea;
In riches as in poverty
Flesh and bones remain;
Black and White
With dreams they die
For in soils
Warm or cold they lie.

115. Lovely the Dance

On a bright sunny day
All you want is a cool stay
And a pal who is a glory
For you need it for a cute story
Oh, how good the moves to me
When they dance, I do see
Sweet also to my memories
And elegant in her mummeries
Are all her little nothings
As lovely to me in all things.

116. Diminished Beauty

You walk in our streets naked
For nothing;
You share your well-made body
Willingly, free of charge;
You are on a mission to expose yourself
More than you need to;
And you are determined to upset morality
Even for one-day glory;
Your beauty is like food,
Good when you hunger,
And naughty with plenty on platter;
Moderation wins hearts,
Even the goddess of Selfishness
In Reason's chamber bows;
Your nakedness is your currency,
To exchange it with virtue,
And to show off in hidden valleys
With consideration.

117. Sex Aren't Love

There is something mysterious about love
And beauty when done with grace above;
For many have had a great sex experience
But it was only a matter of expedience.

When love is made, it brings great happiness,
Because time cures all blame and nappiness.
A woman's body is a lock intricately combined,
Only with patience can it be delicately aligned.

Anyone can win an orgasm through sex
But only love wins hearts and makes flex.
It pays null to rush the art of love-making;
Its end result is nothing but heart-breaking.

Once a sage said: "Weak men force ladies,"
And, "Not all strong men drive Mercedes."
To win the war, you must lose the battle,
For great love happens inside of her chattel.

Men are ready when they erect a tower,
They are feared when they rise to power;
But she is not, even with upright nipples,
And only kind words pacify the ripples.

The golden rule of love-making is in this:
"Love her before you make a kiss,"
And the second is like the first,
"Enter only when she's at her burst."

118. Musonda

This love, that my wings be cast on the sea
This love, the brightest in your eyes I see,
In your hand melts love's melodies at best,
Every morn, I awoke to your palms' first,
You carried a heart of a true mother
And cared for me more than several other,
Yet, you were a silent lover of skins;
When you came under unlike many kins,
I knew you'd carry me through the gravel
To Mibenge where we meant to travel;
Oh, to you I owe an introduction, Musonda,
And tenderly, you did an under-skin agenda.

119. Poetry of Sex

Open; let not your mind blame you
Show me how you are made
Let me tremble in the majesty
Of your nakedness.

Sleep still, stride a bed of roses
Break the limbs, let them stretch wide,
Strip off all; reveal your hidden gem,
Your sanctimonious fantasies;
Close your eyes, and open your heart,
And let me walk you in the paths
Of Nature, the silence of passions.

Awake slowly, like charcoal flames,
And die even slower, as in heated ovens,
In your hair, let me find pasture;
In your eyes, the shining beams of angels;
In your mouth, wonderful are your golden
Jewells of honey;
And in your dimples,
The intense goblets of mixed fruits.

Let me follow the delicate edges
Of your erect nipples,
The pink smells of your upped
And well-sequestered breasts;
Let me sink in the sweet tunnels,
Just below your brazen altar,
Near the triangular Peninsular
Of ecclesiastical sacredness;

Let me get lost in the forest of pubics,
In the dark shadows of your well-watered gardens;
Do not weed, I beg, do not week all,
Let me feel the sharp stings of your
Innocuous venom, the taste of your
Never-ending charms;

Squeeze me, I pray, till my request
Be granted,
Release me from the ephemeral trap,
And lift me to Marineland
To revel in the fear of heights,
The dying sensation of the sky screamers;

Kiss me, kiss me deep, deeper than my tongue
Can speak,
Thrash me with a single blow of your breath,
To open wide the rivers of sweet larva,
The Hotspring of boiling syrup,
Oh, with you only, let me live,
And without you, let me die.

120. Painful Thought

There is a beauty so much dear
A person who so moves thine life
That thou art made to drop a tear;
To breed grief wherein rage is rife

She puts elements in thine soul
The eternal chip that so stings
That thine physical being, and more
From this point forward moves and springs

Beauty is who she plainly is
Bright as the fullest morning star
For the real package is all his
To cause avowed foes hard to spar

She beams with eyes of love and peace,
High weights of concern and vain fights
So, weave jointly into one piece,
That thine hurtly ego within frights

This smile that thou have, O dearest
Takes ruthless tolls on myriad minds
And breathes shivers without rest;
That thy nimble limb wobbly winds

A painful thought, O flawless Ruth
In exile a prince thou rejected
Till late thou stumbled on the truth;
Still, thou art missed; how dejected.

121. Women

Women:
They were meant to be loved
Their bodies look like
They were meant to be loved
Their voices sound like
They were meant to be loved
Their eyes shine like
They were meant to be loved
Their mouths speak like
They were meant to be loved
Their stories tell like
They were meant to be loved
They are weaker than men
For they were meant to be loved
They are made from inside out
Because they were meant to be loved
They have a nature
Soft and hard
That's why they have to be loved
They possess the sweetness
Of honey
But they sting like bees
To show that they were meant to be loved
They walk with a lion's pride
Gyrate with peacock's vanity
Think with a serpent's sharpness
Relate with chameleon skills
Attract like a magnet
And kill with a scorpion's venom.

It is a verity,
They were meant to be loved.

122. So Lucky, So Jackie

So rare, and yet so beautiful
That these two should be found in one
So charmed, so wonderful
That the strongest only should have won
So special to behold, so gracious to have
Oh, so heart-thrusting is your tender love
How that among women you stand alone
So Jackie, so lucky, so much so divine!

123. How Lovely

How lovely, the embraces of my lady
How darling her eyes when they bend
She covers herself in shy fur sturdy
She is all smiles to the very end
Who can argue, she is not gorgeous
Her face does tell it, her heart sings it
But closer, she is diamond for obvious
And in her perpetual bosom, all is fit
How lovely the sweet games of loving
How vital to life the rims of her carving.

124. Ten Out of Ten

Oh,
My all,
I love you
You're cute, too
I yield at your feet
And I am complete
Your mildness wins me
Your allure sets me free
You are, indeed, my power
The scent, hue of my flower
In the silence of your embrace
My nagging doubts you do erase
In the shining beauty of your hands
I hide from false and imperfect brands
Surely, you compare to nothing I've won
Our hearts are matching twins, they beat as one.

125. From Canada with Love

I told you when I was leaving
That I will never forget about you
You were worried, you were angst
I insisted that I had to go far way
You said, "My dear, remember me,"
And I have never forgotten your plea.
Oh, my mother, you are getting older,
And you have earned many grandkids
And acquired enormous wisdom.
From abroad, my dearest mother,
I have sired for you three daughters,
They long to see you, to hug, kiss you.
They ask, "When will we visit nanna?"
And I answer them, "Soon, my loves."
Oh, my mother, you've loved me
Like no-one has or could or would.
I'll keep my promise, I'll bring you here
To see your other family, in Canada.
Stay well, stay healthy, time will come.

126. Pain of Our Departure

I didn't tell you before I left
Though it looked like a theft,
That you loved me, like a son.
I can't ignore what you've done;
You took me in like your own,
You fed me; I didn't feel alone.
I am now established in Canada
And I have daughters by Kanata.
Surely, it is a village of all villages;
It has given me many privileges.
But home is home, Oh, *Mudala*.
We're attached like a parabola.
And those moments we prayed
And in many nations, we played,
You stood tall with me, unflinching.
And I will stand by you, clinching.
Like father and child, we're forever.
Sooner, I'll rekindle our endeavor.
Don't listen to naysayers, cynics.
I love you, ignore all the critics.

127. Friends Forever

You see me when I am naked
And you cover me;
You know that I am weak
And you make me strong;
You understand my doubts
And you believe in me;
You uncover my enemies' plans
And you prove them wrong;
You find me low, and defeated
And you wrap me with love.
You knew I was broke, desperate
And you gave more to have;
You discerned I was getting lost
You kept me in prayers.

128. Love

I long, long	truly for you
I miss you,	and it is true
Oh, come	be my love
Be mine	to have
I love you	yes, I do
My words	are too few
You're my life	my very best

You have no flaws in you, Oh my dearest
Your heart, O my lover, is of pure gold
You're lovely, so tenderly to behold
And you shine, brightly like a star
Yes, truly, so beautiful you are
Oh, my Darling, you're fair
Indeed, Oh, how rare
You're on my mind
You're very kind
My very treat
Cute, sweet
Of rest
Best!
♥

129. Sunshine

You are my sunshine, my one and only
You bring warmth in my shivering soul
You heal my ever-painful heart valves
You elongate my days, shorten my nights
Your whispers in the phone, I repeat all,
And you have char, Oh, loved one
No-one can resist; you're the moon's pal
Surely, you will be mine, I hope and pray.

130. Charsian Song, I

[Gentleman]

You trotted lovingly along Lumumba Road
On your mind, you carried a very big load
It was your floral bright white long dress
That revealed the elegance that you possess.
You stood out among the ecclesiastic class
You were distinct, even in a crowded mass.
You were perfect, made from divine ivory
Your heart as well as your attire, of finery,
No wonder my heart loved and fell for you
Even as years have passed, you remain true.
You're quiet by conduct, but wiser than sages
It always felt like I had known you for ages.
You came as a present wrapped in silicone
You're rare, gentle, gregarious as a pelican.
You said very little, and spoke no single word
I looked round; you had flown away like a bird.

131. Charsian Song, II

[Lady]

Everyone loved you, my dear, yes, they did,
And I knew many who for you made a bid.
I said, "Do I stand a chance, can I try?"
You were a very popular and zealous guy.
My dream came true when you liked me,
When you came very close to my knee.
At first, it was like I was just dreaming;
I believed when me you started esteeming.
You have been my truest lover ever since,
And nothing can otherwise me convince.

132. Charsian Song, III

[*Gentleman*]

Limited by my faith, my love I couldn't show,
And yet, without saying it, you knew so.
You understood that I loved you at first sight,
And from the start, I longed to hold you tight.
Time came, and we sat and talked endlessly,
And your voice resounded in me tenderly.
I couldn't sleep for days, just thinking of you,
Hitherto, I had met many, but you were new.
You struck me as someone intelligent, smart
But then, what I liked most, was your heart.
You sounded as sweet as you had behaved
You were gentle, and you were also saved.
We became friends, and we have been since,
Oh, a charm you've been, a rare, tasty quince.
Before you, I had never known such love,
Such longing forever to behold and to have,
Yet, I was inhibited by the rations of my faith;
"What shall I do; has this become my wraith?"
I pondered, while thinking of a better way,
And, indeed, finally came that romantic day.

133. Charsian Song, IV

[Lady]

You are the one I love, my heart knows
I am the petal of your sanctified rose.
The very day I saw you speak, I knew
To you my soul, heart belong, yes, they do.
I had been loved before, been cared for;
When I met you, my soul declared war.
You were as sweet and gentle as you spoke,
And as serious and blunt as your joke.
Surely, you have captivated all my mind
And to others, my eyes have turned blind.
You're like a hero who has gone on a trip,
Each day, I do long for your returning ship.
Even so I see you in time, hear your voice,
You're still to me, the first and last choice.
The things I have done with you alone,
They rhyme with me perfectly, intone.

134. Charsian Song, V

[Gentleman]

There is only one proof, Oh, my lovely doe
I've not forgotten you in the land of snow,
Nor has my heart stopped beating for you,
For perfect beauties like you, are very few.
Your leg, feet, grub me like boa constrictor,
The pain that I feel, you're the sane inflictor.
Many years have come and have also gone,
Yet, it is your lovely name that I do spawn.
Oh, love, to what can I exactly compare it?
It's like treasure for which one is disparate,
And when he has it, he's nervous to handle,
And only lets it spark brightly like a candle.

135. Charsian Song, VI

[*Lady*]

Surely, I made excuses for you, I know,
Sometimes all I just wanted to say is "hello."
You are the love of my life, my true hero
And I will not always sit in the rear row.
You're always on my lips, in my thoughts,
I know in your heart; I am not of naughts.
Our love knows no limit, it's unconquerable,
And, indeed, it's divine, it's incomparable.

136. Never Left

You live in a planet called Mailaco
The place so divine yet so local
You shine fondly with the wisdom of an angel
For so, I felt it when we tasted thy life gel
How that all these years, fond memories do linger
How that the thought of you will die no longer
For no moment, no comment will erase thy finesse
No tragedy will nudge thy eternal fineness
Forever thy gentle touch will ever be felt;
You're lovely, tightly hold me again like a belt.

137. Kristin

Oh, Kristin, of Canada at Ontario
Oh, how you planned to betray me,
Like a fox, you worked every scenario.
You tried to force me to blindly agree;
And to choose rather to offer on phone
And omit it intentionally in the text.
You've a bitter poisoned heart of stone,
So, in your mind, I was just to be next.
Oh, lucky, luckily, I saw it in between
Before you lied and had me be a scene.

138. 100 Reasons

1. Because you love Jesus
2. Because you are smart
3. Because you know and serve God
4. Because the fear of God is in you
5. Because you pray for others
6. Because you love Church
7. Because you read the Bible
8. Because you're the most forgiving person I know
9. Because you pray regularly
10. Because you have a giving heart
11. Because I have no idea why you love me
12. Because you know my weaknesses but you still love me
13. Because you challenge me to live right
14. Because you correct me when I am wrong
15. Because you chastise me when I am stupid
16. Because you work hard
17. Because you try to understand what I am doing
18. Because you sometimes think of my welfare
19. Because you tolerate my worst habits
20. Because you believe in me
21. Because you think that I am the smartest person you know
22. Because when I am weak you are strong
23. Because you respect me
24. Because you called me "babe!"

25. Because you know my fears and you press me to go on
26. Because you encourage me to work hard
27. Because you compliment me
28. Because you sometimes cook for me
29. Because you insist, I work out although it is tough
30. Because you love healthy and fitness habits
31. Because you love me even if I am broke
32. Because you are willing to relocate with me
33. Because you will not leave me even if have less resources
34. Because you're creative
35. Because I don't worry about financial management; you're a guru
36. Because you have faith that I will always provide
37. Because I feel very accountable to you Because you behave like me sometimes; very stubborn
38. Because you don't give up on a dream, till it is accomplished
39. Because you don't want to beg; you work with your own hands
40. Because when you love something you give it all your strength
41. Because you want to always know where I am
42. Because I call you "Sweetheart" and never realized it is not your name.
43. Because you value my presence
44. Because you speak pleasant sometimes

45. Because you know how I love a cup of honey-lemon tea
46. Because you like competing with me, and I always let you win, deliberately
47. Because I have never known anyone as attentive to details as you, you actually fact-check me
48. Because when I am with you, I feel complete
49. Because I have gone to places where I have never gone with any other person
50. Because when you like something in other men, you want to improve it upon me
51. Because even after knowing you for many years, I still want to know you better
52. Because the more years pass, the more I long for you
53. Because you say sorry when you know you're wrong, rarely with words
54. Because you say "Thank you" when I do or say something for you, unofficially
55. Because you know when to back off from an argument
56. Because you take risks for me
57. Because you do and say everything to make me look good before others
58. Because you go a distance to defend me before the world
59. Because you will do everything for my name to be honored
60. Because you are willing to die for me
61. Because you esteem my opinion
62. Because you bring the best out of me

63. Because no matter where or whom you are with, you are always thinking about me
64. Because you sharpen my character, and intellect
65. Because you are there when I need you, no matter the time or distance
66. Because you don't pretend everything is okay when improvement is needed
67. Because you do give up on habits you know I may not like
68. Because you love children and are concerned about family
69. Because you sometimes sacrifice all you have for others
70. Because you go out of your way to ensure others are well
71. Because you don't pretend to be someone else
72. Because you love shopping (too much, sometimes)
73. Because you invest everything you have in a relationship
74. Because you care deeply for the future
75. Because you care deeply for the earth
76. Because you love knowledge and learning
77. Because you've done everything to make sure that you buy a house or houses
78. Because you devote enormous amount of time searching for cost-saving deals
79. Because I know I can trust you no matter what

80. Because you understand that there is room for improvement
81. Because you're the loveliest soul I know
82. Because you're not just beautiful, you're very humble
83. Because you can be as funny sometimes as you want to be
84. Because you love to make yourself sexy, sometimes
85. Because you make me happy
86. Because you are patience in love-making (you have the grace of patience)
87. Because you value and respect your body
88. Because you respect and honor the marriage bed
89. Because you are the sweetest thing that I know
90. Because you have the warmest heart, ever
91. Because I cannot have enough of you
92. Because I know I need you
93. Because you are my guardian angel
94. Because I can propose you again
95. Because it's like you were made just for me, literally
96. Because I cannot be without you
97. Because you are the answer to my prayers
98. Because you bear children, even if you didn't, I would still love you
99. Because I don't like to see you unhappy
100. Because the only thing that lovelier than love, is you

139. Glorious in Beauty

Lovely like a well-baked sweetery
In soothing attire, she is glittery
Built from angelic elements, she struts
Graceful, spirited and cutely, she thrusts
She does everything right, calm as a well
She is diligent, accomplished as a tail
Glorious in beauty, perfect in manners
She's a trophy wand for winners.

140. Love's Instrument

Make me an instrument of love
Not to desire to be above
May others I consider better
And for those better than me not to feel bitter
That I may seek others to serve
And not my comfort to save
That I should think more highly of all I have met
And not pretend that I am great
If I should be brought to shame
Let it be because what I desire is Your fame
For those less privileged than me
Let me their needs see
All I have learned and achieved, with others may I share
And if anyone is hurt or bereaved, for such may I care
If possible, may I not be known for anything
Other than that, I am trying and I am nothing
May I not only think of my interest
But be concerned with the good of the rest
Teach me to number my days
So, each hour I may follow Your ways
And suffer me not to look down on others
But to treat all as sisters and brothers.

141. Like a Breath

Like breath, I know that you're always there
Like breath, you're present and always here
And yet, like breath, we least think you're there
And like breath, we need you every day here
When life is threatened, and we are short of breath
Down into our souls we search, to the very depth
Oh, Claria, my love, my life, wife of my youth,
Like breath, I need you, that's Valentine's truth.

142. Sweet as Sky is Skype

New as old, so memories of thy childhood haunt
Like a thin leaf, silently waking up from the flaunt
So, our souls neatly weave into ephemeral's deep
So, our thoughts, once novice and thither grip
Oh, sweet to remember are all the words unsaid
Sweet still to know are all the joys unplayed.

143. Like Two Ways

You and I met a long time ago like two ways
We built a relationship that lasts many years
Like two paths, our beginning is in other direction
Like two paths, we have tender, mutual affection
The outgrowths have gone, and also have come
The storms have raged and also become calm,
Yet, your hearts have grown softer and younger
Your memories are louder and now stronger
Because friends like you are hard to come by –
And friendships like ours shall never at all die.
That's why now as ever before, you I cherish
Our dear love and trust will forever flourish
And though time shall end, know this once
My longing of you, will never lose an ounce.

144. Lovely to Have

You can't look at nature and fail to grin at beauty
You can't gaze at peacock and fail to whisper, "Cutie"
The wild sceneries along the banks of the river, flower
The croaking frog, purring fishes in them, shower
There's a memo in the sunrise, and a song when it sets
The moon makes the night glow, the starts its air it wets
You see the zebra graze in the shades, black and white
And hear the lion roar to tenors silhouetted gang fight
Listen to woman's bottoms gyrating inside your head,
Have you pondered she dances to rhythms unheard?
God must have been deliberate, now consider the birds
Their morning melody, minds it wakens, resolves it girds
And these angels called children, O, how lovely to have
For a gift they are, God be thanked, pleasure He gave.

145. Write for You

She came up, smiling, she said,
"Dad, I want to write like you"
Or "read your works, I said."
My daughter has an injection of hope
A lullaby that puts lassitude to sleep,
And she means life can be extended.
I come to the reason I will write,
Oh, my love, once again,
Not for the world to read,
Only if that world meant you;
Not for all to appreciate,
Unless you had said mine was yours.
I write for you, sweet Emmerance,
And you shall love my lines,
Oh, sweet Tashany-Idyllia;
And I never forget your tender heart,
Your lively mind and beautiful face,
For you mean the whole life to me.
And for you, sweet Cuteravive,
My play doll, my endeared doll,
Oh, my dear and flawless Claria,
A wife who is also wise,
My true friend, my moral campus.

146. Ode to Aushi Women

In the area of Luapula
The nut-growing marsh of Mansa
Drums loudly beat on scapula,
Whence flat bottoms are but cancer!

She is just a small tender girl
You can count her black pubic hair
Her chest empty like a funnel
While her nipples are red and bare.

She prods on Bangueulu plateaux
With silly gazelle-like blushes;
She only prefers troupes of twos
With virgin peers in the bushes.

The rare wisdom of her betters
Has not yet charmed her frail figure;
She is shy through her dried fetters
And her lips are out and bigger.

She is not a woman, per say
Her blood is still cold and impure
Because the moon is far away
To chaste her fresh and to endure.

She has not danced *Infunkutu*,
The arrangement of three drums,
The ancient rhythm from Timbuktu;
Nor won the dry skins of wild rams.

She will be taught *Akalela*
To learn how to open taut legs
And she will know *Amalela*
To make kids from fertilized eggs.

They will soak her in Munwa stream
To broaden her pelvis
And fulfill her childhood dream;
To break the curse of a novice.

The sweet juice of soundless rivers
Elongates her womanly shaft
To cure every natural fevers
And purge the lucky winner's haft.

Her sully frame will be made firm
Decked with Kolwe's pure diadems
To date, she has well-run her term
And will earn the prize of rare gems.

Outside, she is cramped with shivers;
Her life's canal is perfected
And her full pulse proudly quivers;
But her self is unaffected.

Her body is bottle in form,
Her nipples are now hard and full,
Her buttocks are firm and uniform
And her waist is mellow to pull!

She has been accepted by Ra
Goddess of the erect solar,
And the shining fruit goes to her,
To court gods of the other polar.

She's joined the Aushi women's core
Who cause charcoal to burn brightly
And make impotent nobles whole,
To mix blood and water rightly.

She can now handle Mandingo,
The killer of angry male lions,
That dancer of the hailed tango
Who with just bare hands breaks irons!

Prefer we the Aushi women
With their ever-protruding backs
Which confuse sanity in men
And accord night the force it lacks.

Their place in humanity
Loses its share in virility,
Gains it in masculinity
And modes it in fertility!

She kills the eyes of on-lookers
And she is not for press showings.
Suitors treasure her like vodkas
And her heart beats higher than wings.

Do not expose her publicly;
Her nude was made for great virtues.
They pass-out rather too quickly;
Those who resist, become statues.

A love son of Luapula soil
Has never known to marry two.
Legend has it that he will toil
And his garden, he will not do.

Oh, these Luapula Aushi curves,
How succulent their deep bosom,
In which mankind vibrates life's waves
And men's desires bloom and blossom!

Sing to her gyrating shifts
And swing through her softly paired rifts.
Mark nimbly her alluring nod
And make safe love in fleshly gold.

BOOK II NATURE'S EXCELLENCE

147. Nature's Love

You can't look at nature and fail to grin at beauty
You can't gaze at a peacock and fail to whisper, "Cutie"
The wild sceneries along the banks of the river, flower
The croaking frog, purring fishes in them, shower
There's a memo in the sunrise, and a song when it sets
The moon makes the night glow, the starts its air it wets
You see the zebra graze in the shades, black and white
And hear the lion roar to tenors silhouetted gang fight
Listen to woman's bottoms gyrating inside your head,
Have you pondered she dances to rhythms unheard?
God must have been deliberate, now consider the birds
Their morning melody, minds it wakens, resolves it girds
And these angels called children, O, how lovely to have
For a gift they are, God be thanked, pleasure He gave.

148. Nature Says It

I look intently at the wonder of nature and sigh
That the creator must be a genius who works
For all the intricacies found in the wild
And the simplicity we may not see
The delicacy of all creativity altogether fancy
And of all that we may overlook;

In the tree trunk we find beauty, just as in a leaf
In birds pecking their wings and dragon flies landing
In animals hides as in their procreativity,
In the snake`s eyes and tongue, in poisons and myrrh
Just as in the streams of quiet waters as in waterfalls
For so all creation in plain view speaks

In man we marvel at such a being as complex,
Yet we see not how all for good come to labor
For nothing in nature compares to imagination`s pond
But yet still we faint at the sight of what is internal
In this we have a pledge life cannot afford to honor
Only that we should live wonders to admire for eternity.

149. When Death Be Sweeter

Our days shall be told as a flower when its petals be withered
Thank the sun, O you lovely blends of Nature's blessed azure
A bird shall not fly when only one of its sides be not feathered
Ask the ant, for it knows where its food comes from for sure
Neither in accumulations nor accomplishments lies our value
But in that eternal gem of service and kindness one to another
In vain we hurt innocence, erecting statue after statue
In this we find true light and joy, in loving each as a brother
O you, your strength you spend on chasing money and fame
Do stop and pause, how much of it shall you take to the grave?
For riches may be desirable, but better still is a good name
They who will say, "I am sorry, forgive me," these are brave
But those who love others as themselves, these will never die
Though they be all but bones, their soul will ever live on high.

150. The Heart

This – life's pumping flesh – deserves another look
The pulsating veins, their militant force they hook
The tenacious aortas, endless ventures they book
The beat they drum, melodious moments they brook
Whence to life, to light and bright purpose it stays
The chanting of its chambers, death on fours it slays
The silence of its valves, the ballet dancer must stop,
The composer's muteness merges to eternal drop
And the source that moves a clock's singing needle,
 Will, today, become a still, stalled, rusting riddle.

151. Saying Sorry

You say, to say sorry is a sign of weakness
I say that, not saying sorry is wickedness
For those who freely forgive one another
Have also won back a sister and a brother
To be good friends for a hundred years
We'd have to bear each other in many ways
I admit, I will wrong you many times over
But I confess, I will always love you forever
Even when you don't think that I mean it
My intention is to build, that is my spirit
For you and you, who I have done wrong to
I ask you now, forgive me, I love you, too.

152. Fruitless Lullaby

Cry thee till night should
Turn to day
And laugh where no rhythms are
On the way
The loves of yesteryear are
Elegant in youthful form
And the singing we make is silenced
By winter's storm
Till we age and only these memories
We shall relish
And in them our sons and daughter
We dare to embellish.

153. Each Face

Each face brings to one a dance,
Each time a story the years have told
For we shun not the first fruits of prime
In ancient, rustic and eventful youth
So much we don't see when we leave
And meet again, and hope springs life.

154. Thank God I'm Black

Since my birth, my mother told me I was me, a human
That on this earth, there was only one race, from one man
That was the faith, the belief I hold on even up to today
Whether in mirth or deep sorrow, in this hope I stay
That I'm black, that I have no regrets, and no lack
Thank God I am no other, thank God I'm black
Growing up as a child, I had no illusion of race, or of color
I frolicked freely into the field, no need of place, or of valor
My dreams were mild, my heart at rest, my vision clear
All around me was beauty-wide, grandeurs and dear
That I'm black, that it mattered less, it left no mark
Thank God I am brother to all, thank God I'm black
Then I grew much older, I was silenced by invisible words
My blood began to get colder, I discovered many worlds
My nights became shorter, my friends fewer, I was lost
My days turned hotter; innocence became tempest-tossed
That I'm black, it mattered more, it cut like a shark's teeth

Thank God I am not another's slave, thank God
I'm not beneath
I am known by many synonyms, black or even
African
Sometimes by antonyms, "of color" or even black
American
I am sung in hymns, though in the rainbow I am
omitted
I am a butler or servant in films, in prison I am
committed
That I'm black, I absorb all colors of people in me,
am not stuck
Thank God I am father to diversity, thank God
I'm black
Now I know, I am proud to be black, I make
white pure
Even more, I fit all shades, I am universal, I make
light sure
And above all, I am tolerant, I embrace cultures, I
forgive
I have a goal – to be everything to all peoples, to
give
That I am black, it is not the same as being
dark
Thank God I am a mother to humanity, thank
God I'm black

155. Moody Toronto Whether

They wake up, day in and night out, in self-denial
And all long, they leave her just how they founder her
She brags of multiple husbands, all still in self-denial
And why not, she determines the day and maps the night
While they sleep, she sneaks into a cold room and turns it low
The men stout, children flout, but senior moult,
The women, her rivals, shout, "Increase heat the more!"
In one day, she changes her moods into three matters
In the morning, men hate her, she frees her cold sores
In long jumpers, pajamas and shovels, men clear the while vomitus
In the afternoon, she extends her long legs, to open her pores
At night, she springs to the South and summers in the East
Her husband, the people, does not know what she is doing
He searches from the swelling North to the dipping West
But he comes up empty, dumped and stops going.

156. Heartcry

Perfection, to you is a garment
That fits my soul;
You're an epitome of beauty infantile
And grace admixed in perfect measure;
Oh, this windily figure who moves hearts
With every step she moves heavens
And in every absence, oh my soul you crash;
Each day I live in the shadow of
Your fond remembrances;
Your heart, that fleshly gem in crimson,
Crafted from marble sinews,
Tender like angels' wings,
And lovely as a queen's chamber;
In your bosom mind and matter consent,
My untrained voice sings a song,
And my hands scribble lover's lines;
You stand as a mighty tower
And those legs taste like honey to behold,
To brag about your love is in order,
To say, "I feel you good" is bolder;
Oh, Heartcry, its poetry, lovely and true
Oh, Heartcry, like a woman, I love.

157. The Mighty Fall

When the mighty fall
So, their arrogance go
In praises and song, they are sung
But forlorn they never again sprung

When the mighty fall
Media houses make more
They mislay when they are low
While in past victory they flow

When the mighty fall
And their worlds with them all
For in their stories, deified
In their fall, they are Satanized

When the mighty fall
Their pomp with them falter
In fame their worthy ever glow
In their shame all their prides swelter

When the mighty fall
Should we also not fall?
We love them in their glory
Shouldn't we lose in their gory?

158. Aren't Just a Number

In this land of many chances
And opportunities
I still feel like just a number
Nay, am not just a number, a color
Nay, have a clan, a tribe, a culture
Nay, says I am not just a number
The medium is the peace
They pander like others are events
And they announce to exclude us
Nay, am not just existing
Nay, I have a talent, a habit
Nay, I have character and manners
The West is color-blind, let them say
The East has people who are persons
And the South is not an island
Let the people of color emerge
And let them be a people, no a number
Aren't just a number
Am a human being.

159. Someone Help

What shall I say
When my mouth is treason
Where can I go
When my home is a prison

Where shall I stay
When I don't have a reason
How can I dream
When chilly winter is my season

How shall I walk
When my land is forsaken
How could I dance
When my feet are but broken

What shall I talk
When my tongue has nev'r spoken
How can I speak
When my soul within is shaken.

160. Fits Any Size

Size does count
But only the size of the heart
In shapes, humans come
And of diverse looks, they balm.

Ugliness is only fiction,
But lovely is every mind
Within every human story
With a Yeoman's history.

Sex is cheaper than love
For with toys

Humans may find pleasure
But only with geniality
Does any size fits.

161. Summer Dammar

The shoes that I am wearing
Have steel toes
And the glass through which I gaze
Is tinted within

I count hours, like accounting for pecks
And the tick of the watch
Stands suspended, like a kite
As if life has given up tryin'

The clothes that I am wearing
Have steel imbedded inside
And the map through which I peep
Will lead me straight home.

162. Sounds

Faces, cold, sullen and morbid
Blood, bold, sour, and sordid
Memory plays on your views
And hear sounds without news.

Hear the rhythm the drums fuse
Tear down the mask they use
Ululate and whistle in Bemba
And set aflame a blinking ember.

Oh, the music of striking laughter
Composition of a native drifter
The shadows eastward tire
To set shaking waists on fire

The land comes awake every night
Daughters line to see sons fight
There is a party within a feast
And winners are crowned with a fist.

163. Diapers

These diapers long gazed upon
As they whimper through time
On mere papers of rare cushion
And the dream of healthy babies

Though the diapers be wet
Through the blinking of mirrors
Their smell breed memories
And in them stories we keep.

Your name is like sticking gum
Your speech is a blubbing charm
Your limbs nimble and tender
And in our hands rests your pure heart.

This summer we tread the mall
Wearing only flaps and little Os
And changing many, many diapers
With love-dots on joyful wipers.

164. Oh, My God

Oh, my God, wow!
What wows is an owl
An owl lives in the trees
The trees grow in a forest
The forest in which birds hide
Hiding from slings and stones
Stones of lime and marbles
Marbles which built the city
The city is Ottawa
Ottawa is in Ontario
Ontario is a province
A province is in Canada
Canada is a country
Country is a kind of music
Music may be hip-hop
Hip-hop is an art
Art is made by brush and paint
Paint is of many colors
Colors may be in orange
Orange is a citrus fruit
Fruit may be sour or sweet
Sweet is like sugar
Sugar is from sugarcane
Sugarcane is grown in Brazil
Brazil won the 2002 World Cup
World Cup was in South Africa
South Africa is in Africa
Africa is a continent
A continent has nations
Nations may be Zambia
Zambia has 13 million people
People have different names
Names like John or Mwewa
Mwewa is in Bemba
Bemba is a tribe

A tribe consists of nationals
Nationals have races
Races may be white or black
Black absorbs light
Light comes from the sun
The sun is in the sky
The sky is in heaven
Heaven is, oh my God,
God's holy throne.

165. Newspapers

North of newly built station and
East of the empty plot of land is
West of the well-known bank, and
South of the coliseum's magic block

People read news everyday
And there is no day without it
Papers are spread out in layers
Early each morning just before
Roads become filled with people
Selling and buying newspapers.

166. Bemba Tales

This bird looks like
My own mother
Even the eyes look like
My own mother
The mouth looks like
My own mother
Even the ears look like
My own mother

Pounded groundnuts
Do you look like
Your mother or father?
For your mother is beautiful
Though you may look like
Your own father,
Resemble your mother
For she is beautiful

This stick is mine
I saw it at *Katenta*
This stick resembles my own
I got it at *Katenta*

This stick of mine has spots
This stick of mine has dots
This stick of mine is speckled
This stick of mine is
Black and white

This stick is dappled
Like a leopard
This stick is stippled
Like a tiger
This stick is freckled
Like a giraffe

This stick is speckled
Like a zebra.

167. Music in Zambia

Nerves are cold, sullen and unexecuted
Energy is sour, squalid and inundated
Memory plays against views
All that is seen are souls without spirit

Miss the rhythm that skins ooze
Hear the sounds of tar-marked drums
Speak with a waist and a hand
And brace awake to pure ecstasy

Music in Zambia is our brew
The sun showers with delight
Shades dance and smug
White flowers gather to cheer

Places are bumpy and brown
Mountains laugh with their chests
Valleys whisper within spaces
And in Zambia music speaks
Louder than echoes.

168. Free Soil

People, people begin to make room
To let the white-shadowed groom
Pass through to his fated doom
To gain shape after one zoom

They are not ashamed to brag
About the newly-scented rag
On which the Queen of hip-hop lags
Followed by boys carrying bags

It is a land where fools carry wallets
And the wisely-born hold mallets
To shape effigies and chisel wood
In order to gain a penny for food

The snake winds lazily in rush hour
As tolled-cars small and large cower
In the heat of slowly-burning oil
Where hearts curse costs of free soil.

169. No Sorry Life

There is nothing light about life
You may make it lighter if you can
The more lightened you become
You know it is not done lightly

Do you carry something heavy?
Do you have hands heavily tied?
Is this life heavier to you?
And the heaviest is lurking still?

You need easier ways to conquer
Refuse to pick on easy routes
And face tough times with ease
Whenever you can, take it easily

All the difficulties of life
Do teach us nothing about difficulty
As when you help in difficult times
You, difficultly, make it to the end.

170. Nests of Newmarket

She looks through the window
In the gravel by green meadows
As her heart dances to the flaps
Of the skipping scarlet macaw

This uniform, so naturally dark
This scream, which shudders nature
These parrots, in their raw colors
Their wings, readily they wag

Here and there moves whimper
Up and down their beaks simper
Side to side raises echoes deeper
Tether to thither lovers get hyper

171. The Way You Are

I love you the way you are
I love your heard
Just the way it is shaped
I love your neck
Just the way it bends
I love your chest
And the mounds it creates
I love your bosom
And the size it is in
I love your legs
For the way you walk
I love your feet
For the way they pierce
I love your hands
They touch softly and charmly
I love you
As perfect when you're you

172. Healing Poesy

When thy senses be disquieted within
Thou reacheth thy hands further
And in thy medicine cabinet
Thou grabeth a bottle of pills full

Thou softeneth thy raging nerves
And silenceth thy panting sinews
With thy stream of healing fluid
And thou resteth fondly well

In these mine warring soul
Oh, poesy, thou healeth me
In these thy words well metered
Thy lines doth sooth mine acuity

173. Canadian Spring

The sun doeth shine steadily in Canuck
The flowers doth wave happily in Kanata
The grass in mountainless prairies
And cars through west speed to east
Spring doeth shine on caffeinated brains
Cows and bears in shades hide
And farmers on pumpkin skins drilleth
To shun devils from spreading colors.

174. Down Recession Street

Down recession street
Nothing out of the ordinary is seen
Green loans and maple trees line-up
And the same old buildings stand

Down recession street
Large Ford cars drive as usual
Trucks and vans stop at red lights
And Esso gas station is busy as always

Down recession street
Chrysler plants are closing down
The work force is reduced to graffiti
And all production is done by managers

Down recession street
Bearing deep semblance to Petawawa
While GM plants shut down in Oshawa
And all look for help from Ottawa

175. Highways

In lanes two and one they drive
As trucks and vans swerve in and out
To and from work hearts race in throbs
As they speed through round abouts

No matter what you wish to do
Not to follow set out traffic rules
Is to risk your safety and survival
For people who drink and drive pay

Do what you can to reach the end
You will not wrong the rear mirrors
Nor offend your sober-rested mind
And thus, you escape unseen errors

Loved ones all need you breathing
For although you drive all alone
You carry in your family and friends
And to arrive alive is your thrive.

176. Money

Learn thee to appreciate money
And change thee thy money attitudes
For thy confusions regardeth money
Breedeth twisted facts of wealth

Know thee that money is existence
Understandeth freedom's next of kin
For as thousands lacketh its power
In poverty countless doth succumb

Educate thyself in providence's drill
Coach thyself in shortages' tricks
For in hard times knowledge winneth
And in thy ignorance death loometh

People ought to hold money in bounty
Every purse boometh with laughter
And in thy plethora hold thee thy pass
To wander the earth till Doomsday.

177. Four + 1 Messengers

They may come from anywhere
The four messengers from hell
In their path and from nowhere
They arrive without a bell

AIDS makes her nest in Africa
H1N1 lays her young in America
SARS leases her spores in Asia
CANCER rests her head in Austrasia

Dig up mass graves in a desert
Deny Hitler a noon dessert
For all race as all color he refuses
Jews and Blacks, he kills with gas fuses

No-one is innocent in Europe
None, when discriminations gallop
America pleads "not guilty" to blood
And Africa is submerged by a flood

COVID-19, thou servest Africa of triage
And saveth mine land a purgatorial viage
But Europe and America thou treatest worse
Thus, forfeit hauling mine land in a hearse.

178. No Author of Tragedy

I am not an author of tragedy
I write what happens in reality
But I will not at all be rigid
When so much lead to cruelty

I am not a critic of mass industry
Nor do I see souls labor like machinery
And I will not keep my mouth dry
Nor only make advocacies summary

I am for humanitarianism
But in the poor name of the victims
Money is collected for many an ism
While kids pair in miserable teams

I am not an opponent of aid
I only tell of hypocrisy as a fact
In the name of butter and bread,
Poverty and profit make a pact.

179. Didn't Feel Like Writing

I didn't feel like writing poetry
For my darling Muse be asleep
To awake a drowsing mind
Takes more skill than rhyming
And the hand that draws and paints
Is saner than an idle clock.

I didn't want to draft a narrative
For the senses be off and dull
To design an end-rhyme epigram
Takes more skill than prosing
And the length of the work itself
Doesn't account for real genius.

180. Shakespeare Unedited

Thou in thy dream saw Shakespeare
In the dead of night saw thou a spear
For the wife of that venerable Macbeth
This lady of vice and untimely birth
Thee in thy dream also saw Portia
In kind and mind as Obama's Sasha
Yet in thy wake watches Sinatra
The nard which played Cleopatra
Whence that night Julius Caesar
In battles trekked he with no visa
To surpass the spoils of Richmond
And to the Senate be gave diamond
Thou wrote on thy knee: Elizabethan
Which thou recanted to biblical Nathan
Who in predictions of David or Pharaoh
Who the priming looks of Romeo
Would dare not crown Richard the Third
For who wore bloody gowns unaided.

181. Filibusting

The plant in and out, empty
The force that work them, grumpy
The tummy groans easy, bumpy
And the sun outside, so hotty
In history we learn, but naughty
The past comes, to haunt, a dumpty.

182. Tear of God

They lash junkets of donor support
On the pained daughters of the soil
All in the hope to redeem a race
Of a people mired in blood

The grim image of black Africa
Illuminated by an over-shined sun
Lamps its toxins of artificial gems
On a land deep in solstice shadows

This aid that always comes late
Given by greased governments
Is only a drop in a gigantean ocean?
As kids and women in tears bask

A tear of God lazily dropped
And who for Africa shall mourn
Who, for broken and forsaken land
Who, for stricken and afflicted band?

183. Move On

I pretended I was a man
Yet, I was a boy in men's seat
I advanced and won a woman
And that I knew the reality

She was wittily and gorgeous
She was focused and mature
She carried herself prodigiously
And moved herself majestically

For a time, I realized my weakness
When I could not provide for her
Since I did not have money
And many plans wasted in the soul

Like a snake, my skin peels off
When I appeal to my best angels
My worst demons only show up
Yet I move on, I search for life.

184. Rise and Go

Listen to me, and hear me
I am not a quitter, not at all
I am a conqueror, and see
I will gain and increase more

Times are hard ahead
But equal I am to the task
I will not cut hair nor beard
Until this proverb I unmask

Those who know this agree
That I have come a long way
That I will not falter by degree
That in the course I will stay

I am a winner and a champion
I will not be down or get low
For winning is my own companion
And all ahead, will fall below.

185. Sleep On

However grievous your day
How much pain it brings
So quick recovery you may
And too dinly sounds it rings

Go to your comfort and inn
Sleep on it and do recoup
As the day draws to its mean
So will the pain a coup

The brave may lose a war
The weak may win a battle
If fatigue took its cruel toll
And pain is allowed to rattle

You will sleep well and sound
As your mind gets good rest
So will your sanity rebound
And your power at its best.

186. Morning Joy

The night with tempest rages
The storms with rage troubles
There is hail and dark rains
And all-around darkness reigns

Sorrow and pain quickly invade
There is neither peace nor joy
All around only tears and fear
And you think life is but veer

You woke up one raining day
You thought it was all over
You wished you could be free
And you found it was not to be

There is a little waking flame
Up on the distant horizon
For all your troubles will tame
And you will win and rise on.

187. Gain in Pain

Whatever you lose
Do not lose your confidence
Wherever you go
Do not leave your hope

In whatever situation
There is a way of escape
In every circumstance
There is good hidden inside

Like a wound, it will heal
And like days, it will pass
For each lost moment
There is a star about to rise

There is no year without a season
There is no delay without a reason
Only death never shares its pain
And after shame there is gain.

188. Investment Principle

There is nothing that may happen
That people will hasty to say
That it was done without purpose
Since nothing happens for nothing

For everything, awful or lawful
Has an underlying meaning
This may not be now apparent
But will reveal itself in time

The law of life is "take and give."
So that in every circumstance,
There is one gift that will offend
And its value grows in silence

So, in whatever you are involved
Where your time and energy are
There is also your future and reward
And greatness in time it will award.

189. Mulock Drive

There beneath a green-faced forest
By the highway astride four-o-four
Our minds conceived lively lines
By the intersection of rushing hearts

In the upper country of Newmarket
By the love of young Mulock Drive
And the enchanting Harry Walker
There we walked with singing pens

Lady who faithfully works
Mother whose children she laps
Wife of a man of many plans
For daily she dropped him there

So long we have religiously come
To these fountains of living pulses
To the land where money sanely brag
And men seldom go on retirement.

190. The Transit

The TTC is not just a bus station
It is a bus destination
And the best Canada's bus stops
With its blue and ember bus tops
To catch a bus, check the bus time
And know about rush hour's bus prime
But do not carry a bus fare
Just sit in a nearby bus chair
And there wait for the bus driver
Who will pull down the bus lever
Which starts to run the bus engine.
None tells of the bus origin
For there is no bus conductor
Nor a transit facilitator.
All persons pre-pay a bus fee
While the driver keeps the bus key.
For once they close off the bus door,
It is time to bus all.

191. The City

Oh, the City; tentacles it spreads like a pregnant octopus;
Women in legs long and spacious coil;
As down the city-centers busy and ness mesh;
Here I walk, Toronto;
Splendous your restaurants;
Missed calls, you mock."

192. City of Livingstone

City of Livingstone, Zambia
Many memories embedded here
In sands so loose and terrains so quiet
By Maramba, sounds of shining colors
The progeny of mixed races;
By Helen Britel, music glows to disco.
Here the route treks to Victoria Falls
The locals called Smokes with Thunder:
The waters boil at ephemeral speed
The winters warmed by rising fumes;
The monkeys sing to tangled thickets
Draining their natural call
On heads of state's bored-head!

City of Livingstone, Zambia
Canopy of Chief Mukuni
Who alone knows the riddle
Of Nyami-nyami, a lady-snake
Who guards the river and waves!
Here civilizations meet nudely
On rapids, kayaks *sea*-saw freely
Women under trees sit nakedly
While men watch so drily

The sun shines briskly at Sun Inn
Here prostitutes meet their match
With sticks that sing, shoes that talk
Business takes on a twist
And a window to the future
Opens widely over Hillcrest skies
Semi broken; semi whole
So, we dingo to *kapentas* partly rotten
To beans with skimmed insects
And meats that are scarce like frost

City of Livingstone, Zambia
No place much better
No season much sweeter.

193. Father's Day

To my daughters this Father's Day:
I am happy to be your father;
I love you like no other.
In deep love, I made you;
And those who make me happy
Like you do, are few.
To be a father is the greatest gift
I have ever received from God;
And I will forever
Love, cherish, and care for you,
No matter what you turn out to be
Even if you don't bring me gold.

194. Dying While Black

They die brutal deaths, these kids
Just for being Black kids.
They are gathered in these prisons
Like chicken packed in small prisons.
They are readied for a mass slaughter,
A deep, dirty, Black slaughter.
Their only crime, because of color
Just because they wear Black color.

They lie in wait, these Blue policemen
And it pleases every policeman.
These prisons are full of human sorrow
Creating creatures that bring sorrow.
When Black goes in saintly and dark
It comes out Whitened, motives dark.
When justice opens its eyes,
Law becomes a whip against Brown eyes.

195. Experience of Songs

A huge White thing in the nimbus
 "Smile, smile" in rhymes of rumpus!
"Why are my son and daughter quiet?"
"They are both in the world, not quite.

"Because I was sold by their soiled son,
And cry out of the summer's sun,
They unclothed into nudity of actuality,
And ignored to say the prose of delight.

"And I am sad; I don't party nor thrill,
They didn't think they hurt my will,
And didn't desecrate the devil's armor,
Who made up a hell of our humor?

196. More than Toys

They are more than toys
They breathe and feel and have wings
And they bring great joys.
They can clearly talk
And far from being only things
They have legs and can walk.

Look how neat their eyes
The moment they come into Earth
And you can't but say, "Yes!"
Tonight, strengthen your faith.
They carry a fruitful porch
Of memories we never knew
And histories we barely watch;
Love babies, and many years, too.

197. Be Happy

No day gives you a chance to smile
Even when you walk for a little while
Or take a thousand and one mile
Because happiness has no style;
It is a thought so nice and fragile.

Be happy in all cheerful moods
And give humankind many goods
For those who hide joy in the woods,
Forego their own daily foods;
And let children starve in the hoods.

198. Stormy August 21

Harshly, it rains along Eglinton;
Hail like sharp-pointing bullets;
Children in mothers' arms buried,
While cell-phones lose potency.

Thunder raves minds and rakes nerves,
The angry roar kills peace in and out,
Pinioning lightning swathes up and down,
Oh heavens, all courage in humans faint!

Driver stops the bus, nowhere
"I can't see outside the bus," squirms all,
Windows sips with fuming liquid venom
And all plans aren't going, anywhere.

"Should have reached Kennedy by now!"
"I by-passed my last destination!"
"I will miss my job appointment!"
Agony, agony, on Ontario's stormy day.

199. Arms of Death

It rushed past by me, so softly and comfortably
I saw the elements faint right before me slowly
And I knew that those who experience it loved it;
Arms of death are graced with soft sponges of life.

This strong feeling of heavy dizziness comes fast
Rarely have chance to wave good-bye to love ones
Senses and thoughts are forever suspended
From ephemeral rays into eternal waves.

Death may be not our enemy, but our transport
We determine the destination by the deeds we did
Good or bad;
This feeling, relaxes all hopes, brings peace
undying.

200. Death Shall Not

Death shall not be my end`s script
Nor the fear thereof my early exit
In life as in death my hopes rest
For my soul in peace finds quest;

Death shall not be solace for thee
If you forget to entrust your fee
In the hands of him who saves
And either fault or sin he waves;

Death shall not be an excuse
For the deeds good you refuse
Always doing trivial assignments,
Neglecting God`s appointments;

Death shall not be the stop of breath
Nor the cover of the coldest earth
For in His heart are many places
To safeguard all in His graces;

Death shall not be the sentence
For those who deal without sense
In life for Jesus' sake, to die to gain
And respite our minds without pain;

Death shall not be for the now
For its pangs at Calvary bow
Seventy plus a promise to live
In this true Word I do believe.

201. Change or the Same

He was going to decide to change
Because he couldn't afford the same
But he was going to meet a challenge
If not, he would hate being the same

"How can I shake this misery," he said
Foes and friends live under the same sun
And from the same toil they are paid
Oh, how unfair it is under the sun!

He dragged himself towards the library
Old and new books shyly stared at him
He had last been here in February
And no-one stood in for him

"All these books are banks of insight"
He was thinking his thoughts aloud
"But they bring me nothing to bite"
He decided to speak up aloud.

202. Why Not Me

As I walk alone,
Along this busy street
Even in this silence
On top of summer's heat
Thoughts torture my poor soul
From within,
Frightful punches in my heart
Begin,
And I sob:
"Why not me?"

I see those who live
In elevated mansions,
They drive elegantly
And wear lurid blouses,
They tint their cars
And possess lots of money,
They are followed by everyone
Like they breed honey.
And within me I glob:
"Why without me?"

I watch men as they play
On technology's best,
Women as they strut streets
In angelic majesty,
I hear the winds blow
At great force to the west,
And all it leaves behind
Is me brownie and dusty.
In anger I ask:
"Why not them?"

I am jealousy of those
Who seem happy with life,
They are accompanied,
By pomp so splendid
In their path,
They leave feasts of pride and strife
And have others wipe
Where they have fended.
With a banger I ask:
"Why only them?"

203. Change with Change

They claim
they will bring change
When all they do
is preach the old message
And their people
don't find this strange;
For you least grow
through the old rug'ed passage.

The people
stare in mesmerizement and wonder
They have the same lines
all their deeming life
And they are confused
and can't ponder;
They feel like they've been
cut with a rust'd knife.

204. No Fundamentalist

I am not a Christian fundamentalist;
I am a Christian,
There is a difference;
I believe in grace as Paul preached it to the
Ephesians,
And I love the inference;
But there are those who use the Bible woefully
amiss,
Such I avoid;
They pick this and for what does not, they dismiss,
That leaves a void;
God truly loves the world and does not exclude,
The good or the bad;
Yet, modern fundamentalists know whom to
include,
And that is sad;
I don't use my faith as a weapon of condemnation,
I use it to help;
Everyone who is human fits into my combination,
And they don't yelp;
There is commonality in every extremity,
Christianity or Marxism;
Every act of love and care for the needy builds
amity,
It mortifies separatism;
Embrace and accept all as composite brotherhood,
Which is veracious;
One world guided by one love and not hatred
would
Be very precious.

205. Fear Nothing

Don't fear anything
But believe every good thing
Don't be diminished
But let everything you touch
Be established
Don't be told you can't
But speak to yourself that they shan't;
Don't look at yourself and say, "Not me"
But look at yourself and shout,
"Nobody but me!"
Don't be overwhelmed by a problem
But overwhelm your problems
With chants of "Awesome!"
Don't be reduced,
But insist that you must be increased.
Don't give up and falter
But keep moving smoothly just like water.
Don't be called a coward,
But let all your effort, energy
And time be a reward.
Don't let the powerful intimidate you
But let God defend
And bring to pass what is due.
Don't die young,
But live large, with a bang.

206. Come What May

The morning comes silently, fresh but expectedly
The past's regrets pass quickly, rather unexpectedly
Surely, there is a design to life, a plan and reasons
And nature prides itself in the symphony of seasons
It is not a neglected error that future ends not in "day",
Only now, and what's gone lets "day" attach that way
Because what has not yet happened doesn't harm
And hope is the reservoir that holds faith's charm
To the stars we clasp candles when the light of life ends
In the sun we witness light's rebirth towards new trends
And today, there will be plenty of memories to embrace
For yesterday is a dot that we cannot afford to trace;
Oh, come what may, the flowers will bud yet again,
May will come, summer is here to relieve the pain.

207. End Shall Last

When my heart shall beat last
And all dreams shall forever cease;
When the drawl shall be cast,
Then all pain shall finally ease.

When rhythm of life ends
The path to Heaven shall begin;
With speed cross timeless bends,
The faithful shall indeed go in.

When music be no more,
All plans shall collapse and vanish;
The trade of daily chore,
Shall be feted, aims shall banish.

When life expels the breath,
And life business begins rest;
To exit from the earth,
This thought fearful, the flight bles'ed.

208. Smells of Coffee

The mornings begin in the usual way
With cars, men and women willing to pay
For freshly-scented, darkly brewed coffee
Which most also imbibe with hard toffee.

It is a touch aware of Canada
Although some citizens of Grenada
Still think about beats of the Caribbean
And share in DNA make of an amphibian.

When my children wake up just everyday
They ask for tea with milk in semi-grey,
Will they also grow up drinking caffeine,
Although it is addictive like morphine?

They stand shoulders high in the Maple trees
Their hands folded into doubles or threes
And they reflect on the goals of hockey,
As they listen to Canuck's top jockey.

209. Insulted in America

They gather around media phones and shades
And insult me because I am not six feet tall.
They gossip of high art, music or movie trades
While me and others petite are left to fall.

They recite them in plots of love novels
And describe their figures of great beauty
But in all my experience and travels
I have found no one as Claria as fluty.

My daughters say that I am handsome
And my wife knows I have great looks,
But in America they think I am not ransom
And they can't narrate me in books.

In America they think all others are not good
They will say no-one from China and Japan is
They gang around basketball for their food
And wouldn't admit others can be fizz.

But I have no regrets to be who I am
In Canada, wisdom reigns higher than heights
And for you, O North, I am up early a.m.
The insults I received; I drowned under weights.

210. Ashen Pebbles

The hilarity of them who thump through the thumb
Of ashen pebbles;
In which they thrum through the stricken crumb
Of sunken fables;
The thrill of them whose thrust falls on numb
Aces of shrunken tables;
Who hung the tongue of a slyly throated lamb
With molten cables

These hard-earned medals will only be metals
Damned to the ghettoes;
These blooms subjected to a loom of broken petals
Gammed without vetoes;
These garlands from the land of our twisted sepals,
Our jammed mementoes;
And the stories of our glories deified in the temples
Of hammed potentials

A throne thrown in jumbled destinations
By a confederation of nations,
These high hopes of childhood hijacked by fate,
Becoming the coveted bait of hate;
And the gentle voice of discrimination
Breeds consternation
In blanket canopied hearts of immigrants,
Enslaved by the lavish junkets of grants.

211. Words of the Departed

Words of the departed loved ones
Will not be forgotten.
Even though they have long left us,
Their words still ring new life.

Like a parrot, we rewind them
And repeat them often.
For they bring sweet memories
Of times and joys we shared.

That sad and gloomy day of loss
When death's messenger knocks,
With these remembrances of love,
We drown them and move on.

212. Do Not Cry

I heard you when you cried
And your face said it all:
"Mommy I miss you," you said
And your voice fainted.

And these words, unedited
Followed, unscripted:

"I feel rejected in this world
Where you have left me.
Mommy, you left me alone.
You were there for me always.
There is no-one by my side.
I miss your kindness
Rest in peace, dear mom."

I was there when you cried
And offered my hank
Then you dried.

213. Dirge of My People

The dirge my people cry,
Oh, these songs they sing
When loved ones are gone
Are full of sorrows
When they are sung.

When they lament silently,
"Oh, you people without mercy,
You have grabbed Chandwe
For no reason at all."

These bring grief and regret
Which touch the soul.

My people dance as they mourn
And sing rhythms of grief.
Their limbs barely move
When sorrow, melody and pain
Are mixed in the pot of loss.

The dirges my people cry;
To placate their dead they try.

214. Friends Gone

Our few days are told as a tale
A remorse fact I now must tell.
Once you hear that pitiless bell;
It has destiny turning pale.

I do recall a few loved friends
Who lamely met their story ends
After that human's nasty fiend,
Their life he denied to extend.

Surely every good turns to waste
When winds bluster by way of west;
Again, people have failed their test
For none comes to detail past taste.

While our deceased leave a picture,
And a voice of their departure,
Sorrow is not a good teacher,
Nor sorry a better preacher.

215. Goodbye to Sara

Joshua used to ignore
The sleeps of her tongue
And Sara never minded
How she used her language.

She told Joshua a story
Of her past date with Peter
And Sara never minded
How she used her language.

One day she told him
That Peter was better a guy
And Sara never minded
How she used her language.

She said Peter was rich
And gave her all she wanted
And Sara never minded
How she used her language.

And Sara told Joshua
To dress like old boyfriends did
And Sara never minded
How she used her language.

One day Joshua met Jane;
Jane was down to earth
And Joshua was happy
Jane understood who Joshua was.

Joshua came back to Sara

To say that it was over
Because Sara never minded
How she used her language.

Goodbye to Sara.

216. The Grip

Dark Shadow
It comes to all like a shadow
And beckons us to enter the door
To take us through eternal meadow
To places prepared for all.

Endless Journey
Tough no one may clearly say
How far on this journey to stay
By the flurries of a clear day
We know don't return our way.

Abode
The spirits of those who depart
For so nature that knows in part
Does tell us they are set apart
For places known by the expert.

Trespass
Though your power in trespass be
One has triumphed over thee
To make safe passage for you and me
When our eyes are closed we see.

Hope
They go each to their very end
In doubt we may know or pretend
But know we in peace they spend
And in hope their faults mend.

217. Elegy to Kenya

O Kenya, hide thy bloody face
And look not on thy bloody mess
Because thy recrimination
Has trodden many a nation.

Thou art now insensitive
To the plight of thy own children
And for women, thou'nt perceptive
For in their ruin thy terrors reign.

By thine western end Eldoret
Thirty-three innocents perish
Butcher'ed at a brutal rate
While skulls prayed in a deaf parish.

Many voices are heard far away
Yet here they fall on aching trust
And no reason will dare to sway
The shame of man's deadly past.

Drums in Africa are beating,
And the children are not dancing.
Women endure in child labor,
To enter worlds they will abhor.

In a butcher's slaughtering sword,
Elections are but a by-word;
And democracy's sunny face
Is mired in anarchy's dire race.

And for the fair arm of the law,
Guns rule and danger guard the poll
While old regimes cling to power,
To destroy liberty's tower.

218. Destiny Killers

Pain runs through his veins
Like a sharp end of a dagger.
Thoughts came out dense
And words were few.

He remembers the dream
He had for his next of kin.
He took his time and money
And worked only for her.

He bought her all school needs
And saved for her college.
He moved her to a better place,
Away from destiny killers.

she broke the law of decency
When she disregarded his efforts;
She met her destiny killer
And cut her destiny short.

219. Life in Circles

Yesterday remains white;
Today it's green
And tomorrow is black.

Life in circles.

In memory lanes we drive
Today your son
And tomorrow your guardian.

Life's imperfidious visage.

We eat, drink and clothe,
We loaf, work and shelter,
That is all there is to life.

Life in circles.

And the unexpected happens:
Servants become bosses
Girls become boys
Beggars become lenders
And hours become minutes.

But when men marry men
Days turn to nights
And it snows all day non-stop;

The circles just continue.

220. Secure

In the middle of the bush
When you leave me behind
I feel very insecure.
When you come back
And talk to me like a friend,
I feel very secure.

When alone at the middle of bushes
Just a thought of you
Makes me secure again.
Whatever you say,
When we are in the thicket
I just believe

And in the shadow of your presence
All my fears just disappear.
I know I am under your care
I really feel very secure.

221. Mad

We all know madmen pick
They may pick up a treasure.
And sane men study
They may study how to die.
At night madmen sleep outside
And worry about nothing.

The sane also sleep at night
In the prison of their own fences.
Madmen pick in garbage bins
And sane men throw therein.

While the sane suffer from ulcers
Madmen never
Take sleeping pills!

Both do die and are forgotten.

222. Unfaithfulness

Once you hear of this word
"Unfaithfulness"
You know there are other things.
Once you become
"Unfaithful"
You know you have been others.
Once you are
"Unfaithful"
You know you've lost yourself.

It is dent to the best plan,
A cancer to healthy cells,
And a crack in one's soul.

223. Cry We Cry

There are many days when we fly
And surely some days we do cry.
There are things we hate and deny
Which our minds daily occupy.

The worst part of us when it comes
All joy and peace it never calms.
We hate it with perfect hatred
Leaving us very frustrated.

Why then is that our own nature
Is much difficult to nurture?
We have dual personalities
Competing for our priorities.

When we think that we have things right
Then our own dreams turn into night
And for our visions and desire
Only shame and pain we acquire.

Yet life must be better I know
For I know good things will be more,
And some day I shall reach glory
To tell my earned and true story.

224. Journey

The journey,
Will begin at Lusaka
Via Harare to
London to Toronto.

Tokyo
Guatemala City
Calgary
Joburg
And the world is conquered.

You can start yours
When you set up goals
Of the destiny you chose
To become your own boss.

O, my Mother,
I hear you miss me.
I am fine, I have a family
And I eat *Imbowa*
I also make *ifisashi*
And I fry *kapenta*.

Rather than say,
"My son left Zambia,"
Mother, say,
"He took Zambia to Ottawa,"
For I will never cease
To be a Mwewa.

225. Never to Forget

Mother,
How can I
How can I forget you?
Why should I
Why should I fail to remember
Mine months in your tummy?
Hopeless
Helpless.
Many times
You met with death in the noon.
You shielded me militantly
And delivered me alive.

Mother,
I forget you today,
I warrant failure
To remember
My own
Birthday.

226. Only Child

I have always known you
My only child.
Even that first day, in my womb
When you wiggled
And that first day on earth
When you giggled.
You will never know
How much joy I felt
The first time
You chuckled.
I always longed to see your face,
Shy, little and delicate;
I held you in my arms
Gave you the first kiss
And you waggled.

I will always love you
My only child.
I was first in your life.
My lips you kissed
And my breasts you sucked
And every time you left me
I jiggled.

You will always be
My only child.

227. Presidential Challenge

Gather you mighty and loyal
To the inaugural of the royal
For in their shadow we live and toil
While our own fate we foil.

The giant claws of mighty dragon
And we their subjects seethe in argon
Of our forgotten intellect
And dance to tunes for us they elect.

They murder more those by order
Than those at periphery of border
Who must plead self-defense
For crimes they only call offence.

A president I will, rather than king
For a precedent is only one thing
To follow the rule they create for him
To borrow peace and kill joy it seem.

There is one boy in all presidents
Who seek the camp of dissidents
To dissent the will of general deal
And rule according to general will.

228. Among Warriors

Days come and go
Each with subtle claws
On them are visages
And dark images.
I see with my mind
The danger they portend
But I still believe
And there is relief
That the humble sky
Towards where I fly
Shall someday be blue
And that is just as true.
The light shall appear
And like a sharp spear
Shall cut across barriers
To be among warriors.

229. Dreams at Lusaka

The statement of one's life:
All in their early childhood
When they are growing up
Have moments of dreaming.

Dreams are not realities at all
And many dreams are sham.
But they plant divine seeds
On which fantasy thrives.

Fantasy itself is very lofty
Always creating impressions
And cosmetics borrow dearly
From illusions of our heads.

Statement are not the same:
They grow like dull flowers
Budding in wrong seasons
Breeding broken petals.

At Lusaka, home of rising stars
Where they emerge from obscurity
To dress in casual and coats
And dance to alien statements.

I want to be a star
The problem is just mine alone
And I share it with no one
Daring to walk the great path.

230. Our Name

A laborer's `annual complaint:
I help others make great money
I escort money into other accounts
I defend the estates in others' names
And forget I have my own assets.

A laborer's complaint of a decade:
Now I have sons and daughters
I have bought them a house and cars
They go to good schools and churches
And I worry if they will succeed.

A laborer does not complain now:
I have a name I cannot recognize
I have existed for all wrong reasons
I have achieved trophies that haunt
But now I live for one name, "Ours."

231. Lost Feelings

What shall I compare life to?
Life is like curio making.
From raw trunks of trees
There come perfect images.
And like a painter does
Thinking in terms of colors
And artists in terms of lines.

So, these feelings we once had
Now long gone and vanished
Can be remade and painted.
New stanzas can be arranged
New themes enacted
And the feeling of love
Does not die though it may fade.

What shall I allude life to?
It is like matter
Which is never lost
But can only converted.
Like dry roses, so are old loves
Down we lay our heads
And we dream and love again.

232. Lights at Christmas

The light burns brightly to the end.
All things look good and very calm.
And wild flowers invade the land
In the presence of mistletoe.

It is Christmas Day in Sameland
Children will open their presents
And sit rounding the twinkling tree
In red oversized pajamas.

This season is very special
And the songs are very unique
People everywhere share in joy
To bring true peace in a vexed world.

These parcels of assorted gifts
Long gathered carefully in thrift
And in malls the jingle bells ring
While kids hum from carols singing.

The poor and needy will reckon
With lack and shortage that beckon
But with help from joyful Santa
They will receive gifts and Fanta.

233. Music in the Sky

I am amazed how that
Above the clouds
That are above a gigantic ocean
Beats resounding melodies
In symphony of superb tunes
And sweet voice of Celine Deon,
And the electric vocals of Richie,
And the vibrancy of Cocker
Together with the beaming
Eloquence of Dolly-
How that these music go
On playing in the landless paths
In those heavens far above.
The sound so beautiful
In those snowy azures,
Bringing earthly pleasure.
These ecstasies are heavily pried for
When the listening becomes intense
And these beats flap the hips of the engine.
There is music in heaven
Bright and beautiful
Drawing a soothing feeling of laughter.
In these skies the busy-ness of life
And the pressure of brewing
Are all swallowed up
Compacted and recycled
And hearts beat in chorus.
Nearing the soils
Melodies begin to faint,
These sweet waves,
Softer than the soul -
And still, there is music in the sky.

234. Bodies

They meet to dance in disco clubs
To rhythms of din and sounds unheard
Surrounded by fumes think and dense
In squeezed scents of melting hot sweat.

Magnolia of silhouetted discs
Play upon dense magnets of volts.
Bodies jive half-naked to singles
While in pure pleasure they shindig.

Lights shine inside moving shadows
Boys flash out identity cards;
Men show off tattoo-tattered backs
And women carpet-comb in wines.

To life and death they toss dense fluids
To delight they tease lethal forms
But they cannot tell who whips them
Nor are they blinded by dim lights.

Throngs of mercurial bodies bump
Skeletons in skirts and pants move
While disc jockeys keep energy
To pick after-party bodily remains.

235. Be Mine

Like a goddess' shining face
You teased me with eyes of grace
To myself I said,
"Who is that
So beautiful that the birds in me
Do chirping?"
Then you turned, faced me
And all the structures of gentleship
In me, did go usurping.
Your prisoner, I am
For your kind manners
Have arrested me
Your ambiance keeps me awake
At the thought of you,
I hobbily shake.
Oh, words do offend me,
For they fail me the right
To describe the beauty I see
Oh, be mine, Native Gem,
For nothing in this world
I would rather have.

236. So Lovely

You are so lovely,
My mind in the night it trails
You so elegantly strut
My right to calmness it fails.
In your piercingly gorgeous eyes
I feel the warmth of soaring angels
In your gentle whisper
In that intoxicating crisper
Which, even in multitudes of voices
None would decipher
My nerves it rejoices,
Your breath scratches me by,
I catch the flaking of confetti,
The shimmering breeze of July,
The flattering words of Rossetti;
You are so lovely,
Oh, bearer of honey gels.

237. IndyGenius

You have captivated me,
Oh, my sister, my love
You have caused my heart
To wake to rhythms of life,
Oh, my dove.
I am losing my mind, Indy
Because of you, O Genius,
You are a force of nature
Like a flying star,
I stand up all night
To watch you fall and rise
Your sweetness, I capture,
Critics' signals, I spar
For your gesture is bright,
And your carriage, so wise.

238. Beauty Pillar

She stands out
As a pillar of beauty
Eyes, the thematic combination
Wows with purity
Her speech, calm,
As though a fountain
Of many waters.
And her visage,
A dream caress
Of many daughters.

239. Native Excellence

Thy worth is not given
Thine worth is taken,
For thy perfection
Is of native excellence
In thy heart and mind
Are splendous bastions
Of passions;
Thy voice effuses the essence
Of exceptional ambiance,
A mark of lovely action
For thine, is the nation.

240. I Have a Witness

I love her,
The whole being
For also I have a witness
If to fall in love comes
With a settling of calmness.
Oh, Shae, your presence
Can bring a raging sea to halt
You're endemic to reason's bellows
And pride you bring
To naught.

241. Dancing Aura

I live for the aura that dances
Around the shape of your lips.
Your set of clean teeth
Just the definition of exhorted divinities,
Sketching the boundaries of heaven,
Each time you speak to me.
Your curved dimple,
Has deeply enchanted me,
A pillow of rosaries
On which I stake my haven.

242. Impossible Love

Impossible love,
How I have longed
For you in close spaces
Oh, Tina, you carry a goddess
A visage, an arm of graces.
Like darkness and light,
We fiercely avoid each other;
Like cloud and rain
We embracingly covet one another.
Let me come,
Even just like a shadow
Your benevolences on a drum
Your embraces to overshadow.

243. Bringer of Joy

All you have ever longed for
Was someone who brings you joy
And in many ways,
That is what I do.
When I first laid an eye on you
I was merely a boy,
Now, I have learned how to please you,
And I am a man, too.

244. After We Met

My eyes fell on you again,
Without the aura of youth.
And through fumes,
The sweetness of your wisdom
Has never left your mouth.
Now, I promise you, again
Without the fear of offence,
That we shall meet as bare-breasted
Combatants,
With no unchaste defences.

245. Love Me One More Time

Love me, love me once more
The children have now left home.
When I met you,
You were a rough-necked ore,
Oh, purified gold,
Let me freely to you come,
To love, not to be loved,
To touch, not to be touched
To the place of perfection
Where old feelings get to be hatched.

246. Love Till Death

You look to him,
But not for him
It is all written all over your chin
You love me, that is a recurring theme
Though you married him,
You still long for me within.

247. Swallow Me

Swallow me,
Wash me clean as snow
In the temple of flowing saliva, now
And hold me,
As tight as a bull constrictor
And in your venomous charm,
Lay me inside your valving restrictor
For there, my pump is free from harm.

248. Overflowing

You poured me
A cup of full water
Oh, the overflow,
Past the fourth quarter
Your mellowly hands
Bubbling with ecstasy
Your hand-made bugle
Charming with fantasy.
Two hearts that met
Two minds that forever are set
Oh, love,
Let me call you as such
For in truth, I love you so much.

249. Among Millions

You wrote me recently
That we had not time
I was already at the train station
There I sat, without a dime
Only a credit card
So, I could not call.
Then as a chilling night did fall
I felt your sacred presence
And abhorred your absence
Oh, girl, among millions
It's only you I like.

250. Weekend of Love

What a weekend, filled with love
And that seat you had me have
When you squeezed towards my side
And left me with nothing inside to hide.
Then we chatted while admirers watched.
It was clear to all that they had been torched.
Yes, ours was a glittering natural force,
And everything about you, comes from
A hallowed source.

251. In New Light

The last time we met at the Parlaver's
We only gave signs unique to lovers.
We never ceased to gaze at each other
With those sweet, soft looks like no other.
Our body language gave all the cyphers
And we traded signals as lax as heifers.
What we feel without any gesture
And how we simply get to bestir,
Oh, it's as if I was made just for you
To see you again, makes all things new.

252. First Voice

It is your voice that I would rather hear
To enable me to your memory to adhere
Oh, love, call me in the wee of the hour
Like in the sprouting stages of a flower,
Chaff me with thine golden vocal cords
As a drink from a fountain out poured;
Let your name be the first word I utter,
For thine is loveliest to say and flutter.

BOOK III PATRONAGE
ULTIMATUM

253. Struggle of My People

Alarms ring loudly deep down within long
We stand decorously secure and strong
Indeed, they enjoy life fewer peers have.
They walk in streets structured with lights above.
Haven't they the better of two worlds in one?
For our black beauties, hearts they have won,
Yet for our kids, I nightly toss bed's ends.
I would not for a morsel damn knees' bends;
Nor for lack of pride shrink from your defence;
Nor at your poor's sight, create a Balaam fence.
Weary talents drain your brain, clan and blood;
In your precocious dead, doomed sorrows flood;
In lavish copp'r, hopes and stocks barely float,
Wryly, your faith rests in your ignored lot.
Freely, your limbs nimble in begging drills;
Drily, lax songs become your simmering pills;
Slyly, rules glue norms to lurid natures.
Does poor peace frolic in vain adventures?
Morrow hides in shadows of green villages;
Mothers grieve in chants of brok'n elegies.
Zambia, loved like a mother who shaped me,
Cherished since I opened my eyes to see.
Our legacy, sign of freedom an' bondage;
Our past, a prayer of a shunned adage;
Let it be said that we had thinking bards,
Let in books, your precious liberty buds;
Let in years to come it be said, "Ours knew"
Although in pride, grand, virtuosos are few;
Struggle is my people's fault-lines of growth,
And to freely prosp'r, our true and bold oath.

254. My Zambia, I Cry

The nation awakes to sounds of mourning
More frequently than it does to mirth
There is music in the air-waves burning
But not to celebration of life or to birth
Bana-Musonda just learned that her job
Will no longer be hers, but foreigners`
Children now run for help to the mob
And begging is part of the national anthem;
Small victories are displayed as mementos
A few malls are idolized as development
And education is a bygone word for ruiners
Inventions are rare and unknown for "them"
Talent is lamped to worst in churches or ghettoes
The nation feels like a chilling firmament
As workers and students alike resort to strikes
Since conditions are bad and the meal hikes
Who shall bring light to a nation in dark
Will the future be as it has been in the past
Are these leaders all look but on the back,
Oh Zambia, O land, stop sliding so fast!
With all that we carry within, we still believe
For Zambia, there is still more hope to re-live.

255. Dreams of Poverty

I wake, tears rolling, in deep sweats,
Dreaming of days gone with big debts,
In pain of worry and harsh nights
When sleep climbs over higher heights.

Dreams of poverty stir my soul,
I fear the day lack will befall
When gloom as a frightful shadow
Becomes a close and common foe.

I run from my footsteps all day,
All my plans have wondered at bay,
Poverty's shame does threaten me
And from my own heartbeats I flee.

The thoughts of days of want do haunt
The feelings of great need also taunt,
I see the pangs of struggle's past
I run and away very fast.

256. Dreams of Africa

I
I dream of Africa, the smells of early rains
I long for the beaches heaving with swamps and fens;
I yearn for the dark long free worms, food for fishes
And I hunger for breams and all native dishes.

II
I miss the songs when new virgins' rites are over
With every step a rare chance to live in clover;
I wish to stand all day watching their curvatures,
When they emerge with tight chonches and fine cultures!

III
I long for your tender bosom, Oh Africa,
I remember busking inside your bright Spica
As I milked in the zephyr of your youthful dawn,
And your *Nshima* maize mixture I had always gnawn.

IV
Oh, the rhythms of Rumba, pleasure of your drum,
In this young and old, day and night, shindig and swam
To the sounds of mirth my ancestors bragged about
Oh, how soundly the children slept after the bout!

V
I often dream of the wastes lying on Cairo Road
Of graffiti and filth garbage across the board,
Of smut of compacted town-center boulevards
Of the uncouth conduct in courtrooms and churchyards.

VI
I didn't enter the portal of the living dead
Nor tasted sweet love in a darkly flowing bed,
Yet, I dream of the best potential of all kids
Of women who dance with opened legs in all nudes.

VII
I have been to the river banks of flowing blood,
To tears spilling over with a weeping flood;
In Africa they teach, "Life once given, it's gone!"
Oh land, without you it feels like I was not born.

VIII
These nights are memorable when I dream of you
These lights are horrible when I forget what you do;
These rights are fallible when I flout the offspring;
These fights are agreeable when I speak your feeling!

IX
The streets of raw Africa are littered with dirt,
The central banks are going to war with yawning debt;
The roads are thwarted with problems of a pothole;
The fields have graves but the sound of music makes whole.

X
I stand at the edge of the rising waterfall
And watch able adventurers drive, dive and free-fall
On the waves of high splashing flurry and glory
Where they burry their heart and mind with no worry.

XI
When I saw the smiling girls at their first instance,
When the bare-breasted women took their early chance,
Their thighs strong and their arms hardened through toil,
Their diamond hands and golden tongues drip silver oil.

XII
The politics of the land are lovely as flute
The speeches of Parliament sound like awful fruit;
The decisions of courts are lithe like a Danseuse
And the banks lend only to those they can abuse.

XIII
The beauty of Africa is a fantasy,
Women keep their pubic gardens smartly fussy;
Men find it in parody of foreign accents
And presidents' pride in signing stately assents.

XIV
The dreams of my homeland are many and intense,
The visions fill my beliefs with divine incense;
The fine blessings and the curse on the savannas
Are shaped like the anxious tendons near the anus.

XV
I dream of your never changing magnificence,
In avant-gardism and now I see your presence.
Your vowel-ended surnames I love to pronounce
And your pure kind-heartedness I like to announce.

257. O Africa

O Africa, I have loved you with pure love
Like an eagle flying up and far in the above
So beats my heart, for the memories of you
O Africa, compared to many, there are a few

You have been my lover, my keeper, my anchor
You secured my undone frame in your banker
And now I remember your infinite loving-kindness
And your unfading and unbridled goodness.

From the lands of the White people, I recount
I look at your history from which fortune I count
That at the beginning of your journey to far here
You kept our promise, "For you, I will be there!"

O Africa, land of unfiltered and sober music
In manners and etiquette, O Africa, you're basic
But the dance of your people my soul it reaps
And your rhythms, a dagger rips mat my heaps.

O Africa, your face never leaves my brown visage
I wait for you, my sense glued to your long image
For blood and tears have run through your soil
The rule of fear has threatened our flowing oil.

I will love you always, O Africa, I will not forget
Your anthem of peace and freedom is my fete
I will never cease to remind you of true loveliness
Of that unadulterated African neighborly selfless

In your brown terrain lies the hope of the earth
In your unplowed villas there I will put my faith
For the children run freely in the early morning
The elegy is no longer our song of mourning.

Africa, should I call you a champion of the sufferer
Or the captain of those who hold the Emperor?
In the art forgiveness, you excel like a frugal god
In endurance, you stand the test like purest gold.

258. Apolitical Theory

Classics
Thou built reason's mind, O Plato,
Shaped brain's wit, thou Aristotle,
And deified politics divine
Whence St. Augustine's city doth shine!

Hobbes
Thou men, equal in body and mind
Court thee that kingly Leviathan
To appease thine life, short and poor
By these contracts, flawed and unsure

Locke
Thou nature in thy undressed state
Do in liberty instruct all;
Our labors with property rewards;
These laws our happiness awards

Machiavelli
Thou double-minds of earthly reign
Partly foxes, partly lions,
Thrust thy trust in beastly powers
To slay virtue on saintly towers

Rousseau
Thou art depraved, O thinking man
And thy good to thy nature tied;
Born free, yet everywhere in chains,
And in forced freedom thine trust earns

259. Hillsboro

Thou city of Hillsboro
By the embers of Wichita
Though thou art only a borough
In thine quiet street once veered a star

Thou art smaller by thy numbers
Yet thou grow the famous and rich
And rarely add to thy members
Desiring thy symbols to reach

Thy people proud and sufficient
Coldly hold to thy horn of race
Whence they gasp like a patient
Cancerously marred in the face

In thine churches emerge a song
Of penance for equality
Whence thy masses in oneness sing
To save thine renowned quality

260. Mibenge

Mibenge, I do remember,
It was here, the root of my roots;
Across the trans-border journey
Crossing the Luapula River.

I do remember my childhood
And our fishing in Mulonga
With all the thickets and bushes
And our ancestors in ashes.

We have come to Mibenge,
The place of childhood scenery
In our fondest memories byes
Where my own beloved father lies.

These earths calmly rest Ngalula
Next to my father's chummy breasts;
In here, I remember innocence.
For tears, unlike memories, dry

Mibenge, where men ever fade
And depart before they can grey.
Mibenge, I remember nuts
A treat only called *intwilo*.

261. Bye-Bye Bishop

The terrain still remain light brown
But we have put on a bright gown.
Several questions of whether
It is only in good weather
That to noble men with big farms
We soon empty all in our arms?

The factual hour will always come
For troubled and torn hearts to calm
And never again to bishops
Will we exist to place our hopes.

We were not meant to live like them
We too have to fulfill our term.
Yet your prayer, O man of God
I will seek in lands far and cold.

262. Eagle's Feathers

They rise up, too strong
And also, very wrong
They awake like they have furlong'd
In comatose for long
They aren't vixen
But with strength of oxen
They mount with wings
Like celestial beings
They wear fake
Only when they command
And with tyrannical demand
They order minions
Into frozen unions
As of callous words with pride
On the weaklings they ride
Until their power is stripped
And with throngs they are whipped
Then they fall, fall, fall
And all fall
It is a mighty and heavy target
For these do forget
That April showers
Bring May flowers
And that the kindness of many
Shouldn't be trodden by any,
Rule kindly, demand justice
For the eagle is big as its feathers
And all bests at ease
Be rewarded with treasures.

263. Mother Zambia

Mother...
Of mound display
An unexplored Eden in Africa;
Full of Nature's best
And an endless of tradition...
(To Zambezi -
To pay an invocative visit:
The people on superstitious gravity)
To you Mother...
Higher vows I pay.
Your soils are veins of life,
The peace
The Joy
The resting
Your people, my people,
Occupied
In structures of thatch
And decorated mad walls!
Your idyllic terrains;
Much more unexploited.
Your virile bushes;
Much less inhabited.
Your smiling hopeful visage
Is the ink that pens this message.

264. South Africa 2010

Oh, Africa, at the tip of the Old Benguanaland,[1]
The land of the Zulus and the Xhosas,
Therein Shaka of the Zulu brought us pride,
Thy gyrateth like none other,
Thou danceth as the goddesses in Brenda Facie,
Or that angel only known as Malope!
In these terrains where Mandela's gongs clearly gluing,
O Africa, south of the continent,
Thou art our blazer.
In that 2010 atmosphere,
Thou hostedth the Great Cup
To the sounds of Beautiful Shakira
And rhythm of Waka-Waka!
Or "This Time for Africa" –
Oh, mother Africa,
Mother of mothers, I honor thee!
From the land of wintry whites and polar bears,
Surely, here in Kanuk's maple groves,
I remember the tropics in their thickets,
Surely, Africa thou art gorgeous, land of my fathers.
Oh, South Africa, be a land of soccer's grandest dribblers,
I surmise, time is now to dribble thine troubles.
And thee, Africa, be to me a trophy,
A garland of victory.
It's time for Africa,
Thou heardeth me, a faint voice from Zambesia
It's time for Africa,
And may the waves of grace to thee,
An orison from our Heavenly Father be.

---

[1] Or Banguanaland, see #269, on p. 297 used interchangeably

265. Africa I Love Despite

Oh Africa, my Africa,
Don't you amaze me
In all wise, you're poor
And sometimes even evil
Other times, you disappoint,
Especially when children you neglect
Your roads are full of potholes,
Some of your housing dilapidated
You keep enjoying other nations things
And you don't pay attention to your own potential
You spend more time copying other people
Than you do trying to improve yourself
BUT I still love you
I am dead in your rhythms,
Especially your Rhumba
Your girls are lovely –
As soft as the feathers of a peacock
Your music – oh my God –
I can indulge in day and night
And your beauty – is true beauty –
The nature, the people
Oh Africa, although you're neglected,
My thoughts are all you
Africa, my Africa, no matter what,
Our love is forever
Africa, till I die, we are two roads that met
And have promised never to part
Oh Africa, my Africa, God shine upon you.

266. The Stairs of Kabwata

I remember the many stairs leading up to fourth home
Here I prayed, we laughed and also, I saw you come
You were so angelic in all ways, you're still an angel
It does not matter "others", or a look from another angle
The Stairs of Kabwata, we were like little children playing
"We're still little, playful children," that's what I am saying
The Stairs of Kabwata, in both our hearts, we know it well
Though long ago, down our hearts, its rhythms still dwell.

267. Canada

Cold and clean
Oh Canada, Canada
Streets of marble
And terrain ever cold.
Your people busy
Subways chilly and clean
And eyes blue and wet.
In these speechless elevators,
Behold avenues,
Swept and candy sellers
Malls crammed and full
And men seem confused.
Canada,
Land of opportunities.
And Canada
Is cold and clean.

268. Black Africa

To you my darling mother,
My one and only
And I don't have another.
My dear family
Has entreated me not to
Ignore history
And our own origins, too.
This is our story
I tell in tears and sorrow
And it offends us
Deep into our bone marrow
After as soon as
They notice that we are black
And color doesn't cheat,
They also think our blood is dark.
We may take the heat,
But we have been strong
To speak to their face
That all along they are wrong
Since we know that race
Speaks volume of variety
And none is superior
Or all-wise in entirety
To think inferior
Of others who are diverse
When you reason in reverse
That today's culture
Is mixed civilization
Of a past nature;
Think Africa's ideation!

Sing you in skins dark
For there's no color as black!

269. I Am a Proud African

I am a proud African,
Let the drums beat, the forest shake and the rivers flow
I am a proud African
There is an eternal blood in me, vigorous and steady
I am a proud African
From the lands flowing with gold and diamonds, lands of my ancestors
I am a proud African
I have built civilizations, toiled for nothing and reaped the wind
I am a proud African
Others mistake me for a bigot, a slave, or a thinkless brat
I am a proud African
I have birthed inventions, and my name is not associated with any
I am a proud African
I am strong, daring, fearless, and my veins drip with ripped marrows
I am a proud African
My wisdom is in my color – dark, black and fits with any variance
I am a proud African
I am the hope of the world, I still treasure the jungle filled with greens
I am a proud African
My shape is a bottle, I treasure the rhythms of my protruding buttocks
I am a proud African
I speak with divine accents, feed with the roles of nature and sleep free
I am a proud African

This is who I am, I don't want to be another, nor serve another
I am a proud African
I love all, never discriminated, never enslaved another race, I am pure
I am a proud African
Generosity is my outer wear, and forgiveness is my inner garment
I am a proud African,
Abused, but never retaliated, cheated but never repatriated
I am a proud African
Others think that I am dull, unsophisticated and clearly brainless
I am a proud African
Tolerance is in my DNA, the past eluded me but the future is mine.

270. Hawaii, I

Oh Hawaii, Hawaii, Hawaii, Hawaii
Oh, island of beauty, beautiful food
Hawaii, Hawaii, Oh Hawaii, Hawaii.
No island is this fancy, no notable wood
I once visited you, Hawaii, Oh Hawaii
With my young but adventurous family
Oh Hawaii, Hawaii, Hawaii, Hawaii,
We raved into your brilliance, how lovely
Oh, Hawaii, Hawaii, Hawaii, Hawaii,
I still feel you, your oceans, your beaches
Oh, Hawaii, Hawaii, Hawaii, Hawaii,
You're a sermon Heaven preaches
The Chikuzees of Hawaii are truly fresh
The Happy Hours frolic with florescence
I see my little ones smile widely afresh
I, myself, feel as if dunked into incense
I am all dancing, drinking and splashing
Oh, Hawaii, Hawaii, Hawaii, I relive you
Till now, I remember, I am all bashing,
I will come again, a paradise you're, too.

271. Hawaii, II

I have been thinking about you,
O Hawaii
Your seashores, your palm trees
and the Asians
The dance,
Oh, these lightened boulevards,
And the clean, green
and spleen environs,
How I miss the evenings
when my loved ones dined
We ate, we drank Champaign
and even danced.
Then we raved into the raving ocean;
I lost the phone – oops.
But got it back in Kitchener,
Ontario, O Canada.
I will come back to your shores,
to bask and hear
Oh, Hawaii, my kids loved it;
my wife enjoyed it.
I love you, O Hawaii,
your divine themes,
your lovely seashores.
We boated of the best,
On the Mighty Pacific Ocean,
smaller but available seas-cruiser.
I held Cuteravive tight;
Emmerance and Tashany adventured.
Then we disembarked
and tasted some sumptuous
pineapples, mangoes, fruits,
Oh love, oh joy, oh hilarity,
I am all for the beauty of the ride.
Invite me again after Covid-19,
and my loved ones I will bring;

O Hawaii, we will be your guests,
the favor to return
And the joy of a life-time
Wherein to indulge.
O Hawaii, the island I clearly,
And love dearly.

272. Los Angeles

Thy art magnificent, O thou city with Angeles
Thou hath no equivalent, serve Domini Angelus
Thy mountainous Bel Air, thy flattened Beverley Hills
Indeed, thy hilly Hollywood, thy unseen Hidden Hills,
These brilliances in their eternally glorious Calabasas
Wouldst Orange County volitionally be "Birth of Jesus"?
Down thy lively lit boulevards mine sweetie droveth
Up at thy vetted Disneyworld, mine little angels roveth
In thy lux hotels, dreams of effulgence hugeth mine soul
In thy fabulous indulgence, mine senses fluently roll
Oh City, a place whereth I would again rather be,
After Covid-19, O City, me orisoneth recover thee.

273. Over the Seas

Here my people, I write
From over the seas, I write
To people dark and lovely,
May I write.

I am yours from abroad
I am a patriot and a child
Your own blood
A product of your need.

To my motherland,
In the fair and brown land
A place of civilization's splendor
And birth place of culture's grandeur.

Here they come to seek fortune
In the lands of fruits and pearls
Where music never lacks in tune
And women keep long hairs.

I am yours from overseas,
My name I have not changed,
Though I be gratified abroad
Yet my wish I will not alter.

My people, I write
And yours still I am
Even from over the seas.

274. Christian Nation

My country is a Christian nation,
A declaration of the century
A transition indeed
To the people in need.

My country is a Christian nation,
A declaration of good faith
A transition indeed
To a people who read.

My country is a Christian nation,
A declaration of trust
A transition indeed
To a people who hate greed.

My country is a Christian nation,
A declaration to God's glory
A transition indeed
To a people great in deed.

275. My Canada

Here my Canada I come.
Once visited forever treasured
Your nakedness is picturesque
Which haunt even in dreams.

Here in my Canada I am
Flesh stuck closer to flesh
Bones big, broad and hard,
Canada, may I call you mine?

Canada, the world's baby-sitter
Hope of the world's destitute
And Canada your open arms
Many a soul you protect.

Here my Canada I come
To breed light from darkness
And brood over unborn bloods
And Canada, I call you mine.

276. Heroes of Freedom

They fought as a band of soldiers;
They died while fighting, as martyrs,
Some are presidents if they lived,
And others have scars to show for.

We meet them daily in grey hairs
These are our truest statesmen,
These our prized gallant fighters,
Pillars on which we live and thrive.

We their brood their glory will save
Never to forget the blood they shed,
And in their footsteps, we will follow,
Attesting to hearts strong and brave.

This freedom so for granted we take
With sword and pain was achieved,
Even when many in pieces returned,
Silently, yet very clearly, they speak.

In libraries their heroism archived,
In pain and anguish they travailed,
These sons of liberty are of renown,
Heroes of peace, our true veterans.

277. Heathrow

Heathrow, Heathrow, Heathrow,
Though bright and ruddy
A detention thou art not
Let me pass, and let me go.

Thy skies in raining tears
Though thy summers be bright
A destination thou art not
Give me a pass, trip thy door.

Heathrow, thou pride of London
Though mine luggage thou lost
A habitation thou art not
Bring me past thee, let me fly.

Heathrow, thy arms wide open
Though terrorists thou perturb
An occupation thou art not
Take my low past, push me high.

278. Over Paris

The skies of the ground beneath
The clouds within which we bracket
And though dull, pale and chalky,
The skies over Paris are bluest.

The envelop that canopies France
Opening its eyes towards Londres
And closing its mind to America
Is frisky, risky, milky and murky!

Oh, the feeling within the steel bird,
Oh, how magnificent it is inside,
Oh, how fearful and uncertain,
How trepid within these tempests!

Over the skies of great Paris
The sun shines lazily pale
In tints of orange and yellow
How relaxed is the air over Paris.

279. Joe Biden

On the flicker of a democratic win,
A due return to sanity will begin,
Even with it the total decay of pride
For virtually four years, the USA denied,
That its internal glory had been faded,
And corruption, its image had degraded.
An unlikely savior be found in Biden
With his election its glory, be widen
O, rejoice, Oh Great Land, rejoice, rejoice
The arrogant's fallen, with their tweeting noise.
For the disgrace is exited, debouched
The legacy of Obama, now whooped.
For whatever happens in Amerika,
Does not remain only in America.

280. Mr. Thairu

Your tag read Richard Thairu,
At Jomo Kenyatta Airport
In the double lines of duty
When you paid no attention.

I am the one you mistreated
A vacationer you offended,
When you pushed me aside
Because like you, I am black.

Your tag said James Smith
At Dallas Fort Worth Airport
In the duty of two lines
When you paid much attention.

I have not forgotten at all
I was only a poor tourist
When you pulled me aside
Since unlike you, I am black.

People will many a time
Judge us by our simple looks
And only God all the time
Writes our truth in his books.

281. Kingdom Within

Man is a kingdom decked within.
The realm therein he aptly rules
With dignity and decorum
And dreams never in short supply.

Your own tender sleep, dreamy man
Will scout for reaching very far
And take you to lands far-away
Lands with plenty and yet unknown.

In your head above, thinking man,
These lands undiscovered are near
Full of treasure and raw riches
And so real and very well-known.

When you came across a signal
And vividly remembered that
You had existed there before now,
It was meetings of intuition.

And so many times you do dream
Of lands and peoples and places
Of plays and drama arenas
And of actors and actresses.

On these arenas and play stages
You have seen yourself escorted
By retinue clad in pure white
Whereas doors everywhere open.

You should never stop to believe
In the dreams of night and of day
For they portend hidden senses
And foretell future realities.

Many days stop me and inquire
And there seem to be conference
Going on in the inside of me.
It is this keeping me searching
For the idyll time and right place
Where the 'I' in me would surface
And join me to self-made heroes.

282. Perfect Full-Stop

Perfect full-stop
When my sentence
Shall be completed,
What will its *predicate* be?
Will it have
A perfect summary of my life?

Many people need where to lean
Someone who looks out just for them
Who has themselves been there before
And by patience and endurance
Has come back home with life's trophies;
This someone must not be the end
But is only a stepping-stone.

Perfect full stop
When my sentence
Shall be completed,
What will its *object* be?
Will it have
A perfect summary of my life?

Many people at life's apex
Do say they began from somewhere
By trying out what was inside them.
Many of them discovered treasures
Of stuff they didn't think existed.
Someday we will find that someone
Who gives us wings with which to fly.

Perfect full stop
When my sentence
Shall be completed,
What will its *subject* be?
Will it have
A perfect summary of my life?

Many dark seasons do appear
To intimidate our courage.
Years of seed-planting will also come
To call for planning and hard work.
Times of helpful disappointment
And radical opposition
Break up eaglets from growing chicks
And make us who we really are.

Perfect full stop
When my sentence
Shall be completed,
What will its *statement* be?
Will it have
A perfect summary of my life?

283. Congo

Congo, thou land of biting gold
Thou crafted my father a home
And gave his son a wife am told
Congo, thou hast shrunken in form!

Thy womb bore many great children
Thy fortunes with them gladly shared
And though to thee they were foreign
Thine barrier was not closed or sheared.

The copper fields of Katanga
By which mine folks thou ably saved
From disgrace and piercing hunger
And their deficiency thou waved.

In thine rivers flow brooding blood
And thine skies drop toxic bullets.
Funeral songs are washed in flood
Horded with parts marred by mallets.

Congo, from my Zambia I call
From my *terra firma* I bawl
Congo, from Canada I declare
End thee thy ugly wars, I decree.

284. Idyll Phonoriah

These sounds
Smell of grapes
And of spices
Of great Indiana.
This is the place
Where we have to discover
Stories yet to be told.

We shall dance
To celebrate an idyll future
Of infectious flavors
And decorations in antique.
It is a country so bright
And land so light.

Oh, Phonoriah
A land so good,
A future so promising.
Oh, Phonoriah,
What an idyll a place.

285. Chitambo

Passing by Chitambo we saw a tomb
Whose epitaph was a dual petition
To the god of the feast of Hecatomb,
Written below was a re-petition.

He passed away with hands in akimbo
After braving the nip of fillaria,
And shunning many calls from the limbo
But was met by a shell of malaria.

This man bemoaned a German war Gotha
And found a panacea in helpful Chuma
Whom he taught the secrets of Golgotha
Whose blood-flow cures the tumor of Guma.

We hear sounds rattle from clouds in Congo
Sending dark and heavy rains of defiance
Smashing civilizations as ingle,
Washing them out without any reliance.

We come home back to village Chitambo
To water the plants of our great Sambo
Whom we rhyme in our book about poetics
Who savors the African politics.

Africa is now a Cinderella
Her beauty should not be spurned as loveless
And a reed-mat shouldn't be her umbrella
And she shouldn't be let to hold sewer gloveless.

286. Mr. Conductor

You drive on tars of Beirut Road
Full of risks and wavy potholes
There you are on your way with loads
Filled with rage and stumbling on poles.

When that woman gullied on you
You almost lost a customer
But today you had just a few
So, you just fixed your sad stoma.

At four every day you get up
And by twenty you are late on
For you rarely capture a nap
Nor find time to answer your phone.

In your busy life friends are few
Since they cannot see or know you
As you leave early and come late
Carrying out routines that you hate.

287. Banguanaland

The vile wars of Banguanaland[2]:
Let me lament for the beloved
And compose a dirge to her plot.

My beloved has a spacious land
Sited between two great waters
Of Indian and Atlantic seas.

She dug it up and cleared out stones
And planted therein dire landmines;
She built a loom and secured it.

She dug around mass shallow graves.
Expecting to bring on power,
But alas, it brought gushing blood.

Dear kindred of civilized worlds
From Cape, to Freetown, to Khartoum,
From London to New York and past:

Did you observe the kid soldiers
Who are forced to drink human blood
And are strained to eat human fresh?

Wambo is factory to limbs;
My beloved's airs are polluted
With gases of ruinous rockets.

Who makes such planes in such plenty?
In whose interest are they shaped?
And who fashion rifles *en* mass?

---

[2] Or Benguanaland, see #246, on p. 270 used interchangeably

Wars fought on my beloved's top soil
Have tainted its fertility
And rendered its earth impotent.

They die unceremoniously
And are buried without prayer
An offence to God, their Creator.

Refugee camps stripe my beloved
Just like the skin of a leopard
And the world believes it is free!

Poverty, like locusts, invades,
Ballots are nothing but a ruse
While laws only favor the rich!

The nations fob watch from a mile
And monitor as man kills man
And thinks it will never haunt them!

People in Banguanaland bawl:
Guiltless children worriedly howl,
But do you hear their hopeless roar?

288. War Sonnet

The gruesome visage of colorless war
And every time it stares its gape of woe
Into the fragile lives of the mortals,
It erodes a million hopes in totals
And render numerous desires devoid.
In gloom man reaps what he tend to avoid,
And in vain he gathers the world to moot
But always overlook war's evil root.
Is it not due to his queer lust and greed,
Of which he has forever vowed to breed
That the scarlet fluid of the innocent
Has flown into a sacrilegious waste?
The joy of life is damped hundred percent;
For gory wars instill, in man the worst.

289. Nuclear Dysfunction

The mighty nations are stockpiling
Hitherto, two wars, heads are filing.
Do they care, when masses be dying,
From poverty, cancer, time is flying.
Thence, state budgets rarely meeting,
Alas, fatal plague i'n't been treating.
For dollars in billions are trending
While armistice efforts aren't ending;
Oh, cursed be all weapons factoring,
Nil, nada, arms made w'd be victoring.
End, don't fashion arms for deathing,
Stop, don't deprive futures, breathing.
Cease those death chambers erecting,
Indeed, choose peace, leaders electing.

290. Rwanda

Rwanda,[3] the core of Africa
Inserted between giant nations
What, shall I recount your sad fate?
The doom of oval-shaped people,
A society of ocean smiles!

Genocide, legacy of war:
A story I must tell with tears,
Rwanda, we will never forget,
We will never remain silent;
We won't deny you compassion!

You are now home to *infamy*,
Your survivors will not forget
The middle of the silent night
Which turned into an awry sight
Of the bloody massacre spree!

Rwanda, trees mature in straight lines,
Character of serenity
And outlook in tranquility,
But your citizens you murder
Hutus and Tutsis, you butcher!

Oh, horror, cry sacrilegious!
The unspeakable has happened,
Woe to the angel of dark Hades;
A strong nation you break apart
Just because their noses are different!

---

[3] Or Ruanda

Rwanda, all innocently slain,
Your tragedy, is disaster,
A flaw in human decency,
A crime against humanity,
And error in human judgment.

291. Worst Antilife Report

Speak to me...
About war being won and lost;
About war separating everlasting friends,
And derailing further the amity of fiends!

Speak to me...
About ominous motives of terrorists;
About the perpetrators of homicides,
And about the perpetuators in genocides!

Speak to me...
About firing at unarmed and helpless people;
About what happens when the masses retire to sleep,
And the workers of anarchy awake to reap!

Speak to me...
About the flawless blood that flows;
About the unborn in volatile wombs,
And when they are born into jaws' tombs!

Speak to me...
About dignity when it is thwarted;
About the rights of the multitudes;
And of those who suffer the wrath of evil attitudes!

Speak to me...
About powers that disregard the song of peace;
About those who rush to pull the swords,
And do not attempt the soft power of words!

Speak to me…
About humans butchered like fowl;
About those in the name of patriotism
And who have done acts worse than nepotism.

292. Colovery

AD. 1 to 3

Oh, scream, retell the awful history
That sadly, became a scotched land's story
The palaces had thinned without pure gold
It wasn't viable to trust methods of old
Even brother had turned against brother
For the throne, siblings murdered each other
What we know today simply as Europe,
No longer was sweetened by fluid syrup
All the people worshiped was Monarchy,
But the strife only led to 'onarchy.

AD. 4 to 13

Armies and warriors massacred villages
The land was littered with crimson pillages
The horse could not breed fast enough
And boys only lived if they became tough.
The age was christened "dark", very dark
There was no guiding light from Moses' ark
The jingle, "Man for himself, God for us,"
Ignored all the teachings of Christ Jesus.
What wrung solid, was the blade of Vikings
Ironsmiths became valued guides to kings.

AD. 13 to 16

When the pangs of hatred and angst perished
The knack for blood winded, life was cherished
It was time to reemerge, rebirth the mind;
The Renaissance, was also very kind.
In art-culture, rose many a scholar;
In economics, vast grew the dollar.
No longer did boys become men early
And women and girls' beauty came fairly.
The pen, rhetoric's wit guided politics
And people were not persuaded by tricks.

AD. 16 to 17

Then came the famed Age of Enlightenment
And the homage to the environment.
The earth was global, and not again flat
And a monarch became a bureaucrat.
Oh, Europe, and unknown America
Soon greed opened up doors to Africa.
Oh, woe, woe to you, my dearest mother
Oh, be aggrieved, dishevel, lament father
You had been discovered, safe wasn't your kids
Your lads'd be auctioned, your land's up for bids.

AD. 18 to 19

Then came the Industrial Revolution
It was by no means a meek solution
For what would be the West's enormous wealth
Would prove to be Africa's burial wreath.
What did provide Capitalists' treasure
Was to become the Natives' displeasure.
My land, was only good but for slavery,
My people caged, shippēd, not for bravery.
Oh, sham, Africa faced brutality –
Over sixty million fatality.

AD. 19 to 20

Those nastily slaughtered in feudalism
Couldn't compare to victims of colonialism
The prior took from, the later occupied.
It's Colovery, both mind and matter died.
What the gun took, the Bible pacified.
Our land, became cursed, color, our war bride.
The grown-ups, were "boys", ladies, sex slaves,
And work, unpaid, lineage buried, no graves.
A byword "Black" became, same as devil,
Our culture, derelict, our pride, deemed evil.

AD. 20 to 23

The cup is half-full, Oh, independence;
The land's, officially, in dependence.
Old masters exchanged hands with corporatists.
Oil, minerals, gone, grieving separatists.
The new masters are called Structuralists,
Ending the glory of agriculturalists.
They trend in grabbing natural resources
And still Africa, is joining forces;
Awake, Oh, sleeper, demand equality,
And let nothing be taken, with illegality.

293. Adventures

Sitting down on McDonald's pallor
At City Schipol International Airport,
In the old land of the Dutch legion:
I wonder that the day rolls away;
I wonder that I should have
Written many lines of rhyme;
I wonder that I have not started
An introduction to a book I would title
Simply as: *Adventures*.

People on scholarships travel far and wide
With cash in their bags;
But I travel with dreams in my head.
I travel on my own volition
In airplanes large and small.
In these unsponsored travels
I land on airports large and small.
In these adventures I look like a
Very Important Person or VIP,
Just like a president or prime minister;
But even though I am not all that,
The adventure, is still mine.

294. Schipol

Runways at Schipol are foggy
Byways, wet and straight and saggy
Weather, damp and dreary at most
Hazing birds and planes in the frost.

Rains fall in bits very softly
Temperatures are rising lofty
And steel shadows come and take off
To move the best in worlds of golf.

The queues, long and coiled like serpents
Flaunting badges of exotic merchants
And from neighborhoods of Deutschland
Cabs pass stunk strippers of Holland.

The simmering breath grapples you
And shakes of hands are far and few
As friends and fiends rub hot shoulders
Fleeing Netherlands from closed borders.

295. Bernados

You need Canada,
And Canada also needs you:

Thus, the anthem rung very early
At the dawn of civilization
At the expense of neglected childhood
When the call that saved Europe
And erected the ladder to prosperity
Was never equaled to elsewhere.

There along the corridors of Liverpool
Naked boys and girls
Squeezed in tiny squirms at Bernados
In need of food and shelter.

And Canada was open
To extend her hand
To the rescue of a genius posterity
And the legacy of goodwill
Which now and always
Great Canada is known by.

By the wood structures in Halifax
By night or by day via Quebec City
And worn-out from ancient labor,
Inhabitants of the world
Found the warmth in work
Denied them from Great Britain
And available to children
Who were neither exclusive workers
Nor *bonafide* members of their families.

296. Brutus

Clap your hands all you people
And shout for joy with a voice of triumph
For the mighty have fallen!
Oh, how they have fallen, the mighty!

Hussein is incarcerated
And Bush is deified
Just like Brutus murdered Caesar
With a sharp blade of a sword.

Saddam has murdered peace
With the face of the Iraq people

And George has butchered morality
With the vanity of the United Nations.

There at the Capitol
Great Julius Caesar fell
At the hands of him that he loved.

And at Capitol Hill
The voice of the Security Council
Is silent, guilty of *vocaphobia*
A disease too hard to cure.

The rhythm of warfare
Has sent conflicting signals:

To aggressors, romanticism
While to the victim, it is realism.

You thought wrong
That the brute quest of Brutus
Did end with the defeat
Of the Triumvirate!

297. Canada, O Country

From east coast to coast to west coast
Three seas, gigantic waters boast
At the confluence of the seasons
Dress'd therein as queen of reasons
Bordered by ten decked retinue
Canada, a group's revenue!

From cold to mild cold to deep cold
Whiter than a glass of pure gold
The hollers of pulping maples
Fall along the trees for apples
To hide the pale-shaded meadows
From shrilly and wintry shadows!

From one nation to another
Here all freely came to gather
From Pacific to Atlantic
Buzz anthems novel and antique
Of "O, Canada, Our Country,"
In both English and French poetry.

298. First Black

Thou hast trodden the path long paved
By the blood of civil rights' throng
Of which Dr. King civil struggles saved
Though the road was dark and long

Thy long walk to white house's glory
Did not in the right's movement begin
Though Selma to Montgomery
An open door it ushered in.

A savior in chic Obama
Rare, wise and uncommonly born;
Fluent in speech and sane in karma
What fêted an event he won?

Over the top of Mount Pisgah
There the good Lord retired Moses
And raised Luther King to trigger
A crown on first of black bosses.

299. Democracy

The womb of democracy has twins:
One is freedom, another is peace
And a nation which enjoys both wins
While those nations devoid of it miss.

There is a session of spanking air,
When people can freely make a choice
From elections held freely and fair,
An exact expression of their voice.

A people in their natures fallen
An apt manager that they must choose
Their liberties portly and swollen
He must further, bribes he must refuse.

There are regimes power abuses
They do contain, and rights they foster.
A rule, fraud it never amuses
While its record proves, by a pollster.

By itself democracy isn't best
Only that all other forms of rule
Which were finer or better or first
Have been inferior and never true.

The strength of a good democracy
Is not in a first-rate theocracy
But in values of institutions
And the rule by its constitutions.

300. Tip of Africa

At the tip of Africa,
What hilarity and grandeur!
The temperate west coasts
Of the lovely eastern grooves,
The sea, the rivers and oceans,
All together weave
Into a lovely impression.

The land of light and beauty;
You have come to South Africa,
The people in carefree moods
In houses paneled and lofty
By black and blue labors.

You hear the sounds of cars
And see the noises they create:
The best places are here
Where life goes to the brim
In the heart of Johannesburg,
The world's city.

Here are buried in Rands, gold
And its display
In splendorous Eaton center.
South of Africa
Is a-free-country,
A continent at the tip of Africa.

301. Epidemics

Oh, *Aids*, menace killer, pale, ugly!
No longer a regular visitor
But an on-the-loose stooge.
You have aggravated immunities
And robbed live communities.

You are an ephemera,
Striking with ephemeral speed,
Among the favorites of men.
You and cancer,
Refuse to grant life its properties
And deny old-age its liberties.

Two displaced beasts
Afflicting joys and inflicting blows;
You have broken human cells
With lethal force
And there is no place, space, or race
Where you have not raked your face.

Assiduous fighting men
Fighters of deadly agendas;
Our patrons in medicine
Refuse to accept your subtle drill
And in time your sting will chill.

302. Inside a Genocide

Sing not on thy bed to thy child
Who thou did not attempt to chide
For the evil that brews within him
Finds a pathway and spills the rim.

They christen it ethnic cleansing
With raised guns and axes they sing
When their fellow man is hunted
While heroic war hymnals chanted

Who dares to scream bloody murder!
To bring the fierce monster under?
Thou discount sounds of genocide
And thy virtue thou cast aside

The guiltless souls of the maimed dead
And sights of remains beheaded
In mass but shallow graves stench
While justice reckons on her bench.

For Rwanda, let the rivers say
And Darfur, the sands will spay
Cambodian fields will not bargain
And halls of gas cry, "Never Again!"

303. Kilimanjaro, the Mound of Gods

Oh Kilimanjaro, on the concourse of the Great Rift
Thou art exalted in the sight of the damned gods
Whence Chishimba concocts her dubious essence
And Musonda proudly pounces on weakened hearts

The peak of Mount Kilimanjaro fluffs in white
As if the gods on good day be enchanted
And the sides are silhouetted with dancing spirits
Whence climbers mysteriously disappear

The rivers that under the mound be stymied
And the oceans from far fret for its grandeur,
To the celebration of the rhythm of death
And the engines of life in sky nets re-appear

This is Mount Kilimanjaro, whence demons stay
The near-end of rising elements and gods spay
For the generations of Masai`s bowls do repay
And Nature, in its symphony, awards heights` pay.

304. No Longer an Alien

I have birthed three gorgeous girls
I have set businesses and rang bells
I've planted seeds of greatness in many
I have not extorted nor cheated any.

I have lectured law in many colleges
I have graduated Canadians of all ages
I have written many books on topics
I have vacated in seasons and tropics.

I have helped the destitute find a way
I've counseled and afflictions taken away
I have broken bread with my enemy
I have cried with those who hated me.

I have bought cars, houses and a garden
I won cases, wheels of justice I've gladden
I have set examples for others to follow
I planned my goals, vision for tomorrow.

Must I still be called an alien, a foreigner?
Mustn't I be elevated, be called an earner?
Mustn't I be celebrated and awarded?
Must I do more, just so I be regarded?

Surely, I'll rise up and be called blessed,
Surely, the stars have aligned, am blest,
For sure, I'll always be found innocent,
For sure, my legacy shall be magnificent.

BOOK IV ALIEN EXTRAORDINAIRE

305. Sweet Name

Sweet is your name to my memory
Smooth to my clean-shaven cheeks.
Did I tell you I knew about you
When in sense and word we rhymed?
You were my morning brightening star
A song I sang when I knew not how.
I saw your face always in phases,
When you smiled without blinking,
And spoke without moving upper lips.

Sound are my dreams when I fall asleep
Saying your name repeatedly and softly.
You were right when you kissed me
And not wrong when I held you back.
But it is your heart that I adore;
Your smiles that dropped spotless love –
For while many friends I have had,
To find one like you is truly hard.

306. Broken Lullaby

Stranger your tongue and tone is a broken lullaby
For before we had time to talk, we said goodbye.

I have met many who look like you, and have said "hi!"
Only to discover they are not you when they sigh.

I have tried to forget about you and reach very high
But when your frame illuminates mine, I say, "my, my!"

We were like sister and a brother when we shared a pie
But you knew to me you were not just but another guy.

One thing you didn't want me to do, I don't know why
You never let me stroke your knuckles or let me try.

You were an angel who brightened my very blue sky
And carved the wings with which I was able to fly.

307. Subway

Thank you, subway,
in which my mind comes to life.
For in you
I hatch poetry beautiful and sensual.
You fill my heart's chamber
with precious thoughts
And chip my hands
with fruitful narratives.
At St. George
myriads disembark in high heels
As bells and sirens
cloud my ripen memory.
I hear the chuckles
of the young nightingales
And pay attention
to the songs they sing.
Kennedy to Kipling
sings my soul in pure verse.
As I recite
the sweet numbers of divine crescendo.
In staccatos of blank and rhymed lines
I find my being
and the reason I live.
Oh, you gods that rule in these darkly tunnels,
Muses who sharpen my linguistic genius –
Stand at Bay when Castle
and Frank broadly view
And all veterans keep
and protect at War-den.
Strange
is when life abundantly flows at Keele,
And while guns and brains
are traded for favor at Jane.

308. Love-Marriage Mystery

Stranger to the world of love and deep feelings
Struggling to understand why we do things.
I saw a girl that I thought would marry me;
I slapped the flakes when it was not to be.
Is it only fantasies that our ideals faint?
Are there proofs that its dreams that we paint?
Reading through lives of human stories,
Realizing that they are just forsaken glories -
For every good two people that will marry,
Foremost will be to kill their ex's and burry.
Yet their memories will never escape at all,
Yelling aloud in their absent-minded chore.
It is the sound of heavy drops of tears,
Eating nerves and awakening myriads of fears.
Why do we change shirts like soccer players?
Willing to live with products of unmet prayers?
Oh, the mystery of marriage and love,
Only God truly knows what's true and above?

309. Goma Lakes

Besides the still waters of the Goma Lakes,
There we strutted silently in search of fortunes.
Movements in sacredly displayed bumble sashes,
In green lands of well-groomed marshlands.
Here in silent thoughts, we hatched future lives;
Our minds ran deeply, our studies gained thrust.
There at the great university uncertainties loomed
As our graduation days grew thinner and closer;
Men and boys here came together of age
While girls and women kicked in tight jeans.

Goma Lakes, our heart and soul:
With every ripple a circle of avowed expectations
And every drop, a thought of anticipated
vocations.
By the serene water fronts, our fears turned to joy
While our vanities told us we were still learners.
The level of every rescinding depth
Summed up our desire to overcome retention,
And fallen branches made our temporary bridges.
Oh, Goma Lakes, where our betters crossed
Before their day of jubilation, they celebrated!

Goma Lakes - your tall straight trees
Shall account for all the plans
Which besides your oasis, have been made.
Your caves of rounded bush and pricking barbs,
Hide deep secrets of broken virginities.
We shall come back to Goma Lakes
To vindicate our pasts now forgotten
And rejoice over pleasures that eluded us
Here at Goma Lakes, we find healing charms;
Besides the Goma Lakes, our hopes live again.
Here, our stories developed plot lines
And secured us from republics of cruel fines.

310. Sun

Sun when you are tiring, do so fast;
When you awake, blow no trumpets.
My people live under brimming rays;
Under the guise of licking roofs!
The meek darked-hearts share space
To rise from rage and pain of struggle,
Seeking for safety in a wrong place!

Sun on my people you shine last;
After exhausting all your strength!
You bring feeble rays of nutrients
To calm minds weak and hands limp.
Children fumble in filthy streets
Begging for food in stinking basins.

Sun, set and don't blame it on the past;
Neglecting hope on the sea of trouble.
Your light turns to mourning
And stories become weapons of failure.
They fall so deep in the pit of misery
And no-one braves to rescue them.

Sun close not your eyes on the just;
Darkness hides its devious deeds
In royal lies and eloquent speeches
While rulers build futures and chalets
Where they hoard pearls and treasure
To feed their gigantic appetites
With empty hearts and packed heads.

311. Mantras

Alien you brag, even spite yourself
That slavery had its part in antiquity.
You rave at the mention of its breaking
Claiming the ancient minds boo-booed.

You are not alone, many are just like you
Who serve frustrated bosses
And pal around with industrial superiors
Who thwart laws of ergonomics.

Rules in the executive boardroom
Ring a different tune from those on the floor.
Pain and its cousin, broken joys
Wrangle incessantly in disgruntled lines.

At shipping and receiving stations
Paper and palm-tracks crambo through coils
Irritating already fragile eardrums
Caused by years of repeated motions.

Breathless hearts pound into warehouses,
Ignoring blood is thinner than diesel,
While shaven bosses lax through idly,
Imbibing coffee and chanting mantras.

312. Wealth

Oh wealth, oh money, oh riches!
Oh mighty, oh power, oh strength!
Oh wealth – do not deny me
Oh money – do not elude me
Oh, if you can, embrace me
Oh, I beg, do not forsake me.

I know the merciless heart of lack
And the miserable hand of poverty
In both, human dignity retreats
And stiff hands of embarrassment rule
Sense and reason take an easy way
And knowledge is a beggar's whip.

I have asked you, lover of none
And beseeched your counsel,
Accepter of all
Because in you,
Wit and foolhardy trust
And fame answers only to you.

313. Chaisa

Chaisa, oh Chaisa, how poor a place
The thought of you breaks my heart
Oh Chaisa, how dusty your streets.

Chaisa, women carry two pairs of shoes
And wish churches have two washrooms
Little army cling to ivory-legged limbs
And would not give up to strong winds.

Chaisa, men travel with polish brushes
And boys wear camouflaged dustcoats.
Chaisa, your houses have no foundations
Catching easy colds from heavy tropics.

How can I forget you, in your lowly hour?
Or forsake you, when you need power?
Chaisa, how can I your desolation ignore
When in dirt and dust you lay low?

314. Northern Hemisphere

I sing to your beautiful skies and days
Oh, universe of the magnificent North!
As a child I only thought of rains
And sun-scorched patches of October.
In visions, wisdom slept pale;
In endless whispers of love.
The posts of the universe in twos posit,
Walking between thickets of dry sands
And reaching white and chilly valleys.
Our minds race infantile fantasies -
Comparing you only to Aphrodite.
A child in terror-ripped village
Vowed to drown the darling of South
Calling her Snow and Mirage.

315. Feeble Rights

It is obvious and I can see it in your mind
As you walk, aimlessly and eyes down.
You are always thinking as you walk
And this you do day and night.
You never straighten up your head
And your steps are always disoriented.
Even in the flurry of spring,
Your eyes are still small and squeezed.
You walk as if you are hiding something
And your own salutes betray you.
You are an alien, better you admit it
Or those who lent you feeble rights
Confiscate the little you have.
The streets on which you trot
Are hard and cold, very cold.
They were manufactured from bitumen
Acquired from the sweat of slave labor
The labor of vindictiveness.
The peace of the world you do not have
And neither do you possess joy.
You claim you stay in a paneled house,
Which is but a refreshing station
And a changing room
To which you only return at mid-night
To munch hard crusts of bread
Since you have no time to cook,
And early in the morning,
You run the monstrous machines
Which neither retire nor rest.

316. Weird Thinking

The plight of an alien is his platitude.
You left your own country with a quest
Hoping to find gold scattered in the
Polished boulevards of trekkersland.
You had thought your own peoples
Were ruined and uncivilized,
You have used the term "backwards"
Time and again, as if your people
Aren't even trying to make progress.
Prisoner of your own weird thinking,
Is almost suitable to you,
And your own languid motives cheat you.
You are never content, never satisfied.
Some people have better manners,
And better manners are bedrocks of
Candid civilizations.
Some people display mature ways of life
And do not ignorantly offend others
In the lands in which they are aliens.
Some are aliens on grants,
The benefits of which will never
Develop their deserted nations.
There were opportunities you never saw
In the land in which you claim
Nothing developmental goes on.
But now you say, how I will be rich
When I return to my own country;
Such hypocrisy is huge,
Since kings are born, and not made.

317. Industrial Towns

I see the rains pouring steadily outside.
The land is being watered for cultivation
And you are wondering why the waste
Since no clear land exists,
Only silhouetted towers and skyscrapers.
No pigsties exist, too,
Only idyll havens
Full of electronically operated motors.
There is no hoe for agriculture, either.
They have combine harvesters,
And long honked tracks and tractors
Which bring in corn, wheat and rice
In bulk supplies for sale and export.
There are transit carriers and long buses
Carrying busy and disheveled men
And blond and brunette women.
Industrial power is auto-run
While human labor works them in shifts
And their din never fades.
Such is the state of affairs in these
Industrial towns where gold is unheard of.
Alien, you only see automobiles
Which are feminine
Since their owners treasure them more
Than they care for their wives.
Cars outnumber the traveling public
And the outnumbered, control traffic rights.
Alien, you see all the beautiful surroundings
And they don't belong to anyone
As owners have not paid for mortgages.

318. Free Existence

An alien, is he only so because of birth?
If we should allow him to obey laws
Just as citizens do,
Can't we also allow him to exist freely?
An alien is a dreamer,
Always dreaming of threats of relocation.
What if he does not have anywhere to go?
If his native land is infested by plagues
Or is invaded by other foreigners,
Or worse still, canopied by battle planes?
Is it only lack or poverty,
That pushes an alien to voyage?
He sees innocent policemen in dreams
Coming towards him and asking for papers,
Demanding that he shows them evidence
That he came in through right means.
By right means, they do not mean
Coming by chartered flights
Or in luxurious greyhounds,
But with authorization by the
Consulate of the nations
Which, too, exist in the alien's country.
They talk about law and order and cops.
They count the alien's steps and
Ensure that he does not exceed the limit.
Yet you seem to understand law and order
And you are more law-abiding than
The citizens of the nation in which
You seek refuge.
If you are law-abiding,
Why do you still think you are a foreigner?

319. Dreams of an Alien

The dreams of an alien are weapons,
Horrendous and lethal.
His night visions are invisible
And well-plotted.
In his dreams, an alien can be free,
Free from fear of relocation and trespass.
In his night visions he can buy a house,
Find great a job and be an executive.
In his dreams all plants are green,
And all roads lead to bliss.
In these exotics all scenes are in summer,
No winter inconveniences,
And all settings are in late spring
With beautiful surroundings and flowers;
And all flowers are either daisies or roses,
And all roses are red and white.
But he wakes up, all about him
Is either blurred or suffocated;
How he longs for the night
When he can fall again and fantasize
And reach places
Too difficult for commoners,
And wear clothes
Too expensive for the jobless.
An alien's dreams are sweet, too.
In the best of deep dreaming,
Ideas are laid and hatched in full,
Bearing green leaves and yellow fruits.
Here he is not imprisoned by his reason
But liberated by it.

320. Schizophrenic

An alien is accused of being schizophrenic,
A mental disorder of ambivalence.
He is made to behave like one
Because he does not have enough sleep.
A man with rights is a small god,
Able to recreate and reproduce.
But a foreigner is like an impotent rich ruler.

"Once there lived an impotent emperor,
Who, due to sheer vanity,
Added one concubine to the numbers yearly.
The thing in between was but a haunch.
The young charmed maidens were wasting
Inside the marble palace.
They peeped through narrow lintels
For the courtiers who wear no silky apparel
And feed on no dignified a table.
Yet they have living hernias.
He was a king with a populous kingdom,
Extending from coast to coast,
And his queens lay flat-bellied
As flat as the king's own dining table!"

So is an alien, in the land in which
His abilities are despised and ignored.
Alien wouldn't despise, the schizophrenic.

321. Hope

An alien counsels, do not underestimate
The power of hope because hope outlives.
Hope in the land where you never wasted
Your umbilical cord.
Hope is a living thing; and has a heart.
Hope passes current inconveniences
And brings valued agendas to the brim.

"I hope in these hopeless terrains
Of landlessness.
In the midst of failure, l have seen success,
And I can reason why.
I walk with eyes down, an open mind and
With eclectic thoughts.
I allow not my independence to betray me."

Though the land where you live is not yours,
Do not despise your economic potential.
It cannot be hijacked, but gives you power,
The ability to procreate and improve others.
Do not be reduced to a pathetic loafer,
And that, not even in your matrimonial bed.
But write books, on poetry or romance
And sell them on the Internet or bookstores
And earn yourself a reasonable living.
In that way, you can sit down
And let your talents feed you.

322. Rich People

The alien advises, there are rich people
And people with riches.
Rich people are rare and few in number
Since they have to have rich minds.
People with riches are large in numbers
But riches find wings and fly away.
People go to work daily, yet only little benefit.
I learned this because
I was once looking for reality's old meaning
And stumbled on several laws of economics.
Streets are filled with movements of workers
Children go to fast restaurants for fatty foods.
They grow up obese or near to it
And are ashamed of themselves.
Others in nations where food is scarce
Deem it a blessing to be fat, even very fat.
When they get skinny,
They are ashamed of themselves
Because society might think
They suffer from incurable diseases.

Tax return brings future rebates.
I regret selling my house in my native land,
And now I move like a shadow
And a destitute in a foreign land.

"Time is Money" is true to the West
And "by grace we survive," is to the South.

323. Critical Thinker

An alien is not a stranger to critical
Thinking; he does engage his mind
In productive reasoning.
Truth is what always wins and stays
Untainted and unadulterated.

"Once there was a man determined
To defeated truth. He introduced his
Arguments with lies and supported
Them with lies. Then one day his
First born son was born and medical
Officials told him that he was a girl.
He disputed the fact with truth
Because he saw that the baby
Had no female features on it
And he would not give his child
A girl's name. From that time on,
He respected truth and vowed
To say the truth and nothing
But the truth: and so, God helped him!"

A truthful plan is not devoid of ideas,
It can only be neglected.
It is truth that foreigners are,
By relativity, very wealthy.
There is truth that they live
To invest since they might be asked to
Leave for their countries.
In your own country, critical thinking
Is rare because all you see is familiar
To you and to everybody else.
You are shaped in a predictable form
And good ideas are not easily conceived.
Good plans are rubies in strange lands.

324. Race of Women

I was a stranger to the race of women
Until I had tied a matrimonial knot.
Beautiful, elegant women are very strange,
And do they really exist in strange lands?
"Beauty is in the eyes of the beholder"
As it applies to women, is very deceptive.
For after one marries and stays with her,
He ceases to see her face,
However pretty it is,
Instead one begins to see her heart,
However hidden it might be.
Women are sophisticated from afar,
Nearer they are not.
Their charm is not on what they put on,
But in what they neglect.
From afar, her lips are red and dripping;
Her eyes are doves and flying;
Her mouth is watery and inviting;
Her curves are divine and enticing;
And her voice is soft, as calm as streams
Of the quiet waters.
But what you don't know about her
Is that she is a mystery,
As unpredictable as a chameleon.
Yet when she comes nearer,
And after you place her in your arms,
She is simply as delicate as rules of begging.
Those eyes are just large globes,
Empty sockets, but lively and beautiful
And strong men have paid for them.
She wears fashions of deceiving splendor
And you learn to love her
For the reality that you don't even know.

325. Idle Mind

Oh, that I should be given something,
Cried an alien.
That I might not stay idle,
Loafing and eating the bread of laxity.
Work is the aim of life,
The bell that awakens conscience.
A worker owns the world in which
He toils and derives satisfaction from it.
In the pockets of work are
Three compartments;
One says *eat*, the other says *shelter*
And the last one says *clothe*.
These compartments are occupied
And when they are empty,
Untold miseries and pain come.
That is why a worker has
Found the bait to attract the three.
A loafer has not.

"One day a crazy man washed his
School books in the sink in order to
Soften his understanding of the subject.
He forgot that there is no nexus
Between paper and grey matter,
Though some papers may be grey.
In another institution of learning
A crazy student was found studying
With lights switched off. After the
Lights were switched on, he was seen
Busy in his books flapping pages
And making notes. Asked why he was
Studying in the dark, he replied that
He had no time to waste, day or night."

326. Time

To be stranger to time is worse than
The sin of immorality.
Immorality, though,
Is a worst state of the heart.
Time helps us to demarcate a day
And helps our days flow smoothly,
And is essential to life.
Yet time brings anxiety and heartaches.
The realization that there is time
Is what forces the lazy to get up
But hard workers are deluded
By the idea that time eludes them!
The guilt that follows moments
Of time wasting are greater than
The pleasures that are achieved
As a result of doing little in much time.
There is time for everything and
No time for nothing.
That is why God has allowed people
To work in their dreams
Even though their bodies are dead.
In a place where everybody works
And time is as vital as the heart's state,
Find strength to spend eight
Or twelve hours of real work.
An alien from the land of the carefree
Will starve to death in a province
Where you earn a dollar hourly,
And not a salary for no work done at all.
Time spent at school is thus appreciated
As long as a salary
Honors your past school efforts.

327. Good and Evil

A stranger warns; do not put your trust in mortal men
Born from the grotesque wombs of women.
Scientists too are not to be overtly trusted.
One of them once said,
"Evil and good are simply hypothetical ideas
And neither bad nor good people exist."
He perceives evil as a mental perspective
And yet our elders, who have seen much,
Dispute the fact as inconsistency.
Evil and good are the sciences of morality,
Which are to be learned empirically
And which also distinguish
Mature men and immature women from
Immature men and mature women.
To deny evil exists is to be evil personified
And to discard thrives to be good,
Is being truly unscientific.
Oh alien, poor alien,
Be a believer in truth and a disbeliever of evil
And in that you will prove the ancient slogan
That Darwin left hanging by simple postulations.
The 'unimpeachable' Evolution Theory is an enigma
To non-scientists and a mental grave to the religious
And both are not to be supposed.
To be professor with no good or bad notion
Is like being ridiculed for walking on the moon,
And this too is as a bath in concentrated acid.

328. Rules of the Game

The alien is sworn to play by
"The Rules of the Game" and I say
Do not despise such cheap propaganda.
These are the essential mores
And dynamic social rules
Which have shaped our world
From time immemorial.
They have maintained a certain amount
Of social order and tranquility
And have squeezed delinquency
From sophisticated social misfits.

Advocates of our legal system
And enforcers of our laws
Are they trained to pursue or
Denigrate our earthly rights?
Do they defend or defeat law?
Do infidels escape while
The innocent are punished,
If it is not so, then tell me?
Cooked defenses are tasty,
More than prosecution procedures.
Acquittals on technicalities
And convictions on insufficiency of
Evidence are all ploys to deny justice
To the men and women who can't talk
Yet we repair mitigations and allow
Evil to flourish in a world
In which felon is lawlessness
While defending of hard cores
Is quintessential professionalism.
Alien, seek to do justice, always.

329. Rundlehorn Drive

The fantastic breeze just on
The onset of summer
In the inner corridor of Rundlehorn Drive
Behind Pinehill Street, Calgary, Alberta
Swells with sounds of remembrance.
The wetlands of Twatotela Crescent,
Overshadowed by light industrial dins,
In the land where God has never retired
And miners never go on annual vacations.
The feeling of summer is
Light to the blind soul
Awakening all the senses of ecstasy
And bringing joy to its full.
Oh, how I love these senses,
The sweet smells of after rains
Which have poured all night long
And soothe our feeling of trepidations.
This breeze is calm
And resonates with unexplained
Greatness and mildness
And Alberta's weather is unpredictable,
A strange reminder of the serenity
Of Zambia in the cold season.

330. Fall from Purity

Why is it that your buttocks are flat,
Like a can of beer, they are empty?
You stuff and staff them
With pieces of pink paper
So that when you walk
No lines follow your contours.
You have been complaining,
That one day you are going to
Dig out the entire road network
Because you have seen enough
Bodies and empty buttocks.
You complain that
Young girls are making you crazy.
That they have no manners because of
The way they dress which
Leave a lot to be desired.
Stop moving, alien,
Because what you have just seen
Is only a drop in an ocean.
You are yet to see
The winter of shameless nudes;
The spring of artificial breasts,
The summer of bizarre heights
And then you will fall from purity.

331. Super Problems

Alien in the nation to which
You have proudly gone to settle,
Do not overlook the value of
Small nations around.
Do not say the land in which
I have graciously sought refuge
Is a super class super power.
For the rulers of the smaller
But peaceful nations
Will hear you and lecture you.
For there must be good leaders
To breed excellent followers.
But with the theory of
International politics
Big nations do not lead
Smaller nations because of
The doctrine of Sovereignty.
Yet the Republic of South Africa
Rules over the kingdoms of
Lesotho and Swaziland
With economic overloads.
The United States of America
Rules over Iraq and Afghanistan
With military overtones.
Alien, superpowers have
Super problems and small nations
May have huge economic potentials.
And do not be fooled:
Big nations will someday collapse
Just like Rome and Egypt did
And smaller nations will rise
Just when you least expect it.

332. Emmerance

This is the word of wisdom
The alien gave to Emmerance
In the land in which
She was born,
A land which became hers
By virtue, of birth,
And the land in which her
Umbilical cord was accurately
Cut and destroyed:

"To be truly free, my daughter,
Acquire knowledge and by it
Gain understanding, discretion,
Goodwill and prudence.

Do not wait for the money lovers
To offer you patterned knowledge,
The world around you shall be
Your classroom and nature
Shall tell you all you need to know.

Read books written by
Passionate researchers and
Do not despise the counsel
Of those who came before you.
Whenever your head gets stuck,
Do not be headstrong,
But rather lift up your eyes
To the skies where He lives.

True freedom, my well beloved,
Lies in knowing who you are
And respecting the rights of others."

333. Clientele

I, an alien and a visitor in the land of
The mortals again and again ask this:
Do politicians play by the rules or against?
They amass lucrative wealth
At the expense of governable masses
And pretend to play patriotism
Only, and only when it befits them
And as quickly as they lose elections
They organize versatile protests.

Protocol.
Politics.
Power.

Apart from their plosive sounds,
What do they share in common, tell me?
They act on the stage of frail promises,
And are cheered for victories
They never initiated.
These are day-time robbers.
What more, should I talk about
Their "honorable titles,"
And the monopoly they demand
On sweat-earned national capital
Which they have grabbed
And registered in their names, far away!
This is strange,
And a chasing after wind.
Liars are attractive and unavoidable.
Extortionists are simple and organized,
No wonder they easily win the hearts
Of hard-working citizens.
Has our world paid lip-service
To the troubles of voiceless masses?

334. Preachers and Politicians

They preach…
They teach
And loudly proclaim.
The pulpit and senate podiums
And parliament and church buildings are one.
The constitution,
And the Bible
Are both enforceable…
And exegesis and legal interpretation
Are similar
And so is the clientele for one,
The clergy,
The same as for the other,
The politician.
Promises…and the Word of God,
Reverberate in the ears of
The "faithfuls" in the name of God.
And the "faith-fools" are sulked
In the name of partisanship.
Actions are taken and judgments passed.
"Believe in the Lord and you will be saved,"
Declares one,
And, "Believe in the loan and receive low rates,"
Demands the other.
Give.
Give.
And "it shall be given back to you,"
Emphasizes the clergyman…
Give up,
Give up!
Give up what: property, rights?
Stresses the politician.

335. Love Theorem

"Falling in love is chemical reaction,"
Retorts the chauvinist.
One can stay in love,
And the other can walk into it,
And marriage is a recipe for disaster
And the bigot does not know.
Love dies. And love lives.
Love is a predictable feeling.
And love has a life span.
And nobody seems to dispute all that,
A twenty first century love theorem
And a blatant one for that matter.
For the older generation,
Marriage is better than flirtation.
But for the novel generation,
Vacillation from partner to partner
Is not a specialization in promiscuity.
Fall in love.
And multiply the falling again and again
And then marry her, for God's sake,
And tell the coward to be brave
And tell him that he should marry!
To live with a woman,
Is definitely very hard indeed,
But to live without her
Is unarguably not what a man needs.
And this is the song, sing it again:
To the stranger, sing organized rhythms
And play the drums to deafness
And loudly declare, that divorce,
Is a tuneless symphony played by
A disorganized orchestra.

336. Money and Politics

Alien, in the foreign land where you go,
Several things you must remember
And one thing you should not forget:
That politics and life are twins;
They have existed alongside each other
For time and time immemorial.
Life is not run by politicians
But politics rule at the center of life
Money and politics
Are two sides of the same coin
Yet politics have hijacked its place
And relegated it to obscurity.
Be no stranger to cash
And embrace the chance to politick
Because money is the weapon of politics
And them that have it
Are tigers in their own jungles.
Business and charities
And non-governmental organizations
And the church and interest groups
Have joined forces, everywhere.
There's no place where their voice
Has not been heard and neither is money's.
Are politicians white washed tombs?
People appoint them; politics promote them.
And I am sure money will demote them.
Alien,
Join politics, like me,
But don't be a politician, like them.

337. Boiling Soul

Why my soul you boil within me?
Why you constantly unsettle yourself?
Should I tread the canyons and deserts
To bring you the peace you deserve?

Peace swings like babies on pendulum
My soul groans like a pigeon
My blood boils furiously like a broiler
While I feel the measure of real drapes.

Is there solace for the troubled soul?
Is there moments when they can rest?
Is there a place quiet and peaceful?
Is there a place for souls in distress?

Yet I am weary and tired of just living
While my peers swim in chocolate dyes
And wear suits of green embroidery.
Is there peace for a man of many plans?

338. Payday

Alien to the feelings that you desire,
To the dreams that pass by in the night.
There you sit in the center of burning fire
To absolve every punch without a fight,
And day lingers like a pitiful tear.
As memory holds her bowels tight
To run from shadows she must not fear.
Do you think night is dark, day bright?
They work better whose respect is for peer
Who frighten fear with a sense of might
And believe payday is very near
To inoculate lack and numb the bite.

339. Woman's Side

A stranger I am to colds, and lengths,
and heights and wides,
To free sight, to climbs, and
To pocking noses.
Mine is not the stature of giants
Nor of the pride of
Easier-spelled names.
And yet in this proudly I stand;
In the bosom of a woman's side,
In the chamber of pulping nerves
And the path of flowing life!

On the wrong tunes, they have played
The dancers have not moved a step
Flat tires are sustained
By enlarging fondling
And soft voices of dying breathe.
There is no known sweetness as these,
No sense as six times these
Hidden fountains!
Their taste no man has ever despised
And in these embraces, dies the might
And surrenders vetted heroes.

340. Bed Chamber

Alien to the ways of the bed chamber
Looking as one battered by seven harmers
Pulsing perfidiously in off and on modes
Being unable in manner or posture to recant.

Alien you neglected the waves of life
Like an impotent king with myriad virgins.
There is purpose in breathing deeply
And intimately in the process of nature.

Men use toys to bridge off the child guy
And women look for glories in gossip.
It is what they never say that hurts;
For women as men, fear to fail in bed.

These lives divine no Viagra's need
Virility rescinding nimbleness to feed
Their agile surging power in force to recede
Reducing procreativity in source and speed.

341. Rulers

When rulers rule, they say great things.
Their voice is heard in motion and pictures;
Their name is called by imperials and kings.
In games by lot pairs crash in fixtures.

The known will soon end in quarterfinals;
The unknown will ascend to the grand trials.
Twelve men will compete for a prize tonight
And a numberless throng will give a cheer.

In their wallets and purses days rejoice
And their work place is a litter of grief.
Here is a man with justice he rules
Guiding minds and ideas to laughing tables.

Swerving chairs and plates in joy will cheer
To mark a season of mended hopes;
This for long has eluded their wishes
But with a vote of confidence will return.

342. Ignorance

I was, ignorant of the race of all
Until I came to Toronto Airport lounge
Then I saw the world in a lamp of glitter.

I was, cheated by the illusions of race
Until I sat on transit's rocket wheels
Then I learned that people exist in colors.

I was, holding on to untruthful legends
Until I entered the mammoth subways
Then I realized variety has a name.

I was, afraid to talk my thoughts aloud
Until at Humber I entered a geniuses' class
Then I saw that brains respect no threats.

I was, disturbed by my foreign accent
Until I spoke words attractive and smooth
Then I knew that I was complete and human.

For the lessons we learn while awake
Strange they may be, yet short and true.

343. Roundness of the Globe

"Do not gaze at me",
Began the alien,
"With those blue and brown eyes of yours.
I also have my own people, with a culture.
We were ten when we were born,
With seven strong boys and three girls.
We leaped through the jungle of life
With fried opinions and hammered lips
And found the world a stratum of classes.
Now I have lost all who were mine,
And that not through bullets or jaw-bones,
But through the roundness of the globe.
Yet I have this to my credit,
I love the smell of ink, and the
Bluntness of a pen, and my hands,
Are strings on a well-tuned violin."

Thus, began and ended the
Curriculum vitae of the alien,
Whose brief account of his own
Qualification and previous occupation,
Does not exceed the thoughts
Of those around him,
And the job that he seeks
Is not in places their qualified delve.

344. Epiloguia

The song of an alien, for the alien,
Has been sung in a foreign land
Where he has not belonged,
And to the people unfamiliar
And unappealing,
From the world of issues.

To munch a large elephant
Is the duty of everybody,
Because by its size, an elephant is huge.
One man picks one piece
And faithfully feeds it to another man
Who was left idling at home,
Yet the glory of the killer is unknown.

To kill a huge beast,
Allow it to swallow you alive first
Lest in-between its teeth you lie grounded.
In the land in which you are,
You are an alien, a visitor, a stranger.
Eat only the portion of your grass
And sleep only on the bed you have made
And plant seeds of benevolence
In order to reap fruits of good will
From honest plants of undaunted justice.

On this earth, we are all aliens
And many will be
The forces of alienation.
Through ink and pain,
We write our experiences
And sow seeds of love in others.

BOOK V DIVINE SUPERIORITY

345. Sonate to Plenty

You don't just own cattle on a thousand hills,
You are in charge of all corporate bills;
Indeed, I now need thousands of moneys,
Your love keeps me warm as myriad honeys;
I go not to bed worry'ng of the next cash,
I'm pleased, I'm endeared by a rainbow dash;
My funds surfeit, my purse swirls to the brim,
With abundance, You fill me to the rim;
Never shall I have problems gaining wealth,
Never shall I worry due to my health;
One who owns gold and silver is my Dad,
He won't allow His son lack or go sad;
My soul, be happy, in God You have shares,
Do find peace, tomorrow for self it cares.

346. Words Fail Me

Oh, Lord God, you created me with all tools
Yet words fail me to declare all your rules
For thou art our God, the only true God
For thou art unique, O Transcendent Lord
For thou art the owner, master, True Sir
And all creation worships you, near and far
Thou art our Holy Father in all wise
For you carest, provideth, and chastise
Oh, Supreme Lord, Despotes, O Kurios
Our All in all, the Almighty, O Theos.

347. Indescribable YOU

How can I praise You,
O sweetest of Heaven,
You,
who dwells in unapproachable haven,
You, who is terrific,
prolific,
and truly omnific
Thy creation, magnific,
and altogether beatific!

348. Ultimate Prayer

Let my future be uncertain, undefined, unclear,
So, I can know the power of Your convincing faith;
Let the sharpest pain lunge through my bleeding flesh,
So, I can appreciate the pleasure of Your healing hand;
Let me suffer loss, be destitute and reel from misery,
So, I can understand the meaning of divine providence;
Let my plans be frustrated, my dreams fail to come true,
So, I can stay true to what You have purposed for my life;
Let me experience disappointment, utter humiliation,
So, I should never put my trust in my own shrewdness;
Let me be rejected, dejected and totally offended,
So, I should learn to love those who despise me;
Let me fail lamentably, suffer invectives and insults,
So, I should endear every victory that comes from You;
Let me taste lack, be broke beyond penniless despair,
So, I should know that every good gift comes from above;
Let me go naked, be vulnerable, homeless and needy,
So, I can crave to abide under the shadow of Your wings;
Let somebody else win, best me, come out ahead of me,

So, I should be contented with the success that is Yours;
Let me die a bitter, painful and an agonizing death,
So, I may wake up whole, in blissful, joyous by and by.

349. Good Grace

You have delivered me from their wolverine claws
You have spoken to their minds and hearts
And You have silenced the trouble-makers
Surely, their grasp is broken, their will shattered
The Giffens, will not for me trouble make
Lord, I am assured of Your never-ending love
I am satisfied with Your everlasting kindness
You have shown me mercy and preserved me
Also, I have watched in the morning hours
And have heart Your tender voice saying,
"It is over, it is over my son, you're free!"
O bless the Lord, bless the Lord O my soul
And do not forget His benefits and good works
For as sure as day and night will reveal themselves
So has the Good Lord manifested His good grace.

350. In Your Mercy, I Trust

You will again deliver me from
The panther's hold,
So, Your eternal wonder I may live to behold;
The Peter's inquiries, You will also render null,
The weapon of a pen, will not be sharp, will remain dull;
You will speak my name in their midst with favor,
All for Your righteousness' sake, not because I am clever;
I have forgiven Hagos, You will reward him with acceptance;
You're my hope, Oh Lord of mercy, my Heavenly entrance;
I know, I will not be disappointed,
For You'll defend me;
I will raise a praise anthem, and from afar only see;
Yes, I'll watch Your divine advocacy, You're my lawyer;
My fear, You'll conquer, O great and mighty destroyer.

351. Essence of Presence

We have wondered away from Your presence
We thought of floundering Your holy essence
Yet, not for a moment did You forsake us
Not for a moment You withdrew Jesus
Father, You saw us when we did not pray
You were acquainted with our vainly play
You did not forget us, not even once
You did not grant our enemy a chance
On our knees, will we bow before this Cross
1340 Not for a time, will we stray from its course.

352. When I Pray

My soul wonders like one lost in deep jungle
I seek for peace my heart so longs for
When I awake, my worries are before me
When I say I should hide, behold I am still here

Taken by the wiles of the world
Pricked by the thorns of the world
Tricked by the lies of the world
Stricken by the tries of the world

My only recourse is to you, dear Lord
When I picked up that Holy Script,
Oh, even in this I am deeply enchanted,
How that the book so simple, breeds solutions divine

How that man in his desperation forsakes it
That woman have begged for fullness apart from it
That in our humiliation we have not gone to it
And our own frailty of life have not discovered it

For me, I toss in bed for hours, hours without end
I reason in the secrets of my thoughts without end
I reflect on the myth of the coming end
Oh, who will decipher beginning from end

For there is no peace one finds in earthly glory
No-one has returned to tell of the end of life
Indeed, we may desire to live but for this life
Yet, within my soul there is faith divine

Within the concourses of my doubts I find belief
Within the worries of life I find a way open
Within this hole, this emptiness of my heart
Within this search my heart hears a voice

I once walked the dry steps of the print of God
Heard the waterfall of glorified saints sing and pray
And led a throng of worshippers to the throne of mercy;
Oh, how my being rejoices for a chance of this!

My soul said, indulge for tomorrow is illusive
Drink and be merry and shun the fear of death
Drown yourself in the pleasure of life
And forget about the fear of the good Lord.

My own views were clear and I said I will attempt all
I will find out what is it that the wicked have mastered,
I will go where they learn and observe them
I will pretend I have no knowledge of the Holy One

I struggled to find my hand at their best skill and power
For with simplicity they acquired pleasure
And with sophistication they braved hearts and souls
And with plain gain they indulged to the very essence.

At no time did they mention of the wrath of Judgment
No-one dared to define the end of all sinners
For to them, the end comes with the last breath,
And they hope only for what mind and brain demand.

They sang of songs of pure earthly joys
They planned for their sons and daughters
They acquired great wealth with all mighty
They knew they would die someday.

I saw that they had a thought of the future, their future
They abhorred any who dared mentioned God
And they looked down upon those who believe
For to them, only shallow minds contemplate God.

Many times, I saw sense in their machinations
Their plans prospered and they lived in luxury
Their ingenuity brought forth innovations
Their brilliance revolutionises technologies.

I said to myself, this is how life should be approached
Without the bondage of a faith that never rewards
The worries of the omissions to an invisible God
And the fears of the Judgment to come.

Just when I began to be comfortable, my soul failed me
My achievements became trophies of a desperate winner
And all those defences I knew kept me safe
Only gave me more sleepless nights and great perturbation

I have come to a place of reconciliation, a place of penance
When I think that I have a legacy, alas, it has no foundation
When I say I will depend on the books I have written
In that I find a small joy and a begging ferment.

For man, there is nothing good but to eat and drink
To enjoy the flowers growing naturally in nature
And to work with one's hands to perfection
While God lends us all a brief existence on earth.

And I walked by the elegant cemetery where death is pensive
There I saw the frailty of man's machinations
I heard the unsaid silences of the traps of living without God
And my heart became a circus of troubled waters.

Who has wisdom to read the invisible ink
To understand that it is a chance of naught
To peg our hopes in things we do
To forget the mercies of the Holy One

Deep down my heart I knew the answer, only imperfect
I knew that from the cheapness of God's love
Flows the priceless trophy of life's desires
For which man may be saved and delivered

It is travesty, that weak men have abused the grace
of God
That money and materialism have ended real
prayer
And all live only to please their bellies
Without giving God His glory

I now understand what I should do: not tomorrow
I will tell God of all my weaknesses: he heals souls
I will disclose my deepest ambitions: he will bear
with me
And I will ask for his forgiveness: he is slow to
anger;
For he abounds in mercy and compassion

Oh God, add more hours to my whimpering years
Do not give my soul to the shackles of the burning
hell,
And let me tell of your wonders like you are
Even when I need it only for a short time

And in these my daily toils, teach me to see the
end
For in much toiling I am still very empty
And in much anticipation,
I gain only frustration
As in one duty there is more tasks waiting

Give me a simple life to enjoy,
a simple life to guard
Give me love for those things that matter to you
And the knowledge of those things that have value
Since only through you can there be true peace

I have three or four adventures I would like to fulfill
Oh Lord, you know they are in line but only of grace
They are the childish ambitions of my life
And if I should achieve them I know they are vanity

Yet give them to me, nevertheless
What is this white which my body so desire
What is this power that my mind will cheer
And this law that I may be nobly sure

In this white, I will know you have been fair to mankind
In this power I will bring to you the glories of earth
And in these I will build for all nations a godly rest;
For in these vanities, let your true wisdom reign

When I pray, I seek for highs higher than spirits
When I pray I see with a clearer lens
When I pray, I heal from all anxieties
When I pray, even bad turns to God's glory

Oh, the mystery of an answered prayer
The strength of one who is a skilled player
Because we all can become only good
When what we feed on is God's love food

353. Jesus Christ

In coming He chose us, promises fulfilled
In living He loved us, all sickness He healed
In dying He saved us, all sin paid for in full
In rising He freed us, for He's faithful
In ascending He held us, many rooms to create
In sitting He prays us, the way is straight
In returning He gathers us, in Him we grow
In judging He rewards us, in Him we glow
In separating He blest us, hearts at ease
In reigning He changes us, His rule is in peace.

354. Works of Charity

For the sake of your secret blessings, don`t pay
There is a rewarder of those who dare to pray
Whose right hand does not interfere with left
And when they gave they quickly left.

Blessed are those who must not show off
When all they did was help the sufferings of
Those who had nothing even to repay
For all the gifts received when they pray.

It is better to give your gifts in secret
Where no-one can dig through the concrete
And hope to find out that it was you
Who gave the way of the blessed few.

God honors the gifts given in love
The ones which are not announced above
So that no-one can know the givers
And such receive all of God`s favors.

355. Cheerful Giver

God loves a cheerful giver;
The one who gives for a purpose,
The purpose greater than just showing off.
There are people in this world who need help.
There are people in need of our help every day
And these people should be the genuine recipients of our gifts.
We should be careful that we are not heaping rewards on those who already have plenty
Or on those who are bent on building their own empires in the name of God.
God has made it very clear that our giving
Should be in secret and not in public making a publicity stunt of it.
When we do such, we pre-empt God`s ability to bless us,
And in that way too, we receive the praises of men
And miss out on true divine rewards.
Seek, and again I say, seek to give,
Especially to those in desperate need,
And God will surely bless you.

356. Mercy and Grace

Mercy withheld from us what we deserve
Grace gave to us what we did not deserve
Lord, it was mercy that saved us from hell
And grace did send us to heaven's well
By mercy I knew that sin's shame was gone
And by grace, I knew that God's will was done
Mercy, how wonderful You sealed the hole
Grace, how amazing Your rule made me whole
So, I bow, with truth that mercy found me
I worship, grace gave me eyes now I see.

357. God and Wine, I

Genesis portrays wine as a social beverage
For merriment and distress relief.
It was drunk at social functions
And it came to be a symbol of blessings
To those who had found favor in the eyes of God.
Its intoxicating effects were not placed to the
gallows. Surely, those who floundered with its effects,
Especially if they took advantage of those who
were very drunk,
Were looked upon with impunity.
Even that did not discount the beckoners of
blessings And God`s endorsement of approval
On those who deservedly earned it.
In the main, wine had come to be a mark of
richness, happiness
And a blessing to be bestowed upon those who
had done good or great things.

358. God and Wine, II

For Noah having been delivered from the flood
And from drowning in the pool of the lost blood
In the land where he was to be newly enchanted
Drunk to nakedness from the vineyard he planted

In the shock of the effects of that brew of wine
Then we awake to reality, to discover if all is fine
For the intoxication does last but for a night
And we should know from thence if all is right

Oh, Melchizedek, thou King of Salem
Thou Priest of the Highest of Jerusalem
For thine wast the gifts of pure wine
And bread baked from the embers of pine!

When God destroyed the cities of Siddim
For the sins of the people had come to Him
He preserved Lot with daughters, no wife
Who made him drunk, and began a life.

From the son`s wine, Isaac drank to bless
From the heirs to the patriarchs, no less
And wine was the thing God would give
To sustain man and his sins to forgive.

O this blood of grapes, sparkling and red
For peers, choice drink and sleep-aid
For gods, trophy, for mortals, a green card
And whose countenance it has made glad

A drink offering to the might gods is wine
A quota given neither with malice nor brine
Yet forbidden in the Tent of Meeting
While the earth gladly takes of its biting.

For a Nazarite shall bear a special swagger
Only separated from all wine's vinegar
Albeit, a shaven Nazarite shan't of wine drink
And from his duties he shall not brink.

The God of heaven has created feelings
And wine to bring cheer and healings
A sweet offering to complement all chances
The best of wine's aroma to fill all senses

And he will love you, bless you and multiply you
He will also bless the fruit of your body, too
He will bless the fruit and wine of your land
And satisfy the works of your laboring hand

The best friend of old, O might wineskin
For to sojourn with you was only akin
Our sons and daughters followed our song
And a curse fell when we didn't store for long

Not only does wine rejoice God and man
It may be restrained for the sake of destiny
To bear sons of valour and mighty warriors
And with wine, no place exists for worriers

It was commonsensical that wine intoxicates
A mourning and sorrowful spirit it differentiates
Yet, when the Lord's Prophet is born
It is given in offering for the holy son.

Ammon's heart is merry with wine, so strike
All who drink it, to mirth as to their own spike
May to danger also they succumb and fall
While such with faint hearts it strengthens all.

The reward of those God has called
To take them to the land of wine and bread
Of olive fruits and well-preserved honey
So, they may live and spend no money.

Of all fine flour, frankincense and oil
To enjoy the chores, they ever toil
Of all choice wines and special spices
And God has broken their sorrow to pieces.

Oh, give me wine, give it to me I pray
And give me silver so I may not spay
For kings and subjects alike may imbibe
And to draught they may never succumb

May we be at liberty to serve different drinks
Even according to how each person thinks
For in golden goblets as in vain receptacles
The royal wine in plenty shall be in spectacles.

To Job, when his sons gather to celebrate
To Job, in wine all their wealth they calibrate
To Job, whose breast is as wine without a vent
To Job, all calamities he cannot prevent!

You have put more rejoicing in my heart
Than when the wine is bound to be an art;
Yet wine that makes people reel and daze is bad
But red well-mixed wine, not forms, makes glad.

So shall your storage be filled with plenty
And with new wine your vats hold abundant;
And not with the wine of violence
Nor with the bread of insolence.

For wine is a mocker, strong drink a brawler
And the unwise reels at it like a fouler
Since the love of wine makes poor
The temptation for it is not for a ruler.

Its wine's duty to cheer the mind and body
But it takes the heart to instruct everybody
On how to control the signs of wantonness
For wine as money may answer to idleness.

Only one is better than wine; your love
And only your love, O my dearest dove
For like wine, your love cheers me up
And shows due course to my heart's map.

Let wine always be sharp, not mixed with water
Let it not be inflammable, making reason falter
Let not your heroism be in intoxicant brews
For judgment it taints, rulers mix-up rules

Oh, cease not making the sounds of joy
But instead, eat and apply anointment oil
For tomorrow we may all be dead
And our memory from the earth may fade

So sad are the days of sorrow, when joy ends
And the new wine mourns, the vine press bends
All the merrymakers stand still and only sigh
And there is none to cheer or make us high

A vineyard beloved and lovely, O sing
Woe to the crown of the prince of gong
For even the priest and prophet reel
And the righteous stumble from its feel.

They are drunk, but not from wine
They stagger, but not from strong drink
They are taken away from the land of wine
From sweet wine, to the land of bitter drink

There is a wine bought without gold
A drink strong and yet I am still told
There is a peace that comes from God
A tomorrow beyond measure or odd.

The Lord has sworn by His right hand
For sure I will not deny you grain fund
Nor subject your wives to enemies` rape
But will preserve you as the juice of grape.

Your bottle shall be filled with wine, not bitterness
For God may repay you with a cup of bitter wine
When you obey the Lord, He'll give you a break
And command wine never to cease for your sake.

Neither shall any priest drink wine in inner court
But in palaces of honor they shall be for support
For it's the Lord who gives new wine and means
From those who forsake him, He lifts no liens.

Men's rulers shouldn't drink at people`s expense
But give to all who have asked for its providence
So that people may drink from grapes they planted
O God for fresh wine`s sake, let not evil be ranted.

For great is God`s goodness to me
And great is his beauty to see
Grain shall make the young men brave
And fresh wine the maidens to thrive

Then as now, new wine is put in new wineskin
And for this new covenant, He must suffer within
For the Holy Spirit will replace the crave for wine
And empower him with graces divine.

For Jesus came drinking wine and eating bread
And do not say that he has a demon, O Israel
For to the infected, pour in wine, reduce the dread
And the afflicted will be saved from fires of hell.

And when the wine was all gone,
The mother of Jesus said to him alone:
"They have no more wine to drink,"
And Jesus made wine in a blink.

When the day of Pentecost came, they were drunk
The outsiders mocked at them as frank
And as early as before it was time for potion
But Peter stood and calmed the commotion.

You may drink wine or eat any food you want
Only do not let it offend a non-participant
And not get drunk with wine, its sin
Be filled with the Spirit and shine.

No longer should you drink only water
You should drink a little wine at altar
But only because of your poor health
And not as a way to accrue wealth.

If thou drinketh, thou shan't be enslaved to wine
Thou shalt never bow to it or to its wile
For thy works of old doth passeth a while
And thou art been born to this fruit of vine.

In the Last Days God shall not destroy the wine
In the days of desolation, He will spare the oil
But Babylon shall fall with all who drank her refine
Oh, to Jesus run, spare your skin from eternal boil.

359. Under Attack

When I was under the attack of my enemy
You still held me up on your shoulders
I never knew of my grievously vane infamy
Until after bitter clouds shook my borders.

I was sinking pretty fast for my own doom
Everywhere I looked, I saw only gloom
Yet in your precious wings I found room
And under in your generous cup, bloom

The rivers of piercing swords rushed through
The fiery fires of raging emotions followed
There was turbulence in my inner brow
And a tempest of sort that my soul hobbled

All along I thought of your love and mercy
I wondered around all things but fancy
And looked for pleasures to satiate my
But you have helped me since infancy

Those who desire to chew me alive
Those who are intent at destroying me
Have increased and no mercy they give
But I will never be afraid, for you I see.

360. He Answers Prayers

There are two kinds of fools on earth
And one of them is me when I doubt
Because each time I pray to God
He answers me as pure as gold

Today I lost a document and searched
Yesterday I needed God`s clear favor
And when I stood before the judge
He vindicated me without a grudge

It was a matter of peace and chaos
So, I looked everywhere for wills
And the night dawned on me sadly
As I prayed, the will appeared gladly

When I was sick of a danger ill
A prophesy came before to warn
And when I asked my wife to pray
I am saying, it was as good as spray

You may have many doubts before
You may even think it is a myth
Yet a simple trust in God is just all
You will ever need to secure more

Take it from me, again, again, again
It is a waste of time and great loss
To avoid matters of prayer in vain
When it comes to answers, God is boss.

361. Religion

I wonder if you go through this everyday
Each time you are confronted with truth
You ask even more questions to nay
Is the entire search for a god or gods worth?

If you live in some jungle in the Amazon
Or you only hear of other sources of truth
Or if you gaze intently on the horizon
Do you feel there is more to this earth?

The inhabitants of the famed civilized world
And the reciters of the ancient riddles
Have been searching for the true word
And all they find are only muddles!

Can we still say that Man is a form of a god
A mere coincidence of nature`s spruced force
Or which generation will declare it bold
That only one belief is the true source?

To deny all facets of human permutation
And to live as though there is no Being
Are all attempts at finding truth`s formation
Even the ancient fumbled over this thing.

The Isms are an excuse for dominating Man
And or the attempts at finding true peace
When will all such works said to be done
Can we still say religion is that or this?

The mystery of God is a matter of belief
And those who organise it very well
Will be held with unpretentious relief
However, with others, we will never tell.

For when the ends of Man's machinations
Are stretched to their ephemeral austerity
Whether by mere chance or sheer imaginations
We still experience but semblance of verity!

So, the advancers masticate rituals as camels
And their followers recite lines they hate
All for the hope of entering divine channels
To render the after-life to its delicate fate

The moment one question is answered
The next question becomes an enigma
And the deeds written in the holy Hansard
May only be placated by a dear redeemer.

Some religions relish the Day of Judgment
When all deeds good and bad will be judged
Others pride in the earthly firmament
That once dead, all things are smudged.

Therefore, we live, not for truth
But for the reality which we know
And therefore, we die, not for faith
But for the truth we never saw

And the question still remains to ask
Who is right and who is wrong
This has become every man's task
Whether we live short or long.

For I live, daily with questions unanswered
And I die, daily with fears beyond the graves
Who will save a poor soul as this of mine?
Only when Jesus shares his side, I'll be fine.

362. Human Love

All the humans are capable of love
All can help to make love reality
All can make love and enjoy love
All the humans are capable of love

All the sexes are capable of love
All they need is to know love
All they have to do is give love
All they have can be real love

All love demands is understanding
All there is to know is to understand
All understanding is rooted in truth
All there is to know love is truth

All feelings are secondary to sex
All muscles and sinews relax in sex
All the traps of life are defeated in sex
All nerves receive new blood in sex

All humans can learn how to fulfil in sex
All they need is to know human anatomy
All they do is touch the right parts
All they get is Nature`s great sensation

All but those who understand can love with sex
All but those who have patience make real sex
All but those who care can love with sex
All but those who have time can enjoy real sex

All except the lazy can hurt with love
All except the quick can hate with sex
All except loafers can love to hate sex
All except loaners have used sex for love

All humans are capable of making love
All humans are capable of hurting with love
All humans are capable having sex
All humans are capable of hating with sex.

363. Favored

Not that I have great words or deeds done
Or that my mind out-thinks all my peers;
It is not due to the trophies I have won
Or as a payment for all my great cheers

It is due to the mercies of the living God
Which have sustained me all this long
And accorded me favors as good as gold
And relieves me from my grave wrong

The mercies of the good and great Lord
Have taken me to heights I never dreamt
And brought me to the fountain of old
That wonderful grace much esteemed

You will hear of the great works of love
All for the kind-hearted who have courage
And of all the favor that comes from above
To all faithful ones in divine marriage

For long I thought I was more than normal
More than the children of earthly glory,
Nay, I came to learn of life`s lessons` formal
That success is also God`s gracious story.

364. The Church

Of adherents and followers, it has over 2.2 billion
Of churches and cathedrals multiply by a million
Of the population of the whole world, about a third
Of all religions, the largest, strongest in the world.
Of faith groups, it runs over thirty-five thousand
Of Christians, world's 33 percent population and
Of half of Christians, are Catholic denominations
Of 100 years, its voice has filtered across nations.

365. Tithe

Our father Abraham thanked God with a tithe
For he finally had victory and could breathe
And these tithes of the land; fruit and seed,
All belonged to the Lord, for all those in need

So, they paid all, never to be found in default
Or they paid a fifth of their own fault
For the herd of the flock belonged to the Lord
Who wanted all to have the fear of God

The Levites were not to inherit anything except tithes;
They lived in homes but where not to own clothes
For the Levites took a tithe from the Israelites,
And made the Temple glorious with many lights

This tithe is just not a tenth of everything
It was an inheritance to servants of the King
To Aaron and his sons, let them eat and rejoice
For they have found favor in God`s voice

They will take the entire tithe into the Tabernacle
With great jubilation and mighty spectacle
Since God has commanded them to obey
And not to debate his holy and sacred way

366. God's Glory

The *Doxa*, the glory,
the nature and acts of God in all their self-manifestation;
And this is what God is and does,
revealed in all of creation and exaltation,
And which has been exhibited
in ways and means God desires to be known.
And particularly in the person of Christ Jesus,
God's Son of glorious renown,
In whom essentially God's glory
has been shone generations after generations.
And made available to men
by means of grace and power to many nations.

To God our Father,
Maker and Sustainer
be all the glory, now and forever.

For in the days of his flesh,
Jesus Christ manifested glory
by deeds and miracles.
And released many from bondage,
captivity,
sickness
and deadly shackles –
At Cana,
where he turned water into pure wine
to feed many a thirsty soul;
At the tomb,
where he raised Lazarus from the dead
and there many eyes saw;
At the Mount of His Glory,
there he taught many of the things to come
And at the Mountain of Transfiguration,
eyes glittered and hearts were calm.

To God our Father,
Maker and Sustainer
be all the glory, now and forever.

His attributes and power
have been revealed through the entire creation,
The world falls short of His righteousness,
character and manifested perfection.
For the might of His glory,
the praise of the glory of His everlasting grace
Has been revealed to the ends of the earth,
to many a nation and race;
The Father of Glory is He,
from whence and to whom all things emanate,
The source of all good things spread wide for all
and to all they illuminate.

To God our Father,
Maker and Sustainer
be all the glory, now and forever.

To date,
and through the lives of those who believe in His
word and name,
And who wait with intent for that blessedness
filled with glory and fame,
the blessedness into which believers are to enter
now and hereafter,
As they are brought into the likeliness of Christ,
and hence thereafter,
to be with Him through the body of His glory,
the brightness of His splendor,
And enchant them forever as their God,
their light and their defender.

To God our Father,
Maker and Sustainer
be all the glory, now and forever.

The Shekinah Glory,
in the pillar of cloud of the Tabernacle's
Holy of Holies,
was only but an emblem
of the glory of the Church
of God's own families,
and will be made manifest
in the appearing of the only
and our Great God,
the Savior Jesus Christ,
whose throne is surrounded by marble and gold,
as one who won His Father's good reputation,
praise and due honor.
Who deserves all our worship,
and must to us all be our favor and banner.

To God our Father,
Maker and Sustainer
be all the glory, now and forever.

367. Incomparable Jesus

He is overall the flame that glitters without end
His palm of comfort holds all he will defend
To the weary I say, "Relax in his balm of peace"
And have his mind of love replace all you miss.

The incomparable Jesus, the Man that I love
Among all creatures He is God and above
For before Him, there was nothing called life
And of many husbands, He has the prefect "wife".

This Jesus whose name makes my head turns
This Christ who saves my every returns
This King from whose kingdom flows power
This Healer who touches me in every hour!

For so I love Him, many times without measure
By His throne are stored for me great treasure
My dear love, my all for now and all eternity
Surely, He`s most excellent amid the fraternity.

368. In the Land of My Enemy

I give You thanks, Heavenly Father,
The Father of Grace, God of Justice,
For to You and for You, belongs praise
You have shown throughout history
That, the only one who remains, is You,
Great and eloquent men have come,
Bright, sophisticated women have gone,
Yet, You alone, continue now and forever.
You stand strong at the door of fairness,
You speak loudly, for the plight of the weak
And You open Your arms, to the hopeless.
As for me, my trust is in You, alone
My confidence comes from Your throne
And in Your love, I take refuge and rest.
Great things You have done, and will do,
Not by me, Oh dear God, only for You,
I have a portion in the land of my enemy,
Your banner over me soars blessedly.

369. Falling though Not Down

Falling to my knees, I am where the heroes of faith passed
You have been kind to me now and in times in the past
I have been like a prisoner in my own thoughts, now am free
I knew in my heart I needed to pray first and only to Thee
Oh Western, the pain was reduced; I first sought the Lord
The Lord gives and the Lord also denies, yet He is God
I praise you Lord, my Father, for you know all things
I give all the glory to you, Almighty, who is King of kings
From now henceforth, all my future into your hands I give
From the hands of the Lord, good we may receive
And even when nothing seems to be there, I still trust
Lord my God, you alone shall be God, the holy, the truest
Who am I that I should doubt your grace; it's sufficient
I *know* your favor has been upon me from times ancient.

370. Windsor

Windsor will take me, to the glory of God
This I attest not that I see, yet I see
For the goodness of his mercy hath shined
He will see me through the down valley
And will bring up to of the mountain
Father, to you my soul looks for help
For my Savior shall rise like a morning star
And my joy, though delayed, will finally come.

371. Fail, Well

Lord, in times past I was a prisoner
I was a slave to a mortal examiner
To a congregation that judged my deeds
To a human master I thought met my needs
To men's opinion for their formality
To people's standards of popularity
Lord, I am sorry in men I put my trust
I am glad you remember that I am dust
Am not ashamed of the Gospel and its Cross,
Christ's my faith, men I love, glory is Yours.

372. Eli, Eli lama Sabachthani

"Eli, Eli lama sabachthani?"
"My God, my God,
Why have you forsaken me?"
How it could be, I asked,
That God His Son He should forsake?
That His only begotten Son's blood
He should allow to be poured as a flood?
These things I pondered to my anguish
Until in prayer He granted my wish
Then I came to learn that God His creature
He had forsaken
But the Father His Son's bones
He would never have broken
"Eli, Eli lama sabachthani?"
I do cry out loud sometimes
When overwhelmed, I drown in world's troubles
And my agony pile up all in doubles
And like God, the thorn in my flesh
He would not remove
But like a Father, His grace is all sufficient.
"Eli, Eli lama sabachthani?"
Now I know, and expect even more
That He loved me, so His face from sin
He turned,
But my peace and eternal life
He gained.

373. Ancient of Days

Oh, Ancient of Days, O Ancient of Days
As my soul from within cheerfully prays
Ancient of Days, that I Thy Creature
Should for a heavenly aorta posture
For a tiny bit of Thy glittery presence
Even before comprehendth I Thy essence
Should tender my limbs gladly to kneel
My vanity and disquiet happily to heal
Ancient of Days, honor, mighty, power
Bid me now to glow in this fine hour
That Thou darling of my eternal pleasure
Not even the world is enough a treasure
Ancient of Days, Thy Law is utterly good
To cease not from praising Thee I should.

374. 2018, a Prayer

I bowed my knees before the Father of my Lord Jesus Christ
Through whose name the entire family in Heaven is named
I came to Him not in my own righteousness,
Which is but like filthy rags; but through Christ Jesus,
My Lord, in whose blood I have redemption
The forgiveness of my sins, and whose name I am saved;

I declared 2018, a Year of Faith, because in this year, I believe
I believe that God You will reveal Yourself to me again
Even more than You have done to me in times past
That I may again see You, hear You and honor You.
That I may love You more than I have ever done before
I asked You to come closer to me and embrace me more;

I only required a simple faith – to believe like a child, not to doubt
To believe, and not to engage in philosophical debates
Father, I asked you to grant me abundant of love for you
And to pray to You, and You will answer me swiftly
I believe that I will see everything with the yeses of faith,

And seek You daily in the secret, in the chamber
of my heart;

I asked for faith to raise my family – to love my
wife more
To be with my children more, and to lead my
family,
I asked for grace to be an active member of the
community –
To find a church where I can be a servant and
contribute
And to engage in ways I have missed in the past
years
So that the glory of God and service of man is my
aim;

I asked for faith, and I will have faith, to believe in
impossible,
To trust God for high goals – high business
profits, high returns,
That my entire venture in 2018 will succeed and
bear fruit,
That I shall achieve, through faith, in all I do with
grace
I prayed, Father, that I should not struggle but
only believe.
I have faith that this will be done for me as I
believe in God;

I prayed for all my enemies to become my friends,
again
All those who have not spoken to me, my old
buddies to return
That my clients will love me and trust me, and I
will do same,
That I will be favored everywhere and given
favorable results

That my cases will win and all my work will prosper
That my hands and works are blessed, will add no trouble;

In this year, I will achieve in excess of $200,000 in business,
I will publish with bigger and well-recognized publishers,
I will have my name in the world recognized by good things,
I will go places and become a citizen with double benefits
I will enjoy everyday life and find satisfaction in my activities
Good doors will open, and bad ones will permanently close;

No weapons of the devil will prosper against me or mine
The Lord, You will be the mountain that surround me
And I will see the destruction of all evil plans against me
You will keep me safe and in assured protection each day
That my family will be healthy and outlive me in years
That I believe in You, and I will not be disappointed.

375. No Shame

Anyone who trusts in You shall not be put to shame
He or she who will believe in the unfailing truth of God
I have been contemplating lately, how amazing God's love
How much He has kept His side of the bargain
The Lord will not abandon His project, not even once
He will bring to pass all that He has promised in His Word
For the Lord's Word is anchor and it is also a sword
I will look to Him, even when the skies be blurry
I will trust on Him, even when the snow should scary
Because He who is in Heaven is mightier than I
He is mightier than all the troubles of the world put together
I will also relish His chastisement, I will embrace His rebuke
For the piercing admonition of His kindness are healing
And the punishment He inflicts are a balm to a faithful soul.
Lord, I have prayed, I have interceded for my enemies
For they will rejoice when they hear of my dilemma,
Yet, I still pray for them – because they understand not
They do not know Your purposes and plans, which I learn

376. My All is Thee

I am well with the Lord's gracious providence
I will not be ashamed in this chosen province
Your Word has come to my beaming heart
You have spoken, and You have set me apart
I will forever be called, "Blessed in the land,"
My offspring shall increase within Your band
In Your presence, I will find lasting pleasure
At Your side daily, I will discover real treasure
And those who fight against me, shall surely falter
Those who remain stubborn, You will scatter
For the kindness of the Lord has graced me
His benefits in this world, I will, indeed, live to see
Oh, joy of understanding that I have everything
The peace of knowing I will be defeated by nothing
Even my accuser will bow before You in shame
The one who stands with me will stand in fame
For if it has not been for the goodness of You
I would have no confidence, no rewards due,
I know that Your mercies will carry me through
Your grace lifts me, and makes me great, too.

377. Again, Again and Again

You have saved me from all my enemies
And also protected me from all infamies
Overwhelmed, surrounded by a critical bust
The rumblings of accusations trike rather fast
Yet, I will trust in You, my ready defender
You'll also comfort me, Your hands are tender
For Zand has brought a false allegation
But You'll acquit me after the investigation
You will also bring to nothing, Giffen's threats.
You will, Oh, merciful God,
Again, again, and again deliver me,
You'll bring to naught Hagos' complaints,
and true praise belongs to Thee.
Because of Your favor, You've silenced all fates
Oh, bless the LORD, O my soul, do not fret
In victory, give praise, His mercy don't forget.

378. His Mercies

Your mercies I trust, do not let my accuser prosper
He had raised an evil hand in falsified allegations
Because he wanted to reap where he did not sow
But You are the defender of my earthly interests,
The Lord, mighty in words, able to silence the proud
In Your hands, I commit this lawyer, deal with him
Not according to Your wrath, but in Your gentleness
Spare his life, correct his mindset that he retreats;
Then he shall hear a voice in his conscious mind
And it shall tell him to forget all his machinations.
You will be praised, O Lord, when his threats die
You will be worshipped for ever and ever and ever,
For You have rewarded me with mercy abundantly
You have prevented it from insurer and regulator
And You have, indeed, heaped great favor upon me;
O Lord, Your lovingkindness in floods I clearly see;
Thank you, O, thank you, my dearest Father,
Words can't express this eternal love for each other.

379. A Wonderful God

I have contemplated on many things, on all fronts
I hide in my imagination; I dwell on all You made
I have pondered on Your essence, power and all
It is an assignment that I have carried in my heart
Whether I am traveling by bus, car or I am flying
I still observe how You have laid all things bare
I look at the invisible elements, such as the air
I see the visible, from soil to oil, flowers to towers
And I am terrified by the truth that I now conceive,
By the power of Your creativity that I perceive;

The skies do tell their perfect story of Your wonder
The things that live around the universe and under
It is clear that You have made elements just fare
You allowed the humans to survive on clean air
And to live just where they are, for it is just enough
Their they can procreate, sometimes cry or laugh
In this world below the ravaging skies all is right
Even the Sun and Moon bring just sufficient light
To cause every activity under the sun to prosper
And nothing is excessive, scarce or improper;

I am amazed at how tiny from Your view we are
We appear larger than a closest distance star
We look far bigger than the largest crawling ants
We sound much noisier than the singing chants.

380. Sweet Story

You have answered my prayers, each and every one
You have made me triumph, and enabled all I have won
Many, Lord, have been my opposition, my obstacles
But at Your feet, Lord, and in Your worthy Tabernacles,
There, I find mercy, and grace to lead me on to victory
Oh, what You have done, I will recite in a sweet story
I will tell my friends and those who care how You care
I will brag about Your perfect golly, which is truly fair
How awesome also are Your attentions towards me
Your daily remembrances that I can daily hear and see
Oh, Lord, in my whispers, You are still standing there
When I silently mutter, my requests You keenly share,
I will stop not to thank You, to bless Your holy name
For You are my true life, apart from You, I am shame.

381. Wow Pleasure

Oh, Lord, real shepherd of my soul
To Thee and for Thee, I bring all
For it has been Thy good pleasure
Why Jesus Thy rarest treasure,
Thou sent Him, for my sins to die
O, watchful shepherd, Thou doesn't lie
Thy good kindness, Thy kind goodness,
In these I find more, and not less.
Thou said, "Worry not, little flock,"
And then I looked, I was in shock.
Yes, it pleased Thee, my Holy God,
It was Thy honor, O dear Lord,
To give us Thy sacred Kingdom;
Praise be to Thy greater wisdom.

382. Lindsay

Oh, Lord, my God, keep safe from Lindsay
For the enemy masquerades as this woman
And in my soul, I have seen her evil intentions
She opposes me in word and in due actions
She investigates my weaknesses and pounces
But You have been my rock, source of my defence
And each time she has manifested, in colleges
You have stopped all her machinations outrightly
You have put her in her own place, for Your glory
Oh, Lord, Your everlasting mercies I daily see
For You will not let her canings to maturity be.

383. Injustice into Victory

I didn't sleep well, Lord,
I agonized all night
Why have You
allowed the wife of my youth,
Why did you permit
The termination of her job?
She is the epitome of hard work,
diligently daily
She has changed her department,
cleanly surely
And yet,
the wicked have celebrated her downfall,
You have seen their machinations,
their own doom.
For me, O Lord, only words
I offer for my dear wife,
I ask You to intervene,
and prove them all wrong
I urge You to come to our rescue,
lift her soul,
O, dear Lord,
let what the devil means for evil
be turned into our song of victory,
our purpose.
And we shall give You continued praise,
O Father
We shall still glory
in Your grace and power.
Because, O Lord,
You will come for us speedily.

How deep Your thoughts and plans,
Oh, God Almighty;
Who would have known Your strategy?
Who would have deciphered Your tactic?

Only now we see,
that You had all along better loots,
for You have satisfied her
with exceptional skills
More than a previous pay
could reward
And more than many hours
could award.

384. Wisdom of Christ

O, the infinite wisdom of Christ Jesus,
The Leader
His supreme prudence in world harvest
His beauty, unmatched – Lily of the Valley, Rose of Sharon
His tremendous creativity in creation, yet Man of Sorrows
O, Merciful High Priest, Messiah who is Prince
A Nazarene, yet King of all kings
He has overcome, O Lord God Omnipotent
And His name is above all names.

385. It's Finished

"It is finished!" Jesus cried on the Cross
For the Lord was on a redemption course
"It is finished!" Jesus completed it all
And paid all our debts in full and more
"It is finished!" was Jesus' victory cry
And it echoed through Hell and up High
"It is finished!" Jesus gave up his breath
And gave us life by grace through faith
"It is finished!" and all sin vanished
And in His blood we are all washed.

386. A Christian Life

My God, do live a Christian life for me
For in myself, I try and fail daily
My flesh works but to please itself only
So, the things I want to do I don't do
Dead desires in my body form a queue
My faculties compete for the gaudy
If I should say that I don't sin, I lie
And the truth of God is far from being nigh
Only in Christ can I live in purity
Dear Spirit, be my steadfast surety.

387. Holier, Lowlier

Oh, that I may be but emptier, lowlier,
And be to my God a vessel holier,
Oh, that I may be to all sin, slower
And to kneel down before His throne, lower,
Oh, that I may to righteousness be, a slave
And to dying to sinful flesh, fast and brave
Oh, that I may pray, daily, and longer
And to grow in my faith a lot stronger
Oh, that I may be unnoticed, unknown,
And be filled but with Christ, and Christ alone.

388. Insult to Mercy

To forgive a perpetual law-breaker
To ignore the persistent faults, too
Is it to insult God, Creator, Maker?
Oh, far be it from me that I be a fool,
Or worse, a pig that it's vomits feed
By not to Your word wisely pay heed,
For You, my sins forgive, time and time
For my salvation, You charged no dime,
My redemption, Your Son's blood poured
Oh, Greater Savior, aren't You also Lord?
For my needs, Your goodness You give
Without hesitation, in me, You to live.

389. Heart of Prayer

I humbly bow my knees to you my Lord
The Creator of all things, Father and God
King of all nations and Chief among tribes
And before Jesus Christ, Scribe of the scribes
Our Lord God and Master, Supreme Deity
To you I bring my requests of piety
To the Merciful Seat of grand glory,
That you should hear me, O Supreme Jury
And be presented with sacred homage,
For yours are the wisdom and all knowledge.

390. Burden of Nations

Now Lord, my eyes are fixed to Heaven
And ask that all nations I be given
Not for me to possess, for Christ to save
And the world sin and misery to waive
I bow to pray for this our world in need
For all the people, Your voice they should heed
Lord, in this day and hour of petition,
I beseech You, save us from perdition
For what nations have in their behavior
Are lost souls in dire need of a Savior.

391. Cantata to Sounds

There is music inside my singing soul,
I feel strong I'm almost reaching my goal;
The firmament above shall be my roof,
And the ground below my theatrical spoof;
Angels gladly welcome me each morning,
I grunt not like one who is in mourning;
My hands will hold riches unthinkable,
My ways meet favors unbelievable;
Oh, I am bursting with exceeding joy,
I am enamored with strength like a boy;
Inside me, there is a stream of waters,
I'm rewarded with smart, gallant daughters;
Oh, Lord, what did I do to deserve these?
Your golly daily this eye of mine sees.

392. Mulungu, God of Africa

I
Oh, give thanks, give thanks to God Omniscient,
The One who is all things, and most sufficient.
In Africa long ago, they knew You as the Omega,
Indeed, in vernacular, this rhymed with mega.

II
Although they had no history of Christianity,
They were not at all devoid of sensible humanity.
They observed Nature, in it they discovered You;
In their customs, it was clearly You they knew.

III
They could be enchanted by how You made them,
They had no doubt it was from You they did stem.
They could be amazed at the meandering of rivers,
But they believed that it was only You who delivers.

IV
They were astounded at the heights of mounds,
But they heard Your voice in surging sounds.
In all these, they never stopped to be thankful;
They knew You're immeasurable, You're tankful.

V
They played drums, flutes and pipes for their God,
They didn't tire to follow, the Protector of Old.
They were flabbergasted by unusual life events;
With libations, they flooded You with presents.

VI
They know You in their mother tongue as Lesa –
And in many dialects, Oh, God, You are Leza.
You're Africa's, You bless her soil, Oh, Nzambi;
You have achieved ascendancy, Oh, Kyumbi.

VII
You're Bore-Bore, kids sing of You, O Mongu.
You're famously known as Yala, Asis, and Mungu.
In dry season, You supply food, O Kalungu
The skies are full of Your splendor, O Mulungu.

VIII
You're big, the biggest, You're called Mukuru.
You busk in Your eternal glory, Unkulunkulu.
You bring the rains and winds, O Ukulunkulu.
You'll rise for Your people, Chindi-Chaimana.

IX
You laid the foundation of the world, Kiibumba,
And beautifully designed its borders, Kabumba.
You unleash Leviathan and slay the Black Mamba,
For You're known as the Dragon Slayer, Pamba.

X
Oh, Most Venerate, You're honored as Yatta.
You're the Great Father, in Bemba, You are Tata,
And by all, worshipped as Zanahary and as Chiuta;
You are Almighty, You roar, Oh, Lion of Judah.

XI
You reign in an unapproachable glory, Nyame,
You have revealed Yourself as Leader, Nyambe;
You display Yourself as Olodumare and Ondo,
For You are the Self-Existing One, Oh, Olo.

XII
Oh Lord God, You rule over kings, O Inkosi,
For as King of kings, You're Inkosi-yama-Nkosi.
You fight battles, and the bounty is theirs, O Tilo
You're worthy to be followed, Oh, Adunbalo.

XIII
And who is like unto You, Oh, Lord Mwari?
Surely their ancestors loved You, as they do, Ori;
From eternity, You've been merciful, Great Wari,
For Yours is the power, the praise and the glory.

XIV
You are decorated, Mighty Warrior, Oh, Rugaga,
You are the lifter of Your people, Oh, Olugbega.
You return triumphantly, O Lord, Great Hero,
And those who hate You, will inherit but zero.

XV
Almighty God, You give all things, Oh, Ruhanga
You drew them in Your palms, Creative Chilenga
For You know the end from the start, Kalunga,
Your love, has not deserted Your lovely Africa.

XVI
You're victorious, glorious, Almighty Modimo,
You're meritorious in deeds, increasing ever more.
All nations of the earth look to You, Oh, Urezwha
And Your goodness is shared by all, Osanobua.

XVII
You are, and can be, many things – You're Oluwa
You do and undo anything, Almighty God Ruwa;
You justify the innocent and the humble, O Suku;
You forgive sins and show endless grace, Chuku.

XVIII
Khuzwane, to describe You, there're no words,
Imana, because You are affected by no swords;
You are the true God and Lord, the Invisible One,
You're the way, truth, life and victory You've won.

XIX
A diversity of people knew You simply as BIG,
For in You all promises, pledges will never renege,
Oh, blessed be Africa, Your land of amazing hope,
Of her, You've spoken in prose, verse and trope.

XX
You've graced Yours with stamina, Great Njinyi,
In their dire need, You've'nt forgotten them, Ngai.
You're their King, Sovereign, their Great Oba;
In Africa, You're like a Mother, *the* loving Baba.

393. Bisrat and Ojo

I'll look to You, from where my helps come
I will pray to You, for You will my life calm
In Your heart, are mercies and compassion
And in Your mind, it is to bring to action.
You will embrace, and not leave him to solo
For Your miracles will be strong with Ojo.
You will conceal Your sons' label so that
It may go well with new counsel with Bisrat.
In this, too, Oh, my Father, You show grace,
By Your kind deeds, You dispel all disgrace.

394. Peter Stehouwer

You will show me favor, Oh, Lord
In the eyes of the man Peter Stehouwer.
You will give him no peace, no sleep
Until he finds me not in breach of rules.
That You, Oh, Lord of love and mercy,
Shall make the Hagos complaint end,
And from the ashes of this investigation,
You will lift me up in grand promotion.
That from hence and forth, glory is Yours
And Yours also are the praises and honor.
For You have vindicated me, this thrice
And given me divine peace, this twice.

395. It's Wichtig

Wake up bones, tendons, muscles and sinews
Stand up marrows and you all tender tissues;
Come out from slumber, Oh, you blood vessels
And jump up and down all you internal entrails.
Tell the central nervous system to stretch up,
Turn on the sensory nerves, let them all dup.
It is time to dance, to shake those many gifts,
Oh, let God enjoy as your central limb shifts.
Do fear no-one, and before none be ashamed,
Let those moves flow, your pride be chained.
It is good to praise Him, to brag, and to shindig,
Oh, my soul, flesh and mind, do it, it's wichtig!

396. Praise in Every Genre

Singers, use your voice to praise Him
Dancers, make every move to praise Him
Poets, compose beauty in praise of Him
Musicians, string numbers in praise of Him
Writers, pen perfect prose to praise of Him
Choreographers, move bodies to praise Him
Ballerinas, step-up, gesture in praise of Him
Drummers, beat the skin to the praise of Him
Gamers, rave up those videos in praise of Him
And players, kill up the talent to praise Him!

397. Earth You've Colored

Each day you light up, is a treasure discovered;
And each night you dim, is a chance to sprawl.
A flower that blooms, the earth You've colored;
And each ray that rises, Your love for me I recall.
Even when the wind blows, I know You're here;
And in the tiniest atom, there I find Your grace.
Your voice is heard clearly in the morning air;
And You reign as LORD in the furthest space.
My mind fails to fathom how You came to be;
And yet I am happy, Your infinite glory I see.

398. Dear My Rarest

I am in love with You, Oh, Jesus
Even as I loved You, as a fetus.
I loved You while in my mother's womb,
Surely, I will still love You in my tomb.
I'll forever love You, before my eyes close,
Before my finite farewell, before I bid adios.
You are always in my head, Sweet Savior
Yes, in my manners, thoughts and havior.
Of all I love, O Christ, You're the rarest
Since I found You, You're my dearest.

399. Afghanistan to Tajikistan

I pray for the state of Afghanistan
To come to Christ, and also Kyrgyzstan
That the light of God will shine on Bhutan
As it touches the state of Pakistan
O Lord God remember Turkmenistan
And save the people of Uzbekistan
That in these nations, O Sovereign Lord,
There will be revival in the things of God
And let the Gospel go to Kazakhstan
And bless the people of Tajikistan.

400. Akrotiri to Laos

Lord through ash you preserved Akrotiri
And through the years, you have built Hungary
Despite the heat, your camels flood Algeria
The Rila Cross is your sign in Bulgaria
Tattoos' worth in American Samoa
As the marks of Jesus Christ make them more
O Lord reveal yourself in Bangladesh
Lord, in Chile, pour out your Spirit afresh
And serve Egypt from turmoil and chaos
As you O Lord from dictators, save Laos.

401. Ethiopia to East-Timor

Lord, in Turkey, let Christianity grow
As You prosper Norway in Euro's role
Let the glory of God shine in Hong Kong
As the Churches' fullness in France belong
O God, let grace not bypass Ethiopia
And Gaza Strip's peace will not be utopia
Lord, keep the ray of hope in East-Timor
In Grand Duchy of Luxembourg, be more
Let Zimbabwe in the Rock put its trust
In Nicaragua, let *La Purísima* point to Christ.

402. West Bank to Western Sahara

May rivers flow in Western Sahara
Unlike the bitter water at Marah,
And let these waters bring eternal life
As you protect West Bank from inner strife
In Samoa, let Christ be its Navigator
As San Marino cuddles its Creator
O Lord, let us be grateful to Suriname
Where we pray for the honor of your name
Let Niger and Saint Kitts-Nevis sing a hymn,
"The Lamb has conquered. we will follow Him!"

403. Andorra to Angola

Let the peace continue in Andorra
And let this also be true in Angola
Lord be the protector of Anguilla
And bring true beauty to Venezuela
Let salvation shine in Guatemala
For Almolonga is a divine parlor
May you give green life in Antarctica
And lavish nature parks in Costa Rica
Lord, the same I pray for Dominica
May God's union be with Madagascar.

404. Argentina to Bosnia-Herzegovina

For sake of the Jews, God bless Argentina
Let love reign in Bosnia-Herzegovina
And rest be born new in Saint Helena
Lord, may racial strains end in Guyana
That the Devil won't prey on French Guiana
I ask that you continue to prosper China
And the economy to bloom in Ghana
O Lord, sanctify Wallis-Futuna
And enhance the fear of God in Botswana
For nations look to you as their banner.

405. Armenia to Estonia

As the high mountains surround Armenia
And as long coastlines along Estonia
Even as Et'hem Beu prayers in Albania
Can be heard towards Papua New Guinea
Lord, let these nations know of your power
And buffer them from a terrible hour
Lord, be King in Syria and Dhekelia
And as nationals meet in Australia
And your arms open wide towards Austria
God, let grace abound too in Eritrea.

406. Barbados to Comoros

As grand lush weddings define Barbados
And nails never made boats of Comoros
O Almighty God, come and wed your Church
That for no other Savior we may search
Let your presence fortify Belarus
And as the giant Barrier Reef of Belize
Is its defense, so protect this nation
And safeguard the long-life of your creation
Lord, bring moderation to Germany
And spurn serfdom from trading in Benin.

407. Antigua and Barbuda to Bermuda

Be no longer a secret to Bermuda
And be known to Antigua and Barbuda
Be the definite boss in Aruba
And be decreed as the God of Cuba
In British Indian Ocean Territory
Be Sovereign, not just God in theory
May they welcome you wholly in Brunei
Make Hutu-Tutsi-Twa one Burundi
And end animism in Burkina Faso
For in Jesus, gentiles are known also.

408. Burma to Panama

You're link of land and sea in Panama
You set the prisoners free in Burma
You're the sunshine that adorns Bahamas
And you are hope of those who are farmers
You heal wounds of genocide-Cambodia
And you lend thinkers with great an idea
You let democracy thrive in India
You stop shipwrecks in Bassas da India
You outlawed all witchcraft in Cameroon
And make rivers flow around Lebanon.

409. Canada to Grenada

You're Governor of friendly Canada
And Governor-General in Grenada
You created beautiful birds of Cape Verde
And keep oceans in place very steady
You care for all the children of the Chad
And you warm up the cold seas of Svalbard
O let Christ be born in Christmas Island
Come, Rock of Ages, to Clipperton Island
And bring Holy Sup to Cocos Islands
And Your beauty, is also Ireland's.

410. Colombia to Zambia

May the Christ be the drug of Colombia
Though small, let Jesus be big in Gambia
Entrench the Declaration in Zambia
As Jesus remains still her real Cambia
That by this, people will find salvation
And from truth there will be no deviation
Lord, equalize land claims in Namibia
Anoint the oil of Saudi Arabia
And be celebrated in Ecuador
As you remain Savior in El-Salvador.

411. Congo to Congo

O Father, I cry for peace of DR Congo
And weep that poverty ends in Congo
O Lord, write in the Book of Life, "Iceland"
That Holocaust be accursed in Poland
Be Upholder of Religion in Thailand,
And make Bangkok into a holy land
Be wealth-broker in Equatorial Guinea
Oh, bring freedom to Conakry's Guinea
Warming the heart of gentle Malawi,
And bring true love to the soul of Fiji.

412. From Island to Island

God, be the blue waters of Cook Islands,
As well as of the British Virgin Islands
Be the great wonder of Coral Sea Islands,
The Trench of Northern Mariana Islands
Be the green parks that'll be truly Greenland's
And end prostitution in Netherlands
Lord, be glaciers that ring Bouvet Island
The real owner of Navassa Island,
The true heaven's slice in Norfolk Island
And the Mighty Shepherd of New Zealand.

413. From Land to Islands

Dear Father, I pray for Glorioso Islands
For Marshall Islands and Paracel Islands
And I pray for Turks and Caicos Islands
For vacant Ashmore and Cartier Islands
And for Europa Island and Finland
These I pray they all become Father's land
For Faroe Islands and Cayman Islands
And for French Southern and Antarctic Lands
Bless them together with Falkland Islands
That Jesus will be praised on their highlands.

414. From Islands to Lands

Lord, hear my prayer for Tromelin Island
And I pray for Juan de Nova Island
I also pray for Solomon Islands
And for Heard Island and McDonald Islands
My prayer, too, is for Spratly Islands,
South Georgia and the South Sandwich Islands,
And for Wake Island and Pitcairn Islands -
For all of these and surrounding islands,
I ask that Jesus be their sole Savior
And that you keep them from bad behavior.

415. From Monarchs to Republics

Lord, rule in the Kingdom of Cote d'Ivoire
And provide true wine of life to Georgia
Lord, bless Central African Republic
And stir up Dominican Republic
As you well-massage the Czech Republic
And govern as Monarchy in Denmark
I pray, end sectarianism in Iraq
Lord, part the fresh Red Sea for Djibouti
And replace turmoil with peace in Haiti
And Egypt - bring New Day to Kiribati.

416. Bahrain to Spain

Lord, let Gabon has no poor like Sweden
And let Your Sovereignty extend to Spain
As I pray that it does the same for Bahrain
And expunge the Holodomor of Ukraine
Lord, end ire amid North and South Sudan
And let Baptism wash the banks of Jordan
O Lord, bless the harmony of Oman
And may the God of Heaven be of Mann
Lord, be the Cherry Blossom in Japan
And prosper but end gods' rule in Taiwan.

417. Greece to The Holy See

How lovely the demesne of Gibraltar
The season-less character of Malta
And the GDP of a barren but rich Qatar
This truly sounds like music from guitar
O, the magnificent inventions of Greece
How that Vatican is a Holy See
How bless'ed the Church is in South Korea
I pray, bring eternal light to North Korea
And may Your Church, Lord, is thrive in Latvia
But let only Your view win in Bolivia.

418. Indonesia via Malaysia

Lord, for Malaysia and Micronesia
For Indonesia and Polynesia
And O Lord, for the Alps of Liechtenstein
And for Libya, Tonga and Jan Mayen
For Great Brazil and also for Iran
I pray for Kenya and Azerbaijan
For Macau, and you cattle-rich Jersey
For Tuvalu and history-rich Guernsey
For Saint Vincent and the Grenadines
Let grace flow, and also for Philippines.

419. Italy to Mali

God, reveal Yourself to Macedonia
To Italy and New Caledonia
To Mali and also Mauritania
To Maldives and to vine-rich Slovenia
To Moldova as well as Lithuania
Be known to Montserrat and Mexico
To Mayotte and to Puerto Rico
To oil-rich Kuwait and to Monaco
To Croatia and the "West" or Morocco
And let these all answer to Your-roll-call.

420. Belgium to Vietnam

Lord, in Nigeria as in Somalia
And in Liberia as in Mongolia
Just like in Nepal as Mozambique
And in Singapore as Martinique
I ask that you do bless them as Peru
And cause your like to shine as in Nauru,
In Guam, in Tokelau and in Russia
In Vietnam, Palau and in Tunisia
In Belgium, Guinea-Bissau and Cyprus
In Niue and the nation of Honduras.

421. UK to US

Let Slovakia and also Switzerland
Let Sri-Lanka and also Swaziland
Let the UK as does also Tanzania
Let the UAE, the US as does Romania
Let the Senegal and also Togo,
Trinidad and Tobago as Portugal
Serbia-Montenegro and South Africa
Let Rwanda, Uganda and Jamaica
Let them all forsake their sinful habits
Let God's glory their cities it inhabits.

422. Paraguay to Uruguay

May the Lord's light shine upon Uruguay
May His great rain pour upon Paraguay
May right be in Vanuatu and Mauritius
Lord, may it be as well as Saint Lucia's
And in Yemen and Netherlands-Antilles
And in Sierra Leone, Reunion and Seychelles
And in Saint Pierre-Miquelon and Guadeloupe
As well as in Sao Tome and Principe
Lord, may they prosper now and forever
And Israel thy chosen, forsake, never.

BOOK VI POETRY OF COVID-19

423. Down Corona Lane

Down the Lane named Corona, lives a virus
It has been gloomily, untimely brought upon us
Down the Lane of Corona, sounds are muted
All routine adventures have been civilly re-routed
There is rarely a person walking,
Neither is there a muse talking
All is quiet, deathly silent, as if life had ended
The way of normalcy, prematurely suspended
Fear proudly prowls an empty street in disguise
And staying at home is seen as damagely wise
Heaven and hell receive more souls
Forever shunting them in eternal thralls
Under the shadow of Corona families thrive
There is more cash on which to sparkly survive
Mobility is a race from room to room, out is rare,
But herein, the art of complete manuscript is there.
Down Corona Lane, same is gone
Down Corona Lame, game is done.

424. Los Angeles

Thou art magnificent, O thou city with Angeles
Thou hath no equivalent, serve Domini Angelus
Thy mountainous Bel Air, thy flattened Beverley Hills
Indeed, thy hilly Hollywood, thy unseen Hidden Hills,
These brilliances in their eternally glorious Calabasas
Wouldst Orange County volitionally be "Birth of Jesus"?
Down thy lively lit boulevards mine sweetie droveth
Up at thy vetted Disneyworld, mine little angels roveth
In thy lux hotels, dreams of effulgence hugeth mine soul
In thy fabulous indulgence, mine senses fluently roll
Oh City, a place whereth I would again rather be,
After Covid-19, O City, me orisoneth rebound thee.

425. I Can't Breathe

"I can't breathe," three words, three last words
Words that have ruined lives, damaged worlds
Oh, Minneapolis, don't you hear him, dying?
His chocked head, cop's knee on his neck, frying?
The indictment, because George Floyd is black?
He didn't walk free, he woke up, all was dark
Oh, cry you all who hate, hate and love, love
Even Eric Garner, his eleven calls, quake above
There is a war raging, xenophobia is the bate
Should looking different be judgmental fate?
Don't tell me White people are racists, nope
I know many noble Whites, many preach hope
Oh, hatred, O Covid-19, you're ruthless killers
You're cowards, you feast on and butcher pillars,
You, ruthless homophobes, you, brutal tribalists,
You're heartless, you're fake, damned nihilists
You target the weak, helpless, you cause misery
Your hearts are deadly, your anger is blistery,
Oh, deny, deny them power and authority,
For they abuse it, wrathing it on the minority.

426. America

America, America, Oh, America, the great
Founded on stolen estate and historical hate
Oh, land, developed by injustice of slave labor
And invigorated by angst one against neighbor
Your soldiers to foreign countries do harm
Saddam and Ghaddafi, you murdered by firearm
But George Floyd, you slaughtered, wrong
Your streets do riot, violence you now prolong
For your president, Trump, knows no clue
His style of leadership, tenders a racist skew
Oh, America, your wealth, rests on Black sweat
Surely, you've weaponized race, with no stet.
Your bigoted police him killed in broad day-light
Your towns lit with gory, nights fill with blight.

427. Pandemic of Racism, I

Declare it all,
say it all,
write it all,
record it all.
My people,
African people,
all over the world,
have been victims
of a pandemic called racism
The characteristics of which are obvious,
namely:
Character is secondary,
the hate monster reigns;
Intellect is third,
the evil of hatred drives agendas;
Love of danger is fourth,
all Blacks are suspects;
And cruelty is last,
Africans must be punished.
From the shores
of Benguanaland,
cries rise,
A mother has just lost a son,
taken by slavers.
A wife is now windowed,
though husband's alive.
And children will grow up
without two parents.
In haciendas of America,
backs reel with pain,
Masters spoil Black thighs,
with no alimony given.
Men and boys
toil endless fields,
with no pay.

428. Pandemic of Racism, II

New immigrants
drive dyeing industrial cranes.
"I can't breathe, my face is gone, please"
falls in death eyes,
this Black man must die.
Oh, Mother,
Oh, my late father,
did you know,
that chickens are killed
with ample dignity,
that animals
have rights activities for them to advocate?
And Derek Chauvin
is charged with third degree.
And is immediately free
on a million dollars bond.
I ask: Where did he get such
with a police officer's salary?
Oh, how unheard of,
for such brutal killing?
An African
would have been lamped with first,
He would have been assigned
death penalty.
And he would have been
gazetted a "demon."

429. Pandemic of Racism, III

Africa,
Africans,
Africans descent nationals,
why have you paid so much,
just for being black?
For over four hundred years,
you've agonized.
For many centuries,
you've been abused.
You've overtly been disregarded
as humans;
Not so long ago,
you were things,
property even.
Not so many years long,
you were flogged.
And not so long ago,
your continent was stolen,
your young healthy ones captured,
taken away.
Your old folks,
beaten,
stricken,
slain
murdered
butchered.
And your hallowed African cultures,
forsaken.
Oh, haters of Blacks,
stop,
cease,
end
terminate;
you aren't
feared

you aren't
not jeered.
Now, guard hard, guard now,
for the ravages of Covid-19
have pointed their lethal noses there
they come; they pay no homage
respect no age
and only take undue advantage.
Brace, O you opiodated governments
and you, who specialize in mismanagements,
and you, whose experience is parley arguments
take steps before the missive come
tell your people, let them be calm
don't spare any intellect
wise leaders them elect
but forget not the ruins of colonialism
and frown upon the dictates of Nazism
if not, Covid could be more deadly
even than slavery and dictatorship
lethargy, do not worship
bravery
not drudgery
but courage
to encourage
the next generation
not to neglect this nation.
You heard of vaccine producers
and of the booster users
and Africa isn't consulted
and Africa is again insulted
before it inoculates its inhabitants
global distribution has been scandalous,
violate
annihilate
and isolate
the pandemic
racism.

430. They Count

They called you floor sweeper,
a toilet cleaner
They did not invite you
to make TV talk
When they gathered
and made future plans
You were deliberately forgotten,
useless
They make you hate your profession,
shameful
At college and university,
you were dung,
least
You were paid less,
working conditions,
worse
You feared to introduce yourself,
you're embarrassed
You became a nurse,
because you couldn't be a doctor
You cleaned people's shit,
and they despised you.
oh, janitor,
oh, grocery seller,
oh, fuel pumper.
No-one loved you,
everybody hated you,
for null
They said,
"You're not an engineer, you're a technician."
They compared you
to a lost cause.
But hypocrites them they celebrated,
ululated.
They called them stars,

paid them billions.
But you are only living
pay-to-pay,
near poverty.
Where are movie stars,
soccer players,
NBA,
NHL?
Where are
"Big Bosses,"
"Big Bishops"
or MLB?
Where are
bright lawyers,
smart judges,
or the showstoppers?
Where are
professors,
airline pilots
or money-managers?
With their big bucks,
they have disappeared,
gone.
Oh, see, a farmer,
made me see another day,
today.
Underpaid mail-delivery guy,
still brought my letter.
Garbage-collector,
still took away my stinking rubbish.,
And the
cable-guy,
TV-announcer,
Internet technician,
still made me watch the world dying,
searching for a cure.
I would go on and on,

I shouldn't, know for sure
that the least among us,
are,
in fact,
the more useful.
And they count, in life or death,
they remain faithful.

431. Courage to Say "No"

The lack of courage to say "No"
It is such rare in our times
It is responsible for many deaths
It has led to many aborted dreams!

The lack of courage to say "No"
Has sold many ideas to the gallows
Has welcomed many to their early graves
Has forced many to give up their visions!

The courage to say "No"
Is responsible for great inventions
Is the DNA that champions are made of
Is the blood that runs in the veins of martyrs!

The courage to say "No"
Makes smart women run away from abusers
Makes wise men avoid endangering families
Makes many survive Covid-19 and other diseases!

Many people are in trouble because they said, "Yes!"
Many souls are dying because they refused to say, "No!"
Weak minds easily say "Yes,"
But strong hearts have learned to also say, "No!"

Stop saying "Yes" to everything
Only say, "Yes", if it is beneficial to you
Do say "No" to nothing,
If it enslaves you to another anew.

432. It'd Be Well, I

The world may look, sound and feel sad.
It seems there is everywhere bad news.
But remember that
He who has begun a good work in you,
Shall not be derailed by the pandemic.
Don't live like those who don't have hope.
Remember: "The LORD is close
To the broken-hearted
And saves those who are crushed in spirit"
Trust also in the Lord, and He shall provide your food:
"The LORD does not let the righteous go hungry..."
During this trying time,
God will not forsake you:
"I was young and now I am old,
Yet I have never seen the righteous forsaken
Or their children begging bread."
You may be alone at home,
But you're not lonely,
Because Jesus is there with you:
"I am with you always, even to the end of the age."

433. It'd Be Well, II

Even if you may develop Covid-19 symptoms,
Don't be afraid, for "God is our refuge and strength,
A very present help in trouble."
And when you're overwhelmed by this pandemic
And don't know what to do,
Pray, call to your loving God:
"In my distress I called upon the Lord,
And cried out to my God;
He heard my voice from His temple,
And my cry came before Him, even to His ears."
And last, God is reminding you, that,
"Tell the righteous it will be well with them…"
And so, shall it be!

434. Canceled

Everything that is not essential is canceled.
This includes education attended in person.
Canceled also is prestigious professional games.
Planes which ace the skies, travel, is canceled.

Nothing that is of essence should be cancelled.
The police. Nurses. Doctors. All healthcare staffs.
Those whose it is their business to save lives –
Grocery stores, gas stations are not canceled.

After days, hair is over-grown, sagging the head.
The crass, the messy, and an undergrowth beard.
Ladies nails cry for a last paint, or they are dead.
Many saloons and barbershops beg to be heard.

Look, the monetary indexes are terribly down.
Dow Industrial breaks many hearts of the rich.
Empty, is every financial bastion downtown.
Many can't flaunt, can't frolic on the beach.

What's not canceled is home, family, and love.
Even religious, spiritual centers, are cancelled.
Luxuries. Business. Courts. Taverns. Suspended.
If contact is not cancelled, life could be ended.

435. Politicians as Leaders

Why do we still make politicians leaders?
They have no clues to complex problems
They don't answer questions, they dodge
When they are called to provide statements,
Nay, they spill eulogies and anecdotes
They're shameless, they meander throughout
For a simple "No" or "Yes", they spin into mazes
As far as they are concerned,
They cause nothing,
They're responsible for nothing,
They didn't do anything
And as for the difficulties at hand,
They only inherited everything.
People everywhere are dying,
Politicians are living,
Everyone is poor and in need,
Politicians are full and flowing
They lead from behind, they sleep in Parliament
They run departments they can't define
They read speeches they did not write
And they are hired without any qualification.
They have one certification,
They are not afraid, to lie -
Only the truth, shall bid Covid bye!

436. Easter Poem

I
The Covid-19 pandemic is all about a disease, a virus
And this just reminds us of the story of our Lord Jesus
His birth, the first wonder of the world, a virgin conception
Herod, trying to kill the Baby, his plan hinged a deception.

II
He grew up normal, like any other child, physically strong
But unlike any other human being, He did nothing wrong
At the age of twelve, He confounded the teachers of law
They tried to dissuade young Jesus, but found no flaw.

III
As He grew up, everything about Him coiled in contrasts
Though He was God, He was also human's special class
And the greatest of these, was the exchanges He made
Though divine, He became mortal, what a price He paid.

IV
Through miracles, He changed the order of entire nature
By parables, He spoke to the intricacy of man, His creature
But through a painful death, He opened a new vista of life
And betrothed Himself to His Church, His body and wife.

V
It is Easter, I want to tell a remorseful, but blissful story
How humility and wounds paved a daggered way to glory
In Israel, the highest of criminality was meted at a cross
It was basest condemnation, lower than ordure, a curse.

VI
The cross, was the sign that you were not at all wanted
You were heavenly waste, and earthly dung, haunted
Hanging there, your crimes, in pain, you bore as trash
In death, devalued, you became lower than rubbish.

VII
How can it be that God, the Father, should subject His Son,
The sinless One, paraded naked, on a tree, in bright sun?
How could a real criminal, a sinner, me and you, go free,
But His beloved didn't allow Him from this cruelty to flee?

VIII
Oh, love, kindness, mercy, justice He made Him to meet
Nailing Him on a tree, sparing not His palms nor His feet
Ignoring His voice, He did not hear His solitary prayer
Only anguish, merciless anguish, His dignity left bare.

IX
Then to our benefit, God His righteousness to us credited
His position in the sight of men, to His shame debited
He took all our sins, past, present and future in His body
His flesh became a large sore, His Word was our antibody.

X
In His wounds, injuries, lesions, cuts, blisters, His life gashed
By the stripes, strips, streaks, lines, all sickness got punished
The scourging plague and infirmity exchanged for wholeness
The torment, terror and setback imputed to us as a bonus.

XI
Then the final blow – death – inflicted on Him *enroute* to Hell
With His own blood, the price, He freed captives from the cell
Proclaimed, "Man is whole, cured, healthy, restored, saved,"
God, to earth and Hades His Son sent, for man He loved.

XII
Oh Covid, you have no power, the worm's itch is quashed
For He is risen from the abyss, His blood their sins washed
Oh, death, oh grave, Satan, by His life your sting is crushed
Those in Him believe, forever their pain, gloom is hushed.

437. Covid War

The nations are at war, not against each other
This is not a battle between brother and brother
There are no flash philosophies, no ideologies
There are no apologies, and no mythologies
The cure is not medical, no antibiotics, either
There is only a social remedy, weapons, neither
The Generals, presidents need no legal authority
The enemy is biological combat, in its full purity
Over forty million people died in First World War
Second World War, had seventy-five million tore
In First, the trigger was a political assassination
In Second, League's failure, economic frustration
Then, only massacres, mass-bombings, genocide,
Now, only disease, starvation, and broken pride
In this war, there're no military ranks, no uniforms
In this war, civilians do chase and weather storms
This isn't a typical war; it has no engagement rules
It respects neither the fighting wise nor fools
Only distances – social, moral, and even spirituals
No need for armaments, armored cars or warrigals
The enemy is invisible – hangs on and to everything
So long as it is visible, to it, this foe will cling
Fear – is its foremost malice, with it, it braces
Tear – has broken rank and cursēd men's faces
Death is common, it is no longer breaking news
Faith is eroding, people's hope now lies in booze
Money – is no longer a god; oil has been debased
Honey is no longer sweet, isolation is the new taste
But one flaw this adversary has, it can't rout unity
If nations, governments bond, bug has no munity!

438. The World in Mourning, First Wave

The sooner the sun rises and sets,
someone has died.
Like vapor they go,
with or without having goodbyed.
There's no funeral home,
no morgue to contain them
There's yelling for grandpa,
for little Moses, it's a shame
There's no crowd to escort
the coronaviroid departed
Only statistics, more news, more bad news,
for the parted
In USA,
they mourned six thousand people today
In Italy,
thirteen thousand people who passed away
Spain lost ten thousand loved ones,
and more counting
While Germany had one thousand plus,
discounting,
In China,
three thousand and more left the earth
In France,
over five thousand couldn't keep life's faith,
They lie without breath about three thousand
in Iran
UK's over-two-thousand bodies
are over and done
And Belgian and Netherlands,
lost over two thousand
Canada, Indonesia,
they put over three-seventy in sand
Close to twenty have died in Africa,
I fear more is to come
Oh, Mother, don't keep silent, let no-one say,

"Be calm!"
For the world is in mourning,
and none is there to soothe.
Oh, no, this pain is gross,
it's worse than extracted tooth.

439. Second Wave, I

It is here, it has been here, it's not going
The Corona Virus, numbers are growing.
By end May, nations had gone in lockdowns
Shutting counties, many small and large towns.
Some countries guarded well, including China
Whiles others the damage wasn't all too minor.
Many people, the aging, have succumbed
Though some, having to live with it, have numbed.
The tow on human mind is in millions,
But the blow on economies, in billions.

440. Second Wave, II

To USA, India, Russia, and Brazil,
It has bequeathed an awful lethal kill.
The nations with female leaders did well,
But those with radical dolts didn't excel.
Africa, except to the South, was spared
Mostly due to strict warnings quickly aired.
Adults and young did not go visiting,
The worker did not do soliciting.
There were restrictions in many a place
And it didn't matter people's class or race.

441. Second Wave, III

Then did begin Trump to thump the trumpet
When he saw his votes begin to plummet.
He and like others forced the re-opening
Before long, the virus had broken in.
The second wave was finally around,
This period, to run everything aground.
The fear of second closure ran amok
And mask mandates began to be in tuck.
The GOP is breaking social distance rules
As millions get ill at rallies and schools.

442. Second Wave, IV

This wave two is dangerously stronger
Many European states get it wronger,
The end seems far away in a distance
With no vaccine, there's threat to existence.
This menace loves and behaves like a flu
So, in Winter and Fall it will accrue.
The goal should be to stop the pandemic,
To reduce its spread, making it less endemic.
To that end, wash hands clean, and stay away;
Do listen to science, wear masks, start today.

443. Dr. Fauci

You may call him anything, US physician
He is nimble, pure, and a true guardian
He will not bulge to theories of ricardian
Nor move an inch to give up his position.

The barrage of political pressure
Underneath the Trump administration;
He's relentless to save the population
From Coronavirus, that wicked thresher.

For very well he knows, life continues
Even when Trump is clearly defeated
So, he stays, till his mission's completed
His foe won't tire him even with bad news.

Oh, Covid, brag not you slew America
But for the foolishness of its leader
And the greed of the misinformed reader;
They endorse the ideals of Amerika.

Oh, let Fauci lead the way, all the way
Till the shot that'll kill Coronavirus fires
And many a crooked politician retires,
Till life yields to normal, and all is okay.

444. They Gather

They gather, in masses, in rallies
As many a death and fatality tallies
They wear no masks, the majority
And those protected, are a minority.
They chant, "Maga," as coffins pie
And repeat slogans, as elderlies die.
Oh, this ruthless public murder,
In their president, they've no girder.
Oh, this total reckless disregard,
The Great Nation, has no guard.
They hug and part, like normal times
No distancing, youth die en primes.

445. Western Virus

The thoroughfare that treks to Covidland
Is plagued by a long, meandering garland.
And silhouettes of broken effigies
Do hang in gory on smitten elegies.
It is the Western Virus, Gravorous,
A descendant of the arbovirus.
Anathemia laments deliriously,
As bell tolls *Invocacio*, serially.
The venom of AIDS conquered, barely,
And mighty Influenza A, lived, rarely.
The deep hand of disease rigged Africa,
But Covid found a home in America.
The rich, brave have him, so do the stars,
He shuts life, is limitless, worse than SARS.

446. To Lock or Not to Lock

A raid of deadly bugs, the world in shambles
To lock or not to lock, the earth gambles;
Nanas are dying and so are young ones,
Every day, daughters are infected, so are sons;
But selfish politicians refuse to accept fate
Their own interests they parade but not of state;
Morgues are inundated, hospitals are overflowing,
And there is no space to lay bodies, overthrowing;
Oh, America, Europe, Africa, and even Asia,
There is much grief inside Eurasia.
No time in history saw an ingesting of bad news,
Everywhere people wake up but with blues;
The enemy, so small, and yet so powerful,
It's sting, so invisible, and yet so hurtful.
Armies of men, fight, mask, by all means possible;
Do stay, find vaccine, make it not transposable.

447. Lamebration

This global winter of discontent's ended,
Oh, may the world celebrate and lament
This lamebration should to our victory sage
For it is not the might, but the proud fall;
The wise in their own understanding,
Who, thicken to moral reason by wealth,
Had forgotten their own nation's health
And corrupted religion with hefty orations.
The Trump has miambly fallen to delirium
Whence Omaha, hundreds left in frozen cold,
Oh, lamebration, then came the vote day,
And they watch a democratic dictator drop.
Oh, Covid, president's pride you do chop.

448. Delta Variant

You defiled the norm and trended into hospitalization;
The original Covid you etched into capitalization.
You became twice more contagious than previous variants
And tortured humanity with immunal blows rather furious.
You increased transmissibility among some vaccinated people
And smashed body defences as water running on a steep hill.
You took advantage of people's conspiracy theorizations
And exploited the rampaging societal lockdown frustrations.
Delta, you behave like a whore, leading to 'hyperlocal outbreaks,'
Wherefore, you rained on civilization lethal micro shelling flakes.
Though you preferred cough and loss of smell to be less common
Yet, you let sore throat and high fever wreak havoc in Ommen.
Once two-dose vaccination was the best protection against you,
Now you want Pfizer-Moderna booster shots, or else you boo.

449. Omicron Variant

You travel at what can only be described as dizzy speed
You leave behind bodies broken, hearts, minds to bleed.
You are unknown, unpredictable, moving like whirlwind,
You empty streets again, freedom, leisure both are pinned.
You're like a common-flu, yet you're lethal and merciless;
You push a hope narrative, yet you're resolutely relentless.
You throw bombs with shrapnel of fatigue and tiredness,
You congest airways and run noses, leaving an entire mess.
Unlike your precursor, you preserve loss of taste and smell
But that's because you rave in the bliss to toll the last knell.
You respect neither age nor health or vaccination status;
You're disdainful, melancholy, as bane as a prickly cactus.
You're one of the seven heads of the Covidic Serpent;
We vow to utterly modify you like a musical mordent.

450. Vaccine Inequalities

Cry, Mother, cry
For the youth of innocence be dictated
Cry, Father, cry,
The hope of a vaccine effect is decadent.

Cry, Mother, cry
For the modest of equivalence be castrated
Cry, Father, cry
The faith in vaccine equality is desiccant.

Cry, Mother, cry
For the age of excellence be frustrated
Cry, Father, cry,
The trust of a vaccine futility is renascent.

Cry, Mother, cry
For the character of valence be cerated
Cry, Father, cry
The love for vaccine boosting is prejudiced.

451. Poorland

The poor, the people and their nations
How they die, in throngs without pulsations
They're victims of socio-economic unequalness
Their only sin, is that they have less and less.

She can't afford a first dose,
Because she has no money
And can't speak of booster dose,
Nor drink from a cup of honey.

The poor people are regarded to be next
Only after the rich have reached their apex
They can't buy medicine within their means;
They would rather use it for rice and beans.

Her only chance of survival is prevention
Because she can't afford isolation,
Or else she dies in detention
Because of dehydration.

452. March 2024

Finally, the bout of Covid is gone
The impossible has at last been done
Cancellation, there is certainly none;
Immunity is as strong as a bone.

We shall once again book for vacation
To, once more, embrace our loved vocation
Joining fellow friends in a precation
And freely breathe without suffocation.

The end is, beyond doubt, very much near
But the start is all right and as much dear
We'll no longer to hug each other fear
And our gullets in public shun to clear.

It is time our dreams once again to love
Fate's satire not to hide behind a glove;
Play's joy to rekindle, freedom to have,
The world is open, grace flows from above.

BOOK VII OTTAWA SPECTACULAR

453. By the Meadows of the Rideau River

Here we drove in our black Mercedes Benz
Whence we gulp caffein with family "n" friends
Awaking to the fresh smell of early Spring
In the bright glow of the wild Eternal Spring,
We frolic to rhythms of Northern Cardinal
As warm blood romp in the ulnar tunnel.
The marvelous thrill hits us right on our faces,
The populace mingle, joining more races.
We stopped, danced to the sips of Manotick,
The meandering alcoves here're fairly heroic;
Here to Moss Kent's freedom dream's fortuitous
With finesse' ambience, we rave quite circuitous.

454. 312

They come and go more frequent than one pees
It is a habit that infects like that of a bowel disease
Some days, it is the man, other times, it is the woman
Each time, they pass as furious and quickly as urine.
Their house is situated on a very busy Ottawa street
But it does not ease the trips which they always repeat.
Here and there, they come bringing two cups of coffee
And thence 'n' thither, they hold a goblet of hot toffee,
But most of the time, they bring nothing with them,
For I don't want to sound like I'm here to condemn
And yet, they come and go, from Monday to Monday,
Without a restful day such as one would on Sunday.
Neighbors, you present yourselves like on TV screen
A mundane style, as one watching a seizure scene.

455. A Hug

Just like yesterday, there in the Scarborough maternity ward,
After seventeen years, I brought her to the university's yard.
Just like then, they were tears of great joy that hit the floor
Now, they are of great delight that sends her to a great chore.
She will learn to be an adult fast, reaching her own decisions,
To ration portions, and budget her own monthly provisions.
She can be anything she wants; a studious student, a doctor
And as roles now shift, I am glad I can still be her life proctor.
She returns to the city in which she first opened her mouth,
Here, she will reason too deeply and end her mental drouth.
The hug, that squeeze she gave out, spoke louder than words;
The sound of it, was the flight of heights of intellectual birds.

456. Air

You may consciously call it,
"The natural equalizer,"
It is here presently in spirit
Over there, it gets wiser.
The whole world breathes the same
And what they exhale,
Every one everywhere will inflame,
And foe as friend will inhale.
Love or hate them
When they cough or fart
And whatever comes from their bum,
You take in, becoming of you, a part.
So, you claim to be better
Than your neighbor, you lie
To them, you're a debtor
And far or near, you're all nigh.
Care what you do when you breathe
It is what another will receive
Whether clean or diseased, they'll sheathe,
And what you hide in it, they'll retrieve.
Air, oh, divine and temporal,
You make one all, and all one,
You're joint and also several
Whoever lives, you she can't shun;
The dead do sublime and to air return
Their fumes daily we consume
No longer should we them to see yearn,
For in the air we breathe, they bloom.
Despise not another, dead or alive;
In the same air you thrive, they live.

457. At Your Wall, O Jerusalem

With joy have I waited to pray by your walls, O Jerusalem
For this, I would pledge to behold the old age, Methusalem
As I lay prostrate from my window by the Ottawa mansion,
When in rhyme I write, carefully calculating each scansion.
To thee, the land that carried my Savior, bid me to come
If I should forget thee, O holy scepter, let me be but a scum,
For in thee the Hope of Glory, walked astride a fitted donkey
Adorned with palm leaves to the brace of revered swanky.
O holy, holy, holy, let my feeble glory to Yours be but dumb,
That in Thy presence, my soiled honor be but a chilling numb,
You, the most glorious, from sweat's drips Thy place traded,
You, the expression of divine beauty, Thy pure majesty faded;
O hosanna, halleluiah, hosanna, to Thee who spread universes,
Let me pray in Thy walls, Thy praises recited in these verses.

458. Balcony Etc.

"It must have a big balcony," she said,
Because the one that sold at the top dollar
Never had one.
"My room should have its own washroom," she insisted,
Because the one which beamed like the sky
Did have only three.
"It should be near the lake, if possible," she thought,
Because, unlike Ottawa, Kitchener is on a ridge.
"It should have three garages," she got excited,
Because the one which opened her heart,
Had two and did not cross a bridge.
"It must be big and spacious," she emphasized
Because what is an upgrade
If one gets exactly the same thing?

459. Barrhaven

At first sight I thought, what is this?
Ottawa, how heav'n it resists?
I took a trip to the suburban
Where residents imbibe bourbon
I said, Wow, a thriving commune
Imperial with business signs in June
Of newly-built, Mattamy takes the boon
Even though all dance to Minto's tune.
Oh, these wide-paved avenues of tar
Neither a mirage nor tan from far,
There's thrift that reigns in Barrhaven,
Not known for fake or charlatan.

460. Bridge by St. Lawrence

"Welcome to Quebec, Begin by St. Lawrence,"
Still, clear thoughts run like a swift occurrence
The route to Montreal passes through here
As the steam from the engine shushes there
This river curves like the beauty of a woman
And gratefully invites like the wink of a man
The above bridge, greets, Queens it represents
Beneath it, are stashes of weeds and presents.
Yet, so tenderly and so soothing is the rush-hour,
To the Capital we return, full of delegated power
St. Lawrence where the royal decided regal
Whence Kanata would fly freely like an eagle.

461. Burning Earth

You who dwell on the earth, O, you all listen
For the command is to subdue, and to glisten
The earth's on fire, and so are its surrounds
The water, air and fauna 'n' flora around
The carbon we spend, the oil 'n' gas we flame
With freedom, we may never them all reclaim.
Yet God blessed them, be fruitful 'n' multiply
But He told them, too, to reply 'n' comply;
To have control and exercise care 'n' restraint,
To use and enjoy the earth with constraint.
See, the earth is burning, due to climate change
The globe is warning, and fast goes the grange.

462. By the Quebec Border

It is nothing, but nothing that divides the borders
There are no walls, no high mounds, no boarders;
It is only a road that crosses invisible lines into Quebec
You need no guide, no maps, and not even deep pecks;
All go through a boring street, not known to jamming
Even this, does not beat drums or even lead to ramming.
O, these brother cities, Ottawa and Quebec at 417
They neither parade nor merge by the concourse of 416;
And both carry with pride, the white and red Kanuck flag
And though one has defeated poverty, it's never seen to brag;
Their waters are one, separated only by native names,
Their motto is a blaze that never sheds its nil-hued flames.

463. Client

You sat there quiet like a deaf bear
Environment's future on your shoulder to bear
You came all the way from Ottawa on rail fare
But you are special, your beauty is fair.
Our eyes met, so did, too, our hearts and souls
Wounds for Mother Nature, festered with deep sores.
We could not hold hands even though you were hot
But we engaged in conversation and our topic was hot.
You were gentle, tender and endearing to see
And you narrated how you had crossed the sea.
Shortly but surely, you drew closer in motion;
We loved, joked and drafted a court motion.

464. Cobourg Traffic Jam

By the three lane drapes overlying the port-city of Cobourg
A jam with antics as intimidating as the villains of Cyborg,
It lies dormant lane to lane like a carnivorous sea trout
Unassuming, dozing, and waiting for its chance to globe-trot,
It is loaded with sedans, trucks, vans, hatchbacks and SUVs,
As the day is too hot, indexes calamitous of massacring UVs,
It slowly begins to unwind, one drive given to yet another
And here, an uncle, aunt, sister, brother, mother or father,
All in gear one to three, the monstrous maze vies in motion
And what a relief, as plans, destinations spring into action.

465. CTV Morning Ottawa

They bring us each morning the best and the latest news
They aren't selective, they pundit to all our dear views
They are nearly almost accurate in all broadcast of weather,
They don't relent, nor even shy away from duty together.
At early morning rush-hour, they stage the vast in traffic
Illuminating the City with flashes of everything geographic.
The Capital, is never without cutting sports information
All that happens on courts, gets the very best affirmation.
Just before a seep of coffee, meet the veteran Rosey Eden;
She is magnificent, known world over, including Sweden.
Awaken to the trumpet melody in Annette Goerner's voice,
And sit there enjoying, for you may have no other choice.
Then recline, be ready for breaking news with Leslie Roberts;
You'll be enlightened to the day's expectations and audits.

466. Daly

It's a dense of mixed persons and minds
Whites, Blacks and races of all kinds
In the sweltering heat of the day
They gather by the tip of Cumberland's way
In one hand a smoke, in the other, food
Some, on bikes, rotate goodbye astride the wood
Other topless males and bottomless female sisters
They gang around passers-by and visitors
Harmless, they crow like pregnant lizards
Looking for space to make beds within blizzards.
You may not call them anything but homeless,
Anything they don't treasure, that's cleanliness.

467. Death of a Monarchy

The day Queen Elizabeth II died, I talked to Amanda
There, outside a Scarborough hostel by the veranda,
We reminisced of lost loves and dried remembrances
Like death, gone desires bear a striking resemblance
To the hour of separation that so frequently attends
To realms of the mortals whom once they did befriend.
This door hinge does open once, and once does shut
For those left behind, it pains, like a dagger it does cut.
Yet, these vivid memories, like trophies forever won
We busk there in, like in a fully bloomed Meridian sun.
"God save the queen," mambos drunkardly to din elegies;
"God save the king," casually dirges to silent melodies.
In chambers of waiting princes, hope sings loudly internal,
In selfless labors, the longest majesty bids leave eternal.

468. Double Deckers

They take you to activities, culture and history
They tell of Ottawa's fame, pomp and a great story
They demo ancestry and also of monuments and heritage
They display of the useful memories on native stage
Hear the bear treads the lakeside and muppet their growl
And listen sensitively to the nagging of the night owl
Be fascinated with the land and nation's sea tours
As the double decker all boredom and maladies it cures.
To the sapphire tune of the most memorable sightseeing ;
In here, repression and oppression you see all freeing.
Oh, these bilingual guides, to the city's pleasure they bend,
And to the world's nice, picturesque view they do trend.

469. Down Stewart 1 Street

The intersection of six roads form a dance here
The highway to Gatineau does also pass there.
But to reach Canada's 417, you must U-turn,
And drive carefully via north till you make a turn.
The mighty Rideau Mall stands astute voluminal;
To the east lies the power's hubs tad abdominal.
The glorious Parliament Hill lurks large in vicinity
And multitudes troll the civic bridge by minute.
The belly of the porous Ottawa University opens
And awards to notable passers each a bow-pen.
But the walk along Stewart Street begins at one,
Here, the climate meets pals full of love and fun.

470. Dream Ruins

They fell, entire pillars, all crumbled down
And great was the fall, heard in the full town
The dream they built, was faulty from the start
The material was fake though shaped by art
And the sad truth is that, they didn't depart
They refused to move out, they could not part
They stayed put within the structure and ruins
They stuck together like limbs of confluens,
Always looking at their broken, failed dream
With neither clue nor spirit to redeem.

471. Drive Me Crazy

You drive me crazy through your twists
You drive me even crazier through your turns.
You throw me off the target by your ups,
You catch me off guard even by your downs.
You rearrange my schedule through your ins;
You make me change course even through your outs.
But you always meet the demands of where I'm driving to
And give me peace of mind of where I am coming from.
When going, I pass you by on one way to give,
On my way back on another lane, you do take
On Ottawa roads, your lifespan is not high
You grow, O pothole, you're always brought low.

472. First Nations

We are on transient plain, on pilgrimage
And from lands to other lands, on passage
Across the traditional territory of Credit First Nation;
An expanse of trees, snow, animals in all its burgeon -
Huron-Wendat, Anishnaabeg, Haudenosaunee,
Mississaugas
Earth of their heroes, detailing their volinous sagas
Issues from the "Dish With One Spoon Wampum
Belt Covenant,"
Which with symbols, they jotted down in agreement.
Their history, almost forgotten, unlike the Epic of
Gilgamesh,
But the dexterity of Musqueam, Tsleil-Waututh and
Squamish,
Here thrive, with drum beats of the nations
of Algonquin,
To shindig, they jump up, down, rethinking theories of
Darwin;
In these prairies, spirit-fused cultures glow past the
temple of pagoda
In the Moh'kins'tsis territories, astride Blackfoot, the
Îyâhé Nakoda,
And the home of the Niitsitapi, tenebrous souls of
Tsuut'ina and Métis,
Whence they blanket, believed to pry guardingly round
the atmos.
In the shadow of ancestral blessings, reside the
Mi'kmaq
In these unceded acreage of the membivous people of
Mi'kma'ki.

In them, we seek peace and friendship together in
perpetuity,
Through them, we share the seen and unknown in
gratuity;
First nations,
Host stations.

473. Food Cheer

The city is dotted with places where to buy food
And all their outlets sell merchandise that is good.
All the tastes from all over the world are all here;
Ottawa is proud that, to the world, it brings cheer.
From Europe, Australia, Asia, Africa and oceans,
And you will find it on boards and TV ad promotions.
I like to sample all the varieties from their roots,
From frozen, to fresh, to salted or tender shoots.
The steak is juicy, well-portioned and sumptuous,
The fish is crispy, inviting, bold and very delicious.
Oh, love chickens and eggs farmed with holy passion,
And here, there is no insistence on cutting rations.
For even the vegetables and fruits come in plenty,
Indeed, yours is to discover, shells are never empty.

474. From Kitchener with Love

A place so welcoming, Oh, city center of Williamsburg,
When we walked by the semi-dense forest by cemetery
Hand in hand, we trotted north and south by Strasberg
To a lamb chopped meal drowned by a cider, we did merry
At the exact convergence of one blue street of West Oak
Astride a children's play park and the region's sports field
And a settlement at the indented elderberry at Blue Oak,
Our destiny, legacy, and sense of arrival, had been sealed.
Kind Kitchener, you've got countless disks at roundabouts,
And myriad experiences of happiness, a full life, no doubts.

475. Full Moon

By the Royalist's town near the port enclave of Batawa
Enroute to the loyalist territory of the Capital Ottawa
There, and along to the nativist region of Gananoque
At a perfect solitaire within the absence of any queue,
Here is the lustre overshadowed by the calming clouds,
In the graceful silhouettes whence we hear clearly loud;
O Full Moon, that you guided us closely and verily on
To the banks where we would hear the Speech Throne,
Thence, only hope and joyous ease thither at Augusta,
To your good spirits we stake chances, not to a busta.

476. Ganja

Surrounded by either neighbors on heavy ganja,
Always leaving me bewildered in a big bang franja
The smell is infectious, almost like second smoke
And like from a pyrrhic dream I found myself awoke.
He puffs it from morn to eve on a makeshift patio
Like smiling *ischial callosities* of a female papio.
A numberless canteens of newly legalized cannabis
Spread the Capital City like the tendons of cannibus
As men, boys, women and girls frequent the places
To seek the high that their usual memory it effaces.
Oh, Ottawa, the metropolis, be not a wonderland
With much *chamba* leads to methods underhand.

477. Hard Knocks

Words – which hurt more than a cut of a knife
And chastisement, that scorns like a frown of a wife
Affect more the reasonable minded
Than it damages a van that's been rear-ended.
For superiors keep positions at the juniors' rebuke
And say words which make them puke.
Oh, mighty dollar, how you diminish grace
And put interests in their demoted place.
Some who manage others ought themselves to be managed
And those who understand character, have now aged;
In the end, it offends dignity to be a dubious boss,
Unless at the Capital, losers prefer to make a toss.

478. Hell's Angels

They called those angels who fell from Heaven, demons
For as sour as their taste, they are usually unlike lemons
On bikes disciplined by shape, shade, and vey high boots,
They grace the highways in delightful mechanical cahoots.
These angels of Hell in moods, deeds, and tendencies, show
With elongated beards bordered by a sulphuretted glow;
Yet, traitors they devour as senselessly as starving gators,
For their rank, notoriety is currency of chivalrial innovators.
The emperor, the order she praises in sobriety of gangland
The empress, he shudders the fear of Hell's brutal brigand.

479. High Commission

You treated me tenderly,
This beautiful story I must tell
With tears of great joy in my eyes.
We traded in niceties gingerly,
And ingratiated ourselves with a good tale
Of our native land and precious byes.
You love our country especially
And you represent its interests without fail
For you don't flinch come lows or highs.
I donated my book fondly
And together, we will rise from poverty whence we fell
Here, in Ottawa, our dream never dies.

480. Hunt Club Road

Talk to my first love about how we met
At junction thirty-two, there we sat and fret;
At mid night, I rave into the veins of my balcony,
Talking to friends like Masudur and Anthony;
And editing texts with numerous type errors,
But the dearest to behold are my wife's mirrors;
In these, her beauty and wit meet their match
And around midday, I am still crafting *The Patch*.
O, Hunt Club Road, where my daughter and I
While watching planes take off and land, ally;
And here, we sit within the aura of green dawns,
While viewing Ottawa's finest, loving the lawns.

481. I Don't Feel Like Writing

I don't feel like writing, which is an oxymoron
I can't put sense to words though I have more on
But I feel like cooking, for my babe, my loved ones
This is satisfying, because I love them with lots of tons
But I still want to write, for the themes come to me
They are ponderous, illuminating, full of glee,
But I still feel like not writing, serve for this poem
Which is but a mimicry, a complaint, a spoem.

482. If Not with You

You are a bother sometimes, even patronizing
You make things hard at times, even chastising.
But you stand as a shrine of emotional support,
A comrade-in-arms, a player in the same court.
If not with you, Ottawa w'd have been opaque
And my chances of climbing to the top, slake.
But your smiles embolden me, even to stand tall,
Your charms invigorate me, even to conquer all.
I would race with a cheetah and tag with a tiger,
And I confess, "I feel whole sleeping beside her."
If not for you, dear love, my glory w'd be a gory,
With you, I am trending to be a success story.

483. Inside the Convoy

They do tell me that the mood was jovial
No child bled nor breachēd their synovial
The neighbors brought wat'r and even latrines
And babies watchēd cartoons on big screens
But Tam'ra Lich's displayed as a rascal
Her manner, posture taken as hascall,
Isn't it absurd, did she truly try a coup?
She's been indicted as if she's a Jew,
But truth is, it's bit of a shaking off,
It didn't amount to the crimes of Adolf;
For freedom many times is reached by force
Not each demo should be flaunted as coarse.

484. Bye-bye Kitchener

Bid we bye to the lovely City of Kitchener
Loved ones and we in you found true honor
Our sweet house first love's harnessing nest,
Home front, shelter and, indeed, loyal crest,
You were enough for us, a bringer of hope
Enlarger of mental maps and inspired scope,
You nursed a family of females and a male,
O the hilarity of clinching a top-cut sale,
Sending a government of joyous restoration
To Ottawa, to extend this firm foundation.
Do sieve through dent and dross, class keep;
Ignite high spirits, bless with gems and sleep.
Decor the fiddling of the nerves with sconces;
Will for us a larger, glitzier haven at once.

485. Jungles of Thought

I walk tall within the jungles of my thought
I have no regrets, no pariah with whom to plot
But only you, for you alone I love with tender care
For you and me have many memories we do share
And forgetting you, is not remembering my depth,
For I have needed you in height and in breadth
O, land, you gave me so much to be grateful for
My three daughters in you I gladly, lovingly bore
And yet, my mother still loves my fine Africa
But my brothers and sister still stick to blastema
Unyielding, and striving to innovate or stand
But they're still mine to love, my true right-hand.

486. Kenneth Kaunda

I heard about your timely death from abroad
You fared well, now rest in the blessings of God.
At the time I wasn't able to attend your funeral
You're rested by the scepter of many a general;
Where Chiluba, the giant of multipartyism is buried
Where Mwanawasa's fight against poverty is carried,
Where Sata's allergies for corruption are unvaried
Where Banda, Lungu and Hichilema's 'll be ferried.
I wonder if they broke your coffin 'n' laid you in reeds
And surrounded your regal head with Mwalule beads,
As the elders did make a deal in Kapwepwe's pride,
Whom they quickly honored 'n' wrapped in a cowhide.
I wanted to be among the mourners of an Africa giant
Who against Apartheid's evils stood boldly defiant.
I hope they did wrap a white kerchief in a wreath;
You preached peace, turning green an African heath.
You dreamed of a united, one country, one nation
You fought colonialism and HIV during your duration.
You harbored Mandela, Machel and freedom fighters;
 You're named among pioneer presidents and writers.
During your life time, you advocated for refugees,
You ate vegetables, had neither wrinkles nor noogies.
A proud nation's father, you were, and in it you died
In your footstool we tend to follow with true pride.
Even though a one-party stands as an arrogant effigy
 That tainted part of your legacy and our self identity.
We are grateful, however, for your militant courage
Against regional civil wars which you did disparage.
Let me your notable life serenade in works of poetry
And put closure and "Say Yes," as to a song by floetry.

You were right, you would live forever in our memories
Which we will gladly hung on walls as Zambia tapestries.

487. Kingston Ontario

There are two feelings that announce themselves by
the view;
The first is a sense of peace that captures the mind,
and joy, too.
Three lanes open up a plane of a rocky split
embarkment entry
And with it, all the good, bad, Black, White history of
the country.
Until recent stories of the Me-too movement revealed
his racism,
And poured scorn on the blotted grandiose of hidden
cynicism,
The confederation's hero, the great patron, John A.
Macdonald,
Was Kingston's favorite standard, was no different
from Donald;
And lying low between Brockville and the naval base
of Batawa
The old capital city's voice is only lower than that of
Ottawa.
We are expected by some racists
to fail
When we are
succeeding;
But they want us to expect them
to succeed
even when they are
failing.

488. Looking for Grace

She is soft and tender, always willing to help
She mixes well as a blender, seasoned like kelp
She is forgiving, always ready to give, not take
She leads to ever living, friends not foes to make
She asks no queries; she accepts all just the same
She offers holy theories, felons she wont defame
She comes before Mercy, love she does promote
She makes Kanata her see, her sins she'll demote
She saves from Hell, and takes even to Heaven
She means for all well, and never claims replevin
She is God's grace; she offers favor unmerited
She is in every place, beauty she has inherited.

489. Married to Two Women

For you, African darling, words are very few
Though not polished or sophisticated, you I love
For your eyes are piercingly cute, Oh you
Who brings down my defences with your doves
And enchants me with your adorable gestures
But your smiles, they fit me like a vesture;
Be not jealousy my love, for I have another
In my travels and searches, I found a suitor
Who is equally as adorable and goes even further,
She is adorned with beauty, and she is cuter.
I'm torn in between, your purity and her dexterity,
And I choose you both, for my progenies' sake,
For in Ottawa, I find comfort with no parity,
In you, Zambia, I have something that's not fake,
Something that is real, virgin and even raw
And for this, I can't ditch you, not at all
For you are my definition of everything awe
Where I lay my ripe eggs in an African kraal.
I love you both, with all tendons of my heart
And nothing can cause me to lose you, to part.

490. Near 1000 Islands

On the valleys of a thousand islands and even more
In the swampy meadows blazing the existential core
To the right and left drawing the ridge after and before
The forage rottenly stretch the earth for novorous spore
As the lumber-jostled terrain braggingly infuse the spore
In elevated Gananoque, natures dress of old they wore,
In elongated jungles astride the leas of Napanee's Nore
Via Heroes' Highway by-passing the bend over Forimore
Enroute the charging chugging of the militant Deseronto
From the Capital through nautical Quinte's to Toronto.

491. Ngalula

You live, you still have breath, resting darling
Your name-sake's done work greatly sterling
For you shouteth not, nor speak out loud not,
Yet, you are missed with dearest kisses a lot
Emmerance shines with excellences in grades
In all modern veneration, she's ace of spades.
To Toronto University for medicine-in-clinic,
By Almighty God's grace, to thrive and picnic.
O Ngalula, our heroness and goddess in silk
Endear us in these lands with honey and milk,
O Ngalula, name that has come to be sacred,
With thy boons, the future's lad's upgraded;
Hail that day in these glorious heaven entered,
On earth, thy good would forever be centrēd.

492. Northumberland

A canopy of the inflicting closeness a bundle of trees erect
A blanket of greens in a cocoon of a sustained tangle grove
To shelter fauna and flora struggling to emerge direct
But a cascade overboard of chirping grass fallen tars it drove.
By Brighton Ontario, dense fossils give way to mutinied coals;
The rescinding glaciers pull back at North and South poles
As humans and tamed animals fight for survival incognito;
It's time to reminisce, time to dismiss, it's time for burrito.
Road-ragers eavesdrop the solid sounds covered in foliage;
Like a green-roof, Northumberland prides in starry rollage.

493. Factions

A clan in disarray, for the uncle who has left us
For a mother we dearly love, keep her well, Jesus
But these children of one ancestral grand parent
Who sap in one dish at Emmasdale without rent
Who went to the profiles mines stones to hunt
And who have one another turned, joy to shunt.
Here, in the land where superstition is silent,
Here, where all is a tribe, there's no assailant.
We mourn a patriarch who shared our goblet
And if God allows, we wouldn't hide our wallet;
For a witch is an abomination before the throne
And solid Ottawa, we'll stand strong as a stone.

494. O

Oh,
My dear Ottawa
At first, I just wanted to say hello
I hoped you'd be where my cottage was
How I have wanted to settle my love in you
I wasn't sure you would my little ones hug, though
I admit, sweeter to my values is the taste in you that is true
But, you are dear to me and mine, the tenderest city that I know
Therefore, when I parked and off I took, I had very modest expectation
Only hope and faith, dear one, only hope and faith that I carried with me
Now I long here to live, to invest, to practice, and to grow many a generation
I long to drive in your long, straight, wide and flat open countryside, to be free
To busk in the glow of elevated civilization, the convergence of sense of friendship
And to frolic in the spur of uncharted territories, the discovery of exhorted beauty
I'll aspire to deserve you, to be endeared to the meaning and wisdom of headship
I'll gladly answer the call to excellence, to dexterity, preparedness and to real duty
Clearly, you have a tender side and a tough side, which I have noted in my writings
To the former, you lavish upon your citizens with the best of greened endearments;

To the later, you station the most alert and well-trained
sentries in camp sightings
Surely, you intend well for your families, for their good
health and enrichments.
You've recognized the territories on which you exist
are sacred to the nations
You've cared for every unceded land as if it was your
own, for it is yours, too.
You've strengthened amity among many races with
improved relations,
And allowed everyone, newer and native, their dreams
to pursue.
O land, how luscious you get each passing decade,
how loamy.
For you are attuned to the dangers of climate change
Indeed, all your virilities you openly show me
Here nothing is odd, nothing's strange
Do make me a promise, O dear
Make all within lovely
Their path, clear
Cuddly;
Oh.

495. Open and Wide

The open country around Ottawa airport
To the foundation of those they transport
The joy of the wide rides airing in open skies
With rhythm they rave minds to premium highs
Within the orchards of laughter and ecstasy
Through rustic homes straddled thence fancy,
Yet, the climax buzzing yonder of infinitum
Wows fans and foes alike on a happy continuum
As clouds and crowds dispel all trace of loneliness
But only exude jam and swaggers in all funniness.

496. Glouster

The sheds of greens, and of more greens
Open-ended they swing softly to sheer, vivid cleans
To intimately arranged butches of straight trees
To sprouts of thick rolls assembled in threes
To shapes of pine-like forests of endeared flora
And to here, the whisper of birds open a pandora
In which silence is treasured more than pure gold
And any role flourishes thousands and one fold,
To long straight roads of extended farming tracts
Where food-drink by hillbillies as a unit interacts
For tractors and trailers here find ready mechanics
Little raccoons and munks at mid-roads rarely panic
Hard work here shines like the sun in delirious fury
But tempers business and pleasure fairly like a jury.

497. Silhouettes of Metcalf

The romp of children's outgoings and honks
At exit, the harrowing of a street named Banks,
Just where Morrisburg and Greely daringly meet
The peddle is placed lazily just under my feet
And walking astride the lone road is a luxy monk
As he steps aside the roadways, I hint a thanks
And quickly I add gas to the engine via John Quinn
As I wonder of Nova Lux' blend of bucolic and gin
And in blissful thoughts of an extended vacation
Which, though, has turned into a dashy staycation,
I wave satisfactorily at the fast winding summer
And towards the eighth line I bend my next goal
Unknown to Metcalfians, I aren't a newcomer'
I am a Can-Zam writer, spirit, body and soul.

498. Open for Heaven

Here in the shadows of the falling maple leafs,
By the chambers of laws and irking beliefs,
I lay my head to rest to wake up to hugging relief
A holy sound fan by my soul undoing a deep reef
This it does well, the expulsion of erring disbelief
Which had barely evaded the evilly feats of a thief.
Oh, Jesus, I pray, be my parish and its own Chief;
Whether morn or eve, to You I'll do all to debrief
For in You, I regain my hope and dump my grief.
My trust is in You, save me from debauchery's seif,
In all frills and huffs, You've been my steady motif.

499. Ottario Lawyer

The most vital documents rest in the briefcase
With all that matters, the relevant is the dossier
It is ever in sight so that the legals can keep pace
In significance, it is just like a holy Bishop's crosier.
There's an open market system of readily clientele
The set of real and chattels waiting to be opened
Those they represent with delight, do know well
And at the law firm, they deal with all scope and
Another branch is abroad for the executive class.
There is more to the practice of law than profits,
One knows that helping one is serving the mass
There is more use than simply briefs at the office.
For justice is better served by an unsedated lawyer
Not given to too much coffee imbibed by the foyer.

500. Ottawa Mission

At the center of a large varsity
There lies an oasis called Mission.
It prides itself harbinger to intercity
At the point of intellectual admission,
The assumed thinkers, on one hand,
And the allegedly futile, on another.
At the end of the day, they form a band
And there, they team up with each other.
See bottles and empty excess containers;
The rich, powerful, head towards the West
While the night lounges get entertainers,
And already tired brains, just go to waste.
But, the Mission goes to entire lengths
To find bread and water, from all depths.

501. Ottawa

A city, a conurbation, camouflage on ancestral corridors
A place of vitality, and given to a punditry of open doors
The hilarity of accentuated haciendas do bloom in here
A land native to nations, capital of the green-plated cheer;
In one-way streets of often patched potholes, brains meet
In seasonal enchantments of broad lights, dignitaries eat,
At six, highways fester with engines igniting and waking,
And at five, a vocal din is silenced into friendly breaking;
Oh, dream, make plans in cleanly maintained environs,
Invite all, love more, brace the towers, embrace sirens.

502. Pizza Friday

There is a thrilling glee that Friday brings
Not the least that work has come to and end
At most there's free chilling for many things
And plans that've hatchēd will have smiley blend
The Morgans, they'll be going to the cinemas
While the rest of the city shift some event
The Horgans, they'll sample budded vanilla;
Kids will get tickets to toboggan at Trent
Acrobats will act at Parley in Ottawa;
We'll have Pizza Friday's joy at the Mwewas.

503. Red and White

They roam the wide and long streets
They never forsake small and narrow drives
Some are longer, others are higher
But the double-decker is the road's king.
At Halloween, they transport candy sweets
At Christmas, many a bright lights thrives
At Easter, they bring hope nigher and nigher
At Canada Day, Natives and locals proudly sing.
There is no ceremony, Transpo can't attend,
Night or day, they ferry love from end to end.
Warm by Winter, they hug with sincere joy,
Ottawa's red and white busses, arēn't coy.

504. Satisfaction Guaranteed

Who would have told me that this prayer worked,
The billows of trouble and worry came upon me
I was sinking, all along it gaped at me and smirked
I was overwhelmed, only despair ahead I did see.
Then, I recalled God and that I could to Him pray,
"Father, I said, here at Ottawa do secure my bids."
The walls of angsts came quickly out of my way
In belief, I see daily all the cracks that prayer rids.
Surely, peace that transcends knowledge is in it,
In it, too, is the divine medicine to cure all fears
Oh, the relief that comes when I do pray, I admit;
The mound of intimidation that easily disappears.
It's a craft neither angels nor devils are privy to,
One finds it terrific if only to pray she really knew.

505. Shandalara

The tero of the noro in the foro of the Boro
The shangrila of the molar unnerve the frigira of the Doro
Askance the chance to the dance of Prancer's inaugural mince
She goes to Lagos in a bogus nandos of the Mongos prince
The emporia of the agmoria in forestria of the warrying gory
She shields the fields with which it builds the wild story
The Zabros of the Narvos in retreat from Wandos to Lindos
Ask Zudu if in Zulu "Zungu" is an epithet of the Zumu's Gundos,
Otherwise ask Mwewa if the shower of the tower at Oshawa
Has the same power as the hawa flower of Ottawa.

506. Sherbrook by Belgrave

Sitting by the park astride Belgrave
I wait for my Eastern African lunch to serve
A "coin" or two I change to pay for parking
And it's "Z693" before I dine out as a king
Oh, Montreal, this visit is so gleefully calm
And many have here to forever stay come
With your treasured white, yellow and blue
And your measured harmony many you glue
To lamb portions I caress every bone in meat
Ottawa to Mount Royal, real friends I meet.

507. Skin Tight

Nowhere else have there been myriads in skin tights
It's like they engage in never-ending clothing fights.
The line is not drawn between what you see and think
There is no contrast with what you eat or you drink
Oh, beautiful they are, these Ottawa women and girls
Who daily display the aura of high ornamented pearls
The era of buggies has slowly vanished from decency
But the show of nature's curves has been of recency
Whence the shape, size of everything is spread for all
Enchanting reason to transient details, big and small.
Oh, Great City, to beauty, we stake our lucky calculus
And to vanity, we bank on vagility and the miraculous.

508. Churches of Ottawa

They ornate the Capital like the strips of a Zebra
At the helm are both the new and old Catholics
On Sundays, you can see prayer fumes in terebra
There, the Syriac, here Latin, Greek and Antioch
They blend hymnals of the Maronite as the Gnostic,
Whence Christian science does fuse Ecumenical
And still rosaries give way to the holy Apostolic.
As praises are heard by the enthused Evangelical;
A myriad saints gather around Eastern Orthodox
These are Oriental, Coptic, and even the Ethiopian
And there's more each time in the offering box.
The faithfuls congregate for worship at Presbyterian,
With impulse, they pray in the Protestant Church
As some relish tastes of Baptist and Anglican liturgy
And for God in Charismatic Churches, they search
As Christian Brethren and Lutherans find synergy.
You see them in their sacred attire at Mennonite
Even when they pray in tongues at Pentecostal
You can see that the light of their faith is bright
To those who wish to join them, they aren't hostile.
On Saturdays, come to the Seventh-day Adventist
Or join the United Churches or even the Wesleyan
Or prefer to pay homage at Unitarian Universalist
Or the Quakers and equalists who are egalitarian.
Others are reformed, unaffiliated and fellowships,
But all are one in Christ, One Father they worship.

509. The Finest

I'd be forgiv'n, Mother and my siblings
For my heart is pure, there are no dribblings,
But this I must say that I've found a niche
My Ottawa's love I'd in no terms ditch
Ev'n thought at Mwewa's we pride in Mpende
My tenets I'd not by any means bend.
For I've found a place, a refuge for my kids
A brace where my egg to recline it bids,
With a father's love and desire of patriot
You I choose, for the sake of compatriot.
Oh, Zambia, Mom who carried me for months,
Oh, Canada, mom who led me in triumphs.

510. The Half Moon

Thy half moon that guideth me
From Montreal to Ottawa's hunt
Throughout as I sped watching
The wind, seas, and a tunic blunt
To the steering, to glee and not to catching
Neither to daring Police I am not outdraw
It be fast, and to each time I craved thee
Directing me towards west
The ecstasy of life meets the engine raw
For then I know that I am but propelling
And to within speed the gauge be impelling
Mine winds from the east.
I love this bird that tames roads and tar
For here mine joy and expression I spend
Taking me places near and far
To the bellowing of Kanuk to thee I attend
As I focus on thy destination, O Ottawa
To music, O, so gloriously African
All troubles disappear this hour
To flavors of asphalt and chickens.

511. The Smell of Rains

I wondered me how it rained scantily
And they called it rain many a family
I missed me the outpouring of the tropics
In Toronto, it was hardly discussed in topics
Till in Ottawa I trekked me to the deluge
The smell of the after-rain, my refuge
Just like I loved it at first fall in Africa
For years pondered me why in America
Only showers fell, and myriads but of snow
And storms, hurricanes that deathly blow.
Nay, the gods be kind to me, and they're
For in here, it pours, scent-like of a star.

512. The Supreme Court

On my rendezvous trip to the helm of Gatineau
Like one who is a seeker, a lover, an inquisitor, a beau
I stumbled upon my life's passion, the highest court,
Here, decked in grey, innocuous, but still a forte,
For here, governments tremble, and reason thrives
Here, many of the nations' histories have archives.
Oh, you parade yourself as dead alligator, all alone
But you're Canada's insurance, its super backbone;
Here, judges create and make the Freeland's laws
And many versions of novel issue framed into clause.
Oh, towers, where the mightiest thinkers converge,
Oh, place, where dross may be falculted or purged.

513. To African Music We Danced

Africa, I remember
Always in the month of December
And sometimes close to September
The surroundings were in full ember
And to music we cheerfully danced
Always on our shoulders we glanced.
We didn't care about the aim they enhanced
But we waited, our time we chanced
Till the dawn of an eclipsed morning
To tears of joy we emerged mourning
Our culturing forced into scorning
But we held onto our Africanism, horning
And though we did not know anything
We prided in our land which was everything
Our heads high we did the carrying
Our targets always in view varying;
And here we are, in Western valor striving
In poshes and Mercedes Benz driving
Our ancestral roots, indeed, reviving
While in modernism and grandeur shining.
Oh, Africa, to Motherland I am enchanted,
My permit to practice law was granted
My view of development was recanted
But my resolve to perfection was replanted.
The music of Africa is in dance free
Boys and girls align in routines of three
And expose themselves in one degree
But all numbers must clearly agree.
These bodies to our rhythm they rhyme
In gyrations they respect no time
The music is so good they chime

And to indulge is not but a crime.
The light of the dark is in the eyes
In the rumble of celebration there's no size
The thin or fat in dance don't surprize
But in moving passions they are allies.
The beauty of the dark-skinned dancer
Is in all wise the best African answer
The tune of the perfect enhancer
The steps of the monogamous chancer.
All come together to the mount of pleasure
To the height of shindig they all treasure
To rest awhile and enjoy some leisure
While at the same time release some pressure.
This is the center of the famed samba
The home of the venerated rumba
To the excellences of the mitumba
And the praise of our holy Kabumba.

514. Tomorrow Land

Four girls, a mother and three daughters
Four ardent lovers of flights above the waters
To delight they brace, in the land of happiness
To Minnie-Mouse they cuddle to tenderness
Their breakfast at Disney Hotel is pure English
To the solos of Cha-Cha they groove in Spanish
As they bravely tour California via a shuttle
Their nature's taste, chivalrous, and subtle
By the teens, they've savored known vacations
By 'varsity, they're gurus of vetted destinations
Ottawa they embarked on Canadian passports
And sooner they return, navigating two airports.

515. Traffic at 6

I opened my door and peeped by the road
Besides my dresser, I checked out the board.
It looked dark outside; it was only five
I got into my car and quickly off I did drive
The traffic by Ottawa piled up by seven
And died out completely by eleven,
But at six, there was hardly any traffic
As government offices closed, to be specific.
Unlike Toronto where lights never fade,
Where night industries never go to bed,
In the Sovereign City, there's respite at best,
Here, both minds and bodies do find rest.

516. Tyendinanga

You remind me of my native land's ruse of Twendenanga
As we pass Trenton's base, near Shannonville's Tyendinanga
Emmerance and Tashany in exploratory modes and reflex
As Cutera wanted to know if Bellevue is as Ottawa, complex
Whereas the cheerful Clarice romances Mercedes' wheels
To the altar of the flying pen and ink my agile mind reels
And to Gospel vibes we intoxicate our supplicating tastes
Then we blush in surreal rays wishing this trip isn't waste;
It's a family on Kanuk's quest to conquer fortune's future,
While raving inside a mixed heritage of a pickled culture.

517. Convenience Store

The lovely ladies who serve at Metcalf Variety
Of course, well-kempt, well-levelled in sobriety
Enters a gentleman who holds a door for strangers
Exits a lady in carefree mood, for none she endangers
Then see a full stock of all-variety juicy meat choices
Even LCBO holds a counter for those it rejoices
But the care of an RBC reserve for the locals' bank,
Would make even die-hards to give an easy thank
A look around, even within seconds, yields glory
A man buys two lottery tickets and he's never sorry
And again all those who have dared to pass by,
Will return, the goodness in it, they can't deny.

518. Many Sides of Manotick

The fate of those who browse neighboring watches,
Till they enter Manotick green zones to visual notches;
The elegancy of conservatory-conscious natures
And the sophistry embedded within by the Creator,
For these speak louder than words for their own
And myriads of tree-covered mansions herein blown;
For the hope of selling good and also of buying fair,
To live and grow herein, in environs, lush and rare,
Awakes a wife of a man of never-ending visions,
An author for whom *anathema* is an indecision,
Oh, believe ye in futures soon to be in your hands,
You will count days, and dollars in thousand grands.

519. Big Mother

She spreads her chest from Ottawa River to Cumberland,
From her middle and outwards, there is no lumberland.
She tightly hugs her mixed kids, from Russel to Nepean
As she cares for many a driver, as well as pedestrians.
In her heart, she embraces the interests of all nations
Without discrimination against those on migrations.
She boasts of a large backyard and widened oval hips,
Just so she could comfort the weak, their issues to fix.
She kisses her little ones, all in one spreading country
And prepares a delicious breakfast, all under one tree.
But she speaks with an accent, to represent all races,
And she welcomes all, wiping clean their marred faces.

520. Double Bic Mac

The trouble that I go through to order Double Big Mac
At one of the locations they denied me having a tic tac;
At another, they accused me of ordering a "quick black,"
While at another, they thought that I said, "Bricks stack."
Wait, poor me, twice I got a classic one for a double
And thrice, I had to throw it in the surrounding rubble.
All I ever wanted was a burger with two sets of meats
So that I could skip the dish or order through Uber Eats.
Until a smiley cashier I stumbled upon at Findley Creek,
With tender voice announced back, "Double Big Mac"?
No sooner I grabbed it, than I sated my starving palate,
Flat on my car seat I fell, as one hit by many a mallet.

521. 417

From Victoria BC to Newfoundland's St. John's,
Canada's longest freeway, it creates many jobs.
This Trans-Canada-Highway, it runs like a racer
Not on marathon, but more like a relay chaser.
Through Ottawa, from Hawkesbury to Arnprior,
It sprints like a dry forest that is fiercely on fire.
Either narrow or wide, on asphalt or concrete,
It's not too early, late, and it takes no backseat.
All that makes living possible, rides with it along
And it never breaks down easily, it's very strong.
It fertilizes the life and soul called Ottawa Valley,
All things thrive, for blessings on it, make a tally.

522. All So Near

She walks alone along the paved sidewalk
And on her smartphone you can hear her talk
She carries a purse with money in her backpack
At the intersection, she stops to eat a snack.
When she sees the green light, she crosses
And at Walmart, she easily purchases rosses.
At the self-serve counter, she scans her card
It goes through, contrary to what she feared.
But she has nowhere to put all her groceries
However, she does not worry at all over these;
She has enough space in the bag on her back
With some creativity, she gets all up stack.
And off she leaves for her home not far
Calmed, she shouts, "Ottawa, all so near."

BOOK VIII VALLEY OF ROSES, A CITY CALLED BEAUTIFUL

523. Valley of Roses

My best Father, my dearest Creator,
For You are magnificently gorgeous,
And majestically glorious in splendor.
You're the universe's endearing Darling,
A City where beautiful is harvested,
In Your favor, my dues have been met,
Your presence, is the zest sustaining me.
You, Lord, You're my Valley of Roses,
For I bow to none other or any bosses.

524. City Called Beautiful

O, my God, today is a day of fast, a day of humility
To You and only You I come, in the name of Jesus,
I have never trusted in any other, thing or person
My eyes have only been for You, Lord my deliverer.
For who can save either by His words or His might?
Only You, my Lord, my Savior, You save brilliantly,
You prepare a sumptuous table for my enjoyment,
You set Your favors, in the City Called Beautiful.

525. Victories after Victory

You have led me through victories after victory,
Not by might or power, but by Your Holy Spirit.
Your grace has been sufficient to me, in all things.
You will again defend me and acquit me early,
You will bring my enemy's accusations to naught,
You will quicken the mind of De Rosa, and save me,
You will soften the feelings of the Law Society,
And You will favor me in my explanations,
That it shall be accepted at first value in entirety;
Oh Lord, the Spirit of God will lead me through,
The power of the Holy One will enlighten my mind,
And with the wit of God and of divine wisdom,
The allegations of those who plan my downfall,
The machinations of those who want me destroyed,
And the conspiracies of those who refuse to talk,
All will be frustrated by means of divine favor.

526. Beauty for Ashes

Hear me, O Lord, when I pray, listen to my prayers;
For You have been faithful to me, and You are good,
May the plans of the wicked all be led astray,
Let Your love and mercy shine brightly on my agenda,
As Your swift sword of protection strongly guard me,
So that those who have meant evil for my future,
Will be brought to nothing if they do not repent.

527. A Feast for the Faithful

You will, O God, also look down on their evil threats,
And punish all those who refuse to obey Your word.
But the faithful and those who seek Your face, O Lord,
For them You shall prepare a feast of satisfaction,
You will also reward them with peace unspeakable,
And shower them with joy as of those who win trophies.
Those I serve diligently who have my contracts,
Lord, let them not rise any accusation, even once,
Let them be satisfied with the work I have provided,
And instead of finishing me, they will promote me.

528. Like Dew in the Morning

And let no future clients be disgruntled over services.
Let it be like dew in the morning, like music to the ear.
And protect and confine me harmless, O Lord,
So that those who designate me to French avocat,
May be fulfilling a divine mission You've commanded,
That through Your help, my graduation may be sure –
Both from the undergraduate and postgraduate.
Then I shall teach nations the fear of the true God,
And sanitize governments of the need for justice,
So that, O Lord, the poor may be fended and protected,
The oppressed may be freed and orphans taken care of.
I will also, with your grace, enlighten the many unschooled,
To point them to the unveiled truth in God our Maker.

529. Flower Every Hour

I pray, God,
For Your matchless wisdom,
Your energy,
So that I may rise like an eagle
And hunt like a lion,
In this, too,
Let there be found meekness
And also gratitude.
For You, Oh, Lord,
Brings me a flower
Every other hour.

530. Unapproachable Glory

Now, Lord,
Hear the supplications that I make:
O Lord, my God,
Is there anything too hard for You?
For You pin Your authority
In mighty universe,
You order nature
So it cannot disobey Your will,
Even animals
All know their station and habitat,
And all creation,
Bows at Your unapproachable glory.

531. Ancient in All, Present for All

You are ancient in all,
And yet present in all of us,
You will create
And You will also destroy at will,
You will make beautiful,
And also dull Your way;
You are God of all nature
And all creations are Yours.
You will shrivel this to its level,
You will make its shape
As one of a ready warrior,
You will put strength in its bones,
Fun in its muscles.
And it shall be said,
"The Lord brings shape to all."

532. Halleluiah, You Always Hear Me

I believe, Lord,
That You have heard my prayer,
Because You always hear me
When I pray,
Even when I pray amiss,
Your grace makes right.
It is well with my soul,
The tables are set with all goods,
The valleys are filled up
To their level plains,
The mountains have risen up,
Shouting, "Halleluiah!"

533. White Flowers

You have put diverse qualities
In human beings,
As You haven't in animals
And the wild bushes,
So that for each excellence
In an animal in the field,
There are more matching it
In a single human being;
All this is how
You have sanctified humanity above all,
And You have seconded man
To be a carrier of Your name,
When You chose him
To bring up Your Son in the world,
O Lord,
Isn't it all this too much,
For a mortal man?

534. Even Time Bows to You

Oh, God, when I consider man,
Whom You love;
Whom You have honored
With titles angels would whimper,
Whom You have provided
With wit for technology,
And wisdom to understand times
And predict futures.
Aren't You the one
Who has made man sophisticated,
Whereas he thinks with his brain,
Deliberates with his mind.
Aren't You the one who has given him
Senses to heal,
And has advanced him
From one epoch to the next.
You alone have done all these,
And You will do even more.

535. Only One God

In times to come,
When my flesh would have been dissolved,
The sons of men
Would have discovered all Your make,
They would have made trips globally
In milliseconds,
And they would have prolonged man's death
To years yonder,
And even their young ones,
Would have learned issues early,
They will be a generation
Of those who may forsake God,
Because they might be tempted,
To think they are gods.
May it never be, O Great God, may it not.

536. Intelligence Supreme

But my prayer, O Lord,
Is that You have preserved remnants,
You have through books
And the Internet supreme knowledge,
So that the daughters
Of men and women
Will read,
And so that
They would not go after their own civilizations;
They will know and trust
The Word of the Living God,
And thereby be blessed
Many more folds than those before.
In this, O Lord,
Be praised,
For You are from everlasting,
And Your dominion
Will keep on growing till eternity.

537. Glad in My Sleep

I will be glad in my sleep,
Knowing that You are still God.
I will also teach my children,
The perpetuity of the Divine,
They will spread like a tornado
In the presence of the Lord,
From one end of the globe,
To the other end of the world.

538. Standing at Two Confluences

O Lord, I am like one,
Who is standing at two confluences;
At one,
You desire me to learn the knowledge of man,
And at the other,
You continue to fill my heart with God,
And in this, dear Lord,
May I be wise not to be silent.
I will not keep quiet,
I will write many more books,
I will leave behind
The wisdom of the loving God.

539. Fountain of Knowledge

Hear me, now my Father,
And do not deny these to me,
That You will make a fountain
Of knowledge to many,
That all who come across me,
May acknowledge Your skill,
And rave
Into Your never-ending magnificence
Forever –
Let even the deaf hear,
The blind see and the mute talk,
For they shall hear, see,
And speak the mysteries of God,
They shall know
That apart from You, Lord,
There is nothing,
But that with You, O Lord,
There is everything we need.

540. Beaming with Delight

O Lord, who is unto You,
Who can compare to You?
There is none,
Nobody can even come closer to You.
You are altogether bright, right,
And beaming with delight.

541. Sings Eternal

My soul sings eternally
To my dearest Lord and God,
My voice within shouts out
To the victories to come,
For You have been enough to me,
And all mine,
Even all that I have
Is from Your gracious hands,
And all I will have or not have,
You have provided all.
May all the glory from men's mouth,
And women's hands,
Be Yours, and Yours also
Be the blessings forever.

542. I am Loved

You are defined by constancy, faithful in all Your ways
So dear Father, I am humbled at the thought of You
To note that You think about me and You love me,
To ponder on this sound contemplation:
That I am loved.
Oh, this revelation, how magnificent, how hilarious.
God who is in Heaven is also here on earth with us,
And He orders all things – seen and unseen the same.

543. Constitution of the Anatomy

How You have listened
To the simple cries of Your people,
You have heard their petition
For mercy and compassion,
For You know that to them,
What is insignificant to You,
Is what troubles their peace
And takes away their stance.
You are aware of their frailties,
That they are dust,
To remember
The constitution of their anatomy,
That although they may brag
And stand tall in regalia,
They are nothing
But powder that is about to be blown.

544. Worthless Scale

Oh, Lord,
You observe all humanity,
You see their weakness
When they are strong,
You reprimand their guile,
When they are venerated,
And You chide their pride
When think they're champions.
Only You, O Lord,
Know their end,
Their perfect full stop;
Only You, dear Lord,
Understands their end from living,
And You have weighed
Their worthless days on the scale.

545. Pedestals of Renown

To You,
All men are just dust that will pass;
Even though they stand proudly
On pedestals of renown,
You count them as chaff
That will be thrown and burned.
For me, O Lord,
I have not despised Your tender mercies,
For in them,
I take refuge and I am comforted.
I know that without Your mercies,
My efforts are nothing.
You will not let me be put to shame,
You will stand with me.
You will not also let
Those who seek my end rejoice,
You will deny them
The consummation of their arrogance.

546. Warrior of Warriors

Now rise up, O mighty One,
The Warrior of warriors,
And spread Your sword
For all Your enemies to tremble,
And vindicate Your servant
Who loves and trusts You.

547. Trust in His Mercy

Do not, O Lord,
Allow the systems of adjudication take place,
And do not
Allow the vales of investigation go on further.
Stop them in their course
So that they can be forgotten,
And let those who pursue them
Lose truck and be bored,
Let them say,
"We've found nothing implicating,
We have stopped."

548. Sweet Name

I will love You, O Lord,
I will say Your sweet name each day,
I will placate myself
As one mesmerized by a young lover,
I will be enchanted
By Your loving smack and be satisfied.
O Lord, it is, indeed, pleasant
To stand still in Your presence,
To learn to listen
To Your tender voice,
And be awestruck.

549. My Genius

Oh, God, my genius,
I would rather
Be closer to You
Than to enjoy myself in evil;
I would prefer the company
Of those who fear You,
To belonging to the barracks
Of all God mockers.

550. Only the Lord

Your name alone is to be feared
Above anything else.
For only the Lord is God,
And only to Him belongs all power.

551. Smirked by God

And in Your everlasting power
I will take refuge and rest,
For I will easily open the mails
And read the contents,
I will also answer him
Who questions and probes me,
I will tell her who is searching
That it is now the end,
For the Lord is good
And He has answered my prayers.
In the mouth of babes and infants,
Oh, You smirk me in an instance.

552. Daddy's Horsy

The Lord has said it clearly,
He has spoken strongly
To my investigators for His sake,
And He has commanded them
To put a stop to contentions.
I am forever thankful
That the Lord has done this,
I am on my knees
To give Him direct homage and praise,
Because to Him and for Him
Belongs all authority.

553. Lovely Like a Rose

Who can comprehend the mind of God,
Our Maker?
Who can ask Him to change His mind
Once He decides,
Who can advise Him,
As if He needed human intervention?

554. Gargantuan Legs

And who can say to Him:
"The Lord errored on such a mission"?
For the universe
Is the work of Your genius,
O Lord,
And the deep of the sea
You created for Your pleasure.
The fishes should roam in spaces
Grandeur and spacious,
Leviathan spreads her gargantuan legs,
Across its precipices.
The small and as well as the big,
Both find their habitat,
The sailor does not know
What lurks beneath the anchor.
Yet, Your eyes are in everything,
You see even in darkest.

555. Wiser than Magicians

You are wiser
Than all the magicians
Of the East,
And in all Your ways,
You excel in tact and strategy.
You are the Lord
Of all the living,
Keeper of all the dead,
To You, for You and unto You,
Belong the now and then,
And at Your silence,
The earth shakes,
And the sky sleeps,
When You shout,
Mountains flatten,
And rivers swirl.

556. Praise Him Early

I give You praise, Lord,
Who neither slumber not rest,
I praise You early
And give You all that define me easily.
The benevolent,
The magnificent,
The admirable, is You.

557. Reclining at His Pavilion

O, Most High,
Today,
Hear my supplication and orison,
Do, O Lord,
Rebuke the one who announces my doom,
Do, O Lord,
Diverge them from their path of blame,
That I may again stand peacefully
In Your presence,
That I may offer again the sacrifice
Of praise to You,
And that I may sing, with joy,
Because of Your victories.
That my soul and flesh
Should recline in Your pavilion,
That I may dance to the tune
Of Your heavenly rhyme.

558. Blessed Generation

My God, my Father,
We are the blessed generation
We are the sons and daughters
Born in peaceful times,
We've measured and achieved
Serenity one with another,
And in our days,
We know the goodness of unity.

CHARLES MWEWA

559. Science of Worship

Let, Oh, Lord posterity,
Remember You,
Those who came before us
Would love our days,
They would busk
In our tranquil glory of sovereignty,
They would admire that for your sake,
The Gospel spreads,
And they would wish
They lived in tandem with science.
Yet, they would scold us
For forsaking Your honor,
They will not take kindly
To our vanity and arrogance,
How that we have taken
The name of God for granted,
And have forfeited Your grace
For the crave of conceit.

560. Law's Magnificence

O Lord, I have reasoned and I have found answers,
That our recluse with justice and loyalty are vane,
For we selectively apply law to fit our positions,
And Counsels and Advocates pander for the tummy.
We have left Government to those who oppress,
And made laws in order to advance rulers' agendas.
The people are not given the right message to follow,
The young are lost and have no moral standards,
The elders have not sat them around wisdom's bench,
And they have no role models to emulate and learn.
Those who forsake the Lord will surely perish,
Their adventures will not be remembered forever,
All they achieved will be burnt in patches of history;
They will be dust in the street and manure for animals.
But those who fear and worship the Lord God,
Their tents will ever stand, their wisdom will remain,
Their children will invent wonders and rule nations,
They'll also take the glory of God as shield of honor.
God, our Lord, You have not left us without hope,
You have shown us how to love by Your holy Son,
And we will praise You in deed and in words.
Be blessed, O Lord, be mentioned in all disciplines,
And be sought after, like precious, much pure gold.

561. Your Excellences

Your excellences make me want to dance, O Lord,
The wealth of Your minerals makes many rich.
You provide rivers of capital under the soil men tread
And dreams of flowers in the wild people rarely grow.
When they sleep, You favor them with fresh dreams,
When they awake, You feed their bellies with goods.
You provide them with strength, their industries run.
When they are sick, You heal them with mere pills,
And when they fall, You lift them up without prayer.
O grace, O the dispensation of those God has favored,
As if what has been done in our times isn't enough,
You've also paid our debts with Your own blood.
You have redeemed us, and crowned us with glory.
Whom have You treated with such favor in all ages?
Whom have You treasured with such grace as us?
And who has not thanked You enough like us?
And who have taken Your free benefits for granted?
O Lord, may You live forever and Your wonder be,
For to You be all the rivers, the seas and the oceans,
And to You alone be all the trees, and the grasslands.
To You also, O Lord, be all the mountains and valleys,
And all the fauna and flora and all creeping things;
You spoke Your Word and created human beings.

562. Blissful Feeling

My spirit is awake in me, though the flesh be weak
And, Father in Heaven, to this blissful feeling I awake,
And yet, not for the feelings, but for the faith in You,
For to believe in what has not been seen or provided,
Is to have faith in the true, the living Father of Grace.
I would have fainted, O Lord, many, many times over,
Until I believed that You are near me, to my soul.
You haven't left me bleak; You haven't forsaken me.
Your Spirit moves me to pray, fast, to wait upon You.
In this, I take tremendous respite and I am at peace.
Because I know, O Father, that You preside over life,
That You are the arbiter of all of nature and all in it,
You issue judgments that are binding on all things,
For all the leanings in the world, are bent towards You;
To guard, direct and order them into compliance,
Even though You still grant them their own free will
And desire that they use it to glorify You alone.
I'll praise You, my Father, I will appraise Your name,
I will also lay down on my face in worship to You,
Among the gods, there is no-one like my Father,
And among the children of men, no-one is worthy.

563. Happiest Pain

It shall go well with me, no matter who targets me,
I can still boast in this: That I know that You, God,
You are merciful, slow to anger and abound in love.
This, though, I do not take for granted, O Father,
And I will not shun Your rebuke and discipline,
If and when it is deserved of me justly and fairly.
But today, O Lord, I am not fairly targeted,
My complainant does want to see me punished,
They want to rejoice in my misfortune and pain,
Because they believe that it will be their revenge.
Yet this I know, Your mercy shines on me brightly,
You've given me plenty for naught, indeed, rightly.

564. My Soul's Show-Stopper

There are those who do not want me to succeed;
You know their machinations, Lord, You see it all.
You will not allow Your son to be unfairly treated,
You'll diffuse their stratagems and obviate their plans.
You will stop them in their tracks and redirect them.
You will frustrate their complaint and bring it to null,
And in that they will be met with justice from Heaven,
For You Lord knows how hard working I have been,
You understand the sleepless nights I invested,
And You are aware of all my efforts to serve them.
You're also just, fair and an impartial adjudicator,
And into Your hands, I would prefer there to fall,
To being abused into the hands of mortal men.
Therefore, I pray, O Just Judge, that You judge me,
And not allow those who seek my end judge me.
For with You, there is mercy and grace in abundance,
And with You, I know I can trust in Your mercies,
Which fortifies my resolve to overcome, like an eagle.

565. Free Freedom

My Lord, my Father, I feel how You feel
I understand how those You have created reject You,
Those who breathe the air that You created,
Those who drink the water You freely allow to flow,
And those who enjoy the sun's rays that warm them,
Yet, they turn against You, and plainly betray You.
They know they're mortal, still they brag about life.
They understand they will die, still they rebel,
And they have the evidence of weakness
And yet they stand tall and challenge their maker.
O Lord, as for me, I know that all things hold by You,
That without You, our pride is nothing but chaff.
You're different, You're merciful, You forgive men.
You still supply Your generosity free without charge,
And You ingratiate the children of men with love.
You care for those who heap ungratefulness on You,
And You keep their children safe at night wholly.
Be praised, O Lord, the merciful, the blessed One,
From beginning of the end to the end of the start.

566. Joyous Peace

Oh peace, mighty and wonderful peace, of God.
Only You, dear Father, can sustain us with peace.
In prayer, we find great joy and unspeakable peace,
In serving You, there is abundance of joyous peace.
If we should follow our own whims and even caprices,
We will be like destitute children who have rebelled,
We will be buffeted by sleepless nights and anguish,
And we will forget what a moment of serenity feels.
But with You, O God, there is plenty of harmony,
As if our entire bodily, souly and spiritual mechanism,
Has been merged at the confluence of eternal bliss.
Give us, O Lord, this peace, this benefit of Heaven,
And fill our hearts with strength, interest and all joy,
So, we dance as we walk, and sing as we speak out,
So, we can embrace each coming challenge with grace,
And endure any wiles the enemy may shoot at us.
Oh, Father, You have given us this peace, this ember,
And we will let it bloom and blossom to its azure base,
We'll give You thanks for the comfort You provide.

567. Darling Savior

You have always been on time, my God, dear Father,
How could I have survived those who seek my fall?
How could I have answered them who question me?
But Your Spirit nagged my spirit, and made me recall,
Your voice was strong in me, it showed me the way,
And Your love made me find out what was needed,
For with Your help, I responded to their missives,
And because You know the details of all my life,
O Lord, You are able to see and know all my dealings.
Therefore, O, Holy Father, now sanctify my answers,
And release Your divine and holy favor in abundance,
So Peter can accept my extensions to the very end,
And because of Your kindness, it shall be all well.
Awake, awake, all peoples of the nations of the earth,
Fear Him, bow before His throne and give Him praise,
For the Lord is constantly fending out for His people,
Good Lord knows all and is present in all our dues.
Be praised again, and again, O Jesus, Darling Savior.

568. Praise Time is Good Time

O God, You're eternal, immortal, invisible, and grand,
You are eternally, highly seated in unimaginable glory,
You're fervently adored by angels and by the 24 elders,
You receive praise and honor every eternal moment,
You speak favor, You breathe life and You give gifts,
Your movements swirl the winds and stay the sun,
The blink of Your eyes creates seasons and days,
Your laughter causes the waves in the oceans to rise.
Even when You're doing nothing, You're still working,
Even when You don't say a word, mountains tremble.
O Lord, how pleasant it is also to say Your name,
To come to the moment of praise and worship You.

569. Church's Glorious

How divinely satisfying it is to belong to Your church,
To hear Your name being stated Sunday to Sunday,
And to be told time and time that, "God is very good!"
Oh God, Lord my Father, I am at the end of the road,
I have exhausted all genius and all that I am capable of,
And I have consulted within wherein I know I'm over.
But, I know whom I have believed in, my Deliverer,
In all the battles I engage, You have allowed them,
I shall emerge winner, for Your name is "Conqueror."

570. Desserts in the Desert

Oh, aren't You the One who makes ways in deserts?
The Lord, who raises the dead and gives back life.
Aren't You the Ancient of Days, the start, the finish?
With You I can scale a mountain and brave the waves,
And with You, dear God, those who see cannot see.
So, even to You now I make this humble petition:
That You cause the Law Society to accept my plea,
That where it is obviously wrong, they should omit,
And that where it is not obvious, they shouldn't see.
In the name of Jesus Christ, my Lord, I now do pray.

571. Mortally Live

If it was a mere mortal man,
Whom I had approached,
And if it was just a human institution alone,
I dealt with,
I would have been despondent,
I would have lost heart,
I also would have fainted
And become as though dead.
But with You,
There is always a way out of the maze,
And with You,
Impossible situations become possible.
For You are God,
The self-made One, the Greatest.

572. Breeze of Victory

The breeze of victory flaps assuredly across my core
And I know that, Lord, You have heard my prayers.
I rejoice in this great triumph, again, You've done it;
You have lightened my soul with a song from above,
And You have permitted me to continue the lesson.
For in everything You've allowed me to pass through,
Oh, Lord, You have prepared a school of experience.
At 7:40 am, August 21st, 2020, You lit up my senses,
You confirmed and brought a great relief to my soul,
I now know that, my Dear Father has answered me,
My Darling Daddy has opened up His vistas of glory,
And has made me very glad with His gracious story,
Whence, I will give Him praise perpetually, forever,
I'll stand in His presence and proclaim, "Halleluiah!"

573. Ten Thousand Halleluiahs

When the Lord begins a work, He brings it to pass.
Though men and evil may stand in its way of progress,
The Lord will overcome all and the end it will succeed.
I have trusted in the Lord; I have put my hope in Him.
With the Lord God is mercy, and blessings forever,
And at the right hand of God, stands my Deliverer.
In my deep, somber and odious agony, He heard me,
In my humble supplications, He came to my rescue.
Indeed, ten thousands fell on my right-hand side,
And, indeed, another thousand on my left side,
But the arm of the Lord stood strong and prevailed,
The Almighty, the Leader of the Hosts of Heaven,
He alone, the LORD Jehovah God, was in command,
And He annihilated them all in order to save me.

574. Beautiful Word

They say it is darkest just before it is dawn
Oh, Lord, I now understand the meaning of it.
It is Your Word, that living and Eternal Word,
That food for my soul, that everlasting diet,
Oh, Lord, without Your Word, how can I live?
You are God who saves, the Lord Wondrous;
For in the time when all seemed falling on me,
When the pangs of injustice, and of betrayal,
When it seemed like my dignity was at stake,
When dark clouds covered my summery days,
And long nights of sleeplessness awakened me,
Oh, Lord, my God, my Father, Your Word,
That spiritual nourishment of life and liberty,
Oh, my dearest Savior, did come to my rescue.
I am whole, and with the eyes of divine faith,
I will see the best of the Lord here on earth.
My pursuers will find no evidence against me,
And I will rest safely into the comfort of God.
Be praised, my faithful God, also be glorified,
You are God who saves, the Lord Wondrous!

575. Spacious Places

My dearest Father,
Do favor Your me
Do grant my wishes, too.
Do bring me to spacious places.
And for those who hate me,
Do give me love to embrace.
You will discourage them,
Oh, Lord, from hurting me,
And You will use them,
As instruments for my good.
For You O Lord,
Shall make all things glow,
Even things done against me
Shall turn out well,
And those who mark me
Shall miss, serving Your purpose.
For to You and for You,
Be all the glory.

576. The Perfect I AM

Many times, I ponder, contemplate on Your mercies,
I think deeply about divine politics and Your own rule,
I see that You're God of all gods, King of all kings,
I know that You have the whole world in Your hands,
You command nature, animals, all manner of the wild,
You instruct mountains and tame all wild beasts,
You tell the weather when to change its course,
You preside over the universe, to guide its movements,
You direct the Heavens and sustain the grasslands,
You're fountain of hope for the hopeless prisoner,
The healer of bodies afflicted by miniature microbes,
Health restorer to those who are buffeted by disease,
The bringer of peace to troubled minds and souls,
The helper of those beaten by the trounces of misery,
The perfecter of the cause of those seeking for justice,
The illuminator of the minds in pursuit of knowledge,
The pathfinder to those lost in jungles and wide seas,
The provider of food to those without means or ends,
Supplier of free water and air in abundance to all souls,
The sojourner together with those in need of direction.
The Father to the fatherless, redeemer of broken lives,
The destroyer of all the aims and plans of the evil one,
Giver of eternal life, taker of the breath He apportions.

577. Good Sharing

You took me from scotched patches
And placed me in snowing shadows,
In glorious dreams from doomed ashes,
From the clutches of damned Thanatos,
Into the tender arms of the gentle Savior,
Oh, Lord, the apostle to faithful Xavier;
You aren't done being good and caring,
And I'm not done yet Your good sharing.

578. God of Everything

You are General of all the generals, my Father
You created everything that is seen or is unseen.
If it was me, I would have repented of the evil I see,
I'd have punished my creation and destroyed it all,
I would have said, "Charles, you can create it again."
I would have lost patience, with the betrayals I see,
I would have slain all nations and whole peoples,
I would have bent or delayed justice for my own sake,
I'd have economized the truth and lie occasionally,
I would have been bossy, arrogant, tilted to reason,
I would've demanded total obedience without excuses,
I would have punished the accused without trial,
I would have denied penance to those who prayed,
I'd have been bored by the petitions of multitudes,
I would have forgotten to follow on my promises,
I would have let the limit rule of the oceans get loose,
I'd have permitted the skies to wreak havoc on earth,
I would have lost heart with sinners and murderers,
I would have not forgiven perpetual law breakers,
I would not listen to those who serve my purpose,
And I would have been an unapproachable deity;
But thank You, my God, that You are not me.
Surely, You are not like any other god or power,
You are fair, just, reasonable, impartial, unbiased,
You give a command to Yourself and You respect it.
You ordained order in the universe, Your rule.
You've been faithful to Your Word from start to end.
You are the same, yesterday, today and forever.
You restrain Your anger, even though You shouldn't.
You tolerate evil-doers even when they sneer You.
You give Your sun and moon to both good and bad.
You supply food, water and air to all, even to infidels.
You bear with injustice, for the sake of Your love.
You are generous with Your mercy, forgiving many.
You answer the prayers of those who make petitions.

You are close to those who are suffering or in pain.
You bind the wounds of those injured by injustice.
You protect children and those who seek Your help.
You defend the weak from powerful investigators.
You acquit those who pray to You of all their charges.
You guide righteously those who seek paths of good.
You do all these, and yet You are God of everything.

579. Master

Oh, Master of the mind and creative powers,
You, O Lord, have the mastery only You can have.
I consider a crow, a hunter's worst nightmare,
First, it lures him towards a more vicious predator,
Then, when he is dead, it prowls on his carcass.
It is star of mimic – no voice can't it duplicate.
Yet, You have given to man all of nature's qualities,
You have set his genius to understand wildlife,
So that only man is able to tame its deadly threats.
Oh Lord, my God, You have made man unique,
For only man can outthink all other luminaries,
Only man has the capacity to reason abstractly,
Only man can exercise his free-will and worship;
Oh Lord, be glorified, be praised for this truth.

580. Battle's Won

My soul is elated, O my Father, my God,
Like one returning from a successful battle,
I hear the sound like rhythms of the war drum,
I perceive the sense as one who had wedded;
Indeed, there is jubilation in my heart's chamber,
There is bliss springing from my inner antennas,
Wherein I see the King's glory, though in part,
The foundation of love captivates my heart,
The bringer of joy enjoins me to laugh loudly,
The pacifier of broken souls assures me boldly;
I can run with a Persian horse and be victorious,
I can mount terrains and the win will be glorious;
Oh Lord, You have strengthened my resolve,
My problems You have also promised to solve;
I can do all things through the power of Christ,
I can do this by His strength, which I've priced;
For the Lord is my victory and my glory,
He has also become my success story.

581. More Desirable

Your Wisdom reads: "A good name is
More desirable than great riches,
To be esteemed, better than silver or gold."
Oh, Lord, my God, there are those out there
Who seek to see me destroyed or devalued.
They will rejoice to see me fall or diminish,
They will laugh loudly; they will drink wines.
But You, O Lord God, protests my interests,
You are my willing guardian and my fortress.
You will whisper my name to my accusers,
You'll frustrate the work of my mortal foe,
You will bring honey out of the lion's shell.
Oh, Lord, You taste like the sweetest fruit,
When You speak, You are a soothing balm.
My hope is in You, shall not be disappointed;
For You are very good, O Lord, very good.
May all Your works bow down in adoration;
May all creation rave in Your amazing grace.

582. Life's Fountain

Of Your teachings, Father, let it echo piercingly,
  They're a life's fountain; they save from death.
  My Father, You have pre-empted death's pang,
  You have given us double portion of blessings.
  If I live, it is because of Your purposes to fulfill,
If I die, I'll awake again in Your glorious presence.
O death, You are my vehicle to my glorious home,
  You'll be needed like sweet comfort when time is;
  For now, however, I embrace the treasure of life,
  The joy of getting up in the morning and praise,
The hilarity of whispering His name before sunset,
The rare honor of observing His creation's marvels,
  And the miracle of family, the bliss of laughter.
Oh, Lord, my Father, I love You, I am in Your mind,
  For You have become my everything, my omen.
  To You be honor – in all its glories and beauties,
  To You also be majesty, in all flurries and duties.

583. Sweet Meandering

The river meanders across rocks and flatlands
It goes from one end to the other end freely.
It dances, yells, cries, laughs, even gets silent.
You have filled it with fishes, insects and reptiles.
You have tamed it with Your grace and life-force.
You have caused its neighbors to benefit from it,
And You've preserved Your creation through it.
It trusts You exclusively, to guide and protect it.
It does not worry about changes in the climate,
Because You are the source of its water springs.
Oh, Lord, let me be like a river of flowing waters;
Let me bring life wherever I go, wherever I am,
And let me trust You easily and unflinchingly.
For You know how to resolve every dilemma;
You'll figure out the best way to end an impasse,
And You will bring victory in ways unthinkable.
I rest, O Lord, I rest in Your everlasting arms.
I take refuge in Your sure eternal life's rotunda;
For You will take care of all my businesses,
You will deal with everything that concerns me.
Oh, my being, trust Your God unconditionally,
And praise Him for His endless guidance, Amen.

584. Power's Hour

My Father, I am living at the edge of faith,
I am barely hiding in the fringes of grace.
I see a danger lurking, I hear voices of despair,
My soul is disquieted in me, I am at my end.
But what keeps me afloat is this trust I have,
This belief that no matter how the darkness,
Your presence will shine through to a blissful end.
You are the Lord who saved Joseph from a well;
The Lord who rescued Moses from Pharaoh's bars;
The God who saved Daniel from lions' wrath;
The power that parted the Red Sea into dry land.
You, O Lord, is the master at setting up traps,
And the genius at untangling evil's stratagems.
I will not fear what is planned ahead of me,
I will face my accusers with the Lord's strength,
And Lord, You will deliver me from all claims,
For You, O God, have saved me before twice,
And I know You will deliver me this thrice.
My Lord saves from fiery fires, dying waters,
He shows up for those in trouble, never falters.
As the Scripture declares: "There is a river,
Whose streams make glad the City of God,
The holy place where the Highest dwells.
God is in the midst of her, she will not fall;
God will help her at the break of day.
Nations are in uproar, kingdoms fall;
He lifts his voice, the earth melts."

585. O Immanuel

You are God's Son, You are Immanuel,
You are right now with me; I will not fear.
Though there be nothing in my bank account,
Though the fridge be empty with no food,
Though I am told, "It's over, you are fired,"
And though my businesses fail to earn profit;
Yet, I will not despair, I will not be shaken,
My faith in God of Love shan't be broken,
My trust in His mercies will not be forsaken,
And my resolve in His grace won't be shrunken.
When I am afraid, I will run to You and be safe,
In Your presence, I will find comfort and refuge,
You'll order Your mercies to blanket over me,
And Your divine wings will carry me to safety.
For You, God Almighty, You're my hiding place,
You, O Lord, You satisfy me with Your grace,
You, Lord Supreme, do keep me firm in the race,
And You, the Glorious One, do brighten my face.

586. Calmly Flowers

You thrill my heart, O Lord, with Your wonders.
You perplex me, You amaze me, You enthrall me.
Can a man worry and gain anything from such?
Can a woman fret and by so doing grow an inch?
Oh, Lord, the way You do things is above reproach;
You answer prayers in ways too high to realize.
You make my faithlessness look trivial, irrelevant;
You defeat my own lack of strong belief in You.
Since it is You, Lord, who put words in my mouth,
You, Sovereign Lord, who design my faith's pattern,
And then directs me to utter those sacred words,
Even answering me in methods too fantastic for me.
I know that You have ordered a defence for me,
And spoken favorably of me for all to follow suit.
I am glad, O Lord, for Your mercies and kindness,
I give You praise for Your miracles and goodness.
I boast in Your favor, I glow in the glory of Your love
And I am charmed by the good things from above.

587. Sun of Sweetness

You lead me, You open my eyes, O Lord
Even before a danger comes, I am aware.
You make me know my adversary's plans,
You remind me of important deadlines,
Oh, Lord, Your Spirit lives within me,
He guides me to the truth for Jesus' sake,
And He directs my faculties into blessings.
Oh, open, open the heavens wide for us,
Oh, Lord, seal, seal all the wicked clefts,
And disregard the works of the evil one.
For to the one who obeys Your precepts,
Him who puts His trust in Your commands,
To such a person, Your favor will increase,
His enemies will quickly see their destruction,
And their memory on earth shall perish.

588. Shadow of Sweetness

The woman who loves Your voice,
She who is attentive to Your directives,
Oh, Lord, nothing good shall You withhold,
And You will make their children fruitful,
You will satisfy their sons with virgins,
And decorate their souls with loveliness.

589. Sea of Sunsets

Oh, Heaven above, seas below, and earth,
Oh, you cloud that moves when He does,
And you sun's rays that adorn His coming,
Do stand still, and the King of Glory,
The LORD, He who is majestic in power,
The True Master, Ancient of Days,
The Maker of All, shall whisper His love,
Through the Holy Spirit that He gave;
Be sanctified, O Lord of life above,
Abandon not our legacies to the grave.

590. Moon of Mercy

I thank You, Oh, dear Lord and God
I thank You, that You answer prayers.
You pay attention to every petition
And You miss no supplication.
You are also infinitely a good listener
And when You speak, You are clear.
Thank you, Oh, Victorious One –
Thank You for You always hear prayer.

591. Seasons of Sunrise

Oh, Lord God, I have revered Your name.
I glory in the glow of Your amazing fame.
I've gone out to frolic like a well-fed calf,
For You have done all well on my behalf.
Oh, God, You are my sun of righteousness,
The aura augmenting my morning, flawless.
I am healed by Your holy and rising rays,
I am perfected by Your love in all my ways.
You will make all things work for my good;
I love You, my foibles You've understood.
Surely, goodness and mercy shall follow,
And Your gentleness shall be my pillow.
Oh, Lord, it is Your love that defends me,
You're glorious, all praise belongs to Thee.

592. Center of the Sun

Oh, Lord, my God, my Father, my hope.
I love what I do, O Lord God, Almighty.
I love practicing the law, advising clients.
I love also working on long submissions;
I love arguing the law, applying it to facts.
I enjoy the miracle of justice and its power.
I'll do it for nothing if I would not choose,
And I'd give the world its just demands.
But, Lord, my practice has been threatened.
Oh, Hagos has brought a pernicious claim
And complained in order to thwart my work.
I pray, Lord, do not allow this to succeed.
I pray, curtail its tale and bring it to nothing.
That, Oh God, You give no sleep to Peter,
And You cause him to find no fault in me.
That the complaint be terminated instantly,
That after reading my answer, it be stopped.
I thank You, Lord, because You've heard me.

593. Palm of Pleasure

I will eat, I will drink, I will dance, I will play
I will worship, I will praise, I will adore, I'll pray
I will say it very loud, "The Lord has answered me."
I will describe in vivid terms for all to see
I will not be afraid any more of nerves, instinct
I will be clear, I will not meander, I'll be succinct
I will believe, I will behave and I will be still
I will not fret, be pompous, or not tell what I feel
I will react as if the victory is here, because it is
I will be excited, I will rejoice, I rave in this:
"I will see great accomplishments in this land,
I will be above and not below, you understand?"
I'll be exonerated just as he begins to investigate
I'll be welcomed by great notice at the gate
I'll be all these, because I've found favor in God
I'll continue flourishing, for the sake of the Lord.
I'll state it again, "It's well with me and my soul"
I'll re-state it, "I'll go up and win, that's my goal."

594. Fountain of Floras

The reason the gardens brag with flowers;
The sun in its elegance shines ever brighter;
The moon, like a bride descending for her groom;
The stars, oh, how gleamy they flatter seasons;
The planets, as they majestically orbit the globe;
The universe, wide, how marvelous Your works;
The plants, the rainbow can still learn a lesson;
The trees, with ornamental basics they grace life;
The grass, a carpet well modeled in Persian style;
The animals that walk the endless wides and forests;
The day that comes to light it all and begin it again.

595. Garden of Glory

You created man for Your pleasure, Oh, God,
And before him, You have spread Your creations,
So that he may thank you for Your effluvious acts,
And praise You for all the wonders before him,
To the end that his essence is only efficacious in You,
And his existence is for the glory of Your glory.

596. Garden of Gold

When I wake up in the morning,
Let Your simmering presence guide me,
Let Your sweet embraces caress me,
And let Your sweet voice be the first I hear.
When I get to bed in the evening night,
May Your glory my chamber fill to brim,
May Your name be the last noun I utter,
And may You be the center of my dreams,
So, I may, even in my immortal state praise.
For You have beautified my soul with love,
And filled my mind with melodies above!

597. Garden of Goodness

Let me never fail to consider Your works;
Let me never ignore the singing of nightingales;
Let me never be in a hurry to smell flowers;
Let me never briskly investigate Your nature;
Let me never be too busy to walk the gardens;
Let me never spare a moment thinking of beauty;
Let me never go to bed without saying, "Thanks";
Let me never be ungrateful to Your endowments;
Let me never succumb to pride and dishonor Thee;
Let me never be awkward in analyzing Your wisdom;
Let me never forget the reason You made me;
Let me never stop worshipping before Thy throne;
Let me never be satisfied with what the world offers;
Let me never say, "It's enough of God," no, never.

598. Cradle of Flowers

Oh, Lord, who is my Father
Surely, there's none I love, no other
But You have been my all
I can't complain or ask for more
Like a bird, I'll not be electrocuted
Even if I may sit on a live electric wire,
Because my roots are not on this earth,
My strength is in Heaven, Your dwelling
In there,
I suspend freely among troubles,
I can't be harmed;
I recline in holy bubbles.

599. Brilliance's Boulevard

I will be confident in Your hope
I have a pathway, I can escape
Even though I run out of legal genius,
I will always find a divine solution,
For You, Oh, Lord, transcend reason
You, will save me in every season.

600. Tower of Power

You are my mighty tower
In You, I'm safe every hour
I can be threatened by all,
But instead, I gain even more.
When my enemy takes a dollar
I regain more, Oh, my restorer
Under Your strong wide pillar,
I will find peace, Oh my healer.
The danger that comes from evil,
The wiles that fly from the devil,
Will not brush even a skin tore,
For God my Savior, is my core.

601. Garden in Eden

Your ways are set in a lovely garden
There, You spread a table for my honor
You also arrange the colors in wisdom
And call for me a feast and a breather.
I am overwhelmed by Your great love,
I am awed by Your great symmetry.
I walk tall, I stand wide, and I sit grandly,
I have been blessed beyond measure,
Your presence, Oh, Lord, is my treasure.

602. God Spring

You are a spring
Of cool, calm waters
You bring me
To drink when I'm thirsty
You let me relax
In the midst of turmoil
And I see the victory of the Lord,
I hear the melodies
Of angels flapping.
I am aware of the beauty they bring.
Oh God, am I not satisfied with You?
Haven't I received all good things from You?
Am I not blessed yonder my risky hopes?
Oh, Lord, mountains may be flattened,
And valleys may be filled to the brim,
Yet, Your love for me is constant;
It is set in the Rock of Ages,
Beneath a rockfest stream,
Where I run to receive rest
And find peace and comfort
In my dire times of need.

603. Little Munks Praise

Through Your grace, I sing out loud
You have answered man's quandary
You have saved him from his quagmire
You did it by giving Your amazing grace
How could I, a person born in sin,
A sinister-tilted, selfish-minded recluse,
How did I find favor in Your sight?
How did I claim a share in Your bequest?
And how, honestly, did I get accepted?
It's all because of Your grace, Oh, grace,
Grace that provides for the chipmunks,
And renders free services to all creation.
Your grace, indeed, is amazing, how else?

604. Sunbelt of His Presence

My God, nothing,
Absolutely nothing
Can separate me from Your love,
My Father, nothing can take me away
From the dream of God's salvation.
I love Your presence, it feels my soul
And I am all for You, to my very core.

605. Fall into Fondness

Then sings my soul, and my flesh dances
All these winds and airs are my chances
The mighty shining sun and beaming moon
And the protection that comes at noon,
All these, Oh, Lord, are for my pleasure;
For You have assigned for me all treasure
And have aligned the elements in nature
So, they weave for me a future by filature;
Oh, Your wonders overwhelm my senses,
And Your providence has made my fences;
I am as one who has achieved great victory,
Those who trust You, You'll record in history.
Surely, amid many troubles, my soul'll frolic
And in the end, I'll win, my riches'll rollick.

606. Step into Splendor

Oh, Lord, You're the wow in my memory
Oh, Lord, You're the cool in my faculties
Oh, Lord, You're the glee in my acuity
Oh, Lord, You're the glow in my intellect;
You satisfy me with Your grace portion
And put my mind at unimaginable peace
With Your campus, I am always in motion
For Your voice sets my heart at ease.
I love You, O Lord, my endearing charm,
I'll mount Your pavilion to kiss Your arm!

607. Ultimate Trapper

I have been young, and I am now mid-age
And I have seen how amazing Thy dealings
That, Lord, Thou art the Ultimate Trapper:
Thou would raise a man only to drop him;
Thou would elevate a woman to her loss;
Thou would give a man wealth, then he dies;
Thou promotest one, so they fall gravely ill;
Oh, man, woman, God has thee in His palms;
He provideth much, so He can take all away;
And Thou doest all such for Thy own glory
Thou trickest tricksters, Thou art fearable!

CHARLES MWEWA

608. Wonderful Grace

A farmer sows his seeds
And spreads them wide for birds;
A chef makes her bread
And throws the left-overs outside;
Smaller fishes are in abundance,
And the shark, whale feed on them;
The sun shines on all persons,
Even on those who curse God;
There's no discrimination with air,
It is available to all the living;
The flowers are in the wild,
So that they can beautify the earth;
There's always a river, a lake
Whenever humans have settled;
The night comes,
To all to rest and recharge.
Your grace is truly wonderful,
Your thoughts, very beautiful,
Your dealings, awesomely affable,
Your mercies, indeed, remarkable.

609. Music to My Ears

You're like music to my ears
Just a thought of You, brings tears;
Your name sounds sweetly, melodily,
Your voice is enchanting, unmorbidly;
Again, and again, You prove Your love,
You shield me from danger, like a glove;
Surely, I am not afraid,
You have my complete aid;
My portion is reserved for beauty,
You're calmly like the beaches of Djibouti;
Oh, Lord, be close to me
Let me Your face daily see.

610. Villa in the Valley

You have promised us mansions
Whenin we shall rest for eternity
There, we shall sing "Halleluiah!"
And there, we shall dance perpetually.
There is a stream flowing therein,
Wherein Thy mercies never end;
Whereas now we sorrow and mourn,
There cometh a time wherewith,
And whereof we shalt be gleeth,
Whereabout we'd be immortalized.
Oh, glory, glory, glory be to God,
For Thy power granteth us all things,
Our destination, the streets of gold,
Oh, glory, glory to the King of kings.

611. Morning for Mourning

A wow You have given me
This morning;
Indeed, joy You've portioned me
Instead of mourning;
For the chips have fallen
Where they may be;
And all the heavenly glory
Belongs to Thee;
I am ready for all actions
And tomorrow will not matter;
Thy peace that guards my soul,
Brought by the petition I did utter;
Those who put trust in You,
Will never be put to shame;
For sure, those who love You
Will endure no blame;
They will mount up with wings,
They'll survive all things.

612. Star of Siavonga

I will tell the world
Of Your grand wonders
I will fashion poesy
To celebrate Thy genes
And I will sing with words
The beauty Thou art mounted.
For You're immortal, invisible
Thou art also unconquerable,
The mountains bow before You,
And seas bellow at Thy roar
Even valleys level when You rise,
For Thy power is invincible
Your authority, undeniable.
Let the stars once again stand
Let them stoop at Thy hand.

613. Glint in the Darkness

Do not be angry with us, O God
Do not invoke Your wrath, O Lord
If You should be agitated, we fall
If You should be nagged, we blow
Keep us closer to You, dear Father
And sustain our lives like a Mother
Tender us, embrace us, cuddle us
Oh, do all that for the sake of Jesus.

614. Suspended on Nothing

You've suspended the earth on nothing
You erected its specifics with words only
You needed no ladder to work its details
You finished all its complexities in six days.
Since creation, no accident has transpired,
Since creation, all that happens it predicted,
Since creation, Nature's rules never defiled,
Since creation, its structure has been intact.
Be magnified, O Lord, You're wonderful,
Be dignified, O God, You're always faithful,
Be amplified, O Father, You're graceful,
Be deified, O Creator, You're praiseful.

615. Heavens Declare

The heavens declare the glory of God
The moon speaks of His mercy and truth
And the stars announce his eternal grace.
The clouds acknowledge His kindness
And the sun supplies His everlasting light.

616. Mwansabanga

Oh, Lord, my God, whom I love dearly
In my mother-tongue, You're Maliotola!
You're Shimukuntwa pakakala, niwe Lesa!
Oh, Shakashaka kuba fiteba eee,
You're Chinshonko umutamba manika,
You're Mwansabanga, niwe Kalunga,
You deserve amalumbo nensombo!
Even today, favor me doubly, Oh, Daddy,
And make the dates December 1st to the 8th,
Oh, Lord, resonate and be just suitable,
Let, Oh, Lord, no discrepancies exist,
And let the Society and compliant agree,
And be glorified, Oh, Lord, my God
For Your mercy and grace, I will behold!

617. Valley of the Doll

In the valley of the doll, let me adore You
Let me, like a child, simply fall at Your feet,
And let me, like a dear cute babe, flaunt,
Oh, let me go bananas, let me express my all,
I love You – Oh, love You, love You, dearly.
Though unseen, I see You in my faith regime,
I know how You embrace me, how You care.
Oh, my Darling Daddy, You must be gorgeous,
You must be beautiful, beyond description.
I am awed by what You say, in my ears,
I and I will forever, and ever, love You.

618. Darling Father

Many people are mistaken, O lord
They think that showing off pays
They are gossiping among themselves,
They are saying: "Charles is not himself,"
And those who knew me in my youth,
Are trying to gauge whether I've backslidden;
Oh, Lord, You know how with time,
I have come to love You – to know You.
When I was a youth, I acted to men to see,
I prayed long and eloquent prayers,
And people everywhere ululated me.
But as I grow up, Oh, Darling Father,
I have learned how to please You, You alone,
And I like it this way, Oh, my Daddy,
I like that I can secretly praise and worship,
Oh, yes, without any human adulation,
And Lord, I know, You value my petition,
And You love it when I do it just for You.
Be magnified, Lord, You're highly valued,
You're more valuable than gold,
More enduring than diamonds,
And as for me, loving You is my daily food.

619. Flowers of Beauty

Flowers are beautiful, so is You
The voice of birds and animals
Do reverberate inside my ears,
And I know that You are near.
For me, You're more than flowers,
And for me, You're more than life.
Until I meet You, Oh, my Darling,
I won't be ashamed, Oh, Beautiful,
I won't hide the force Who is in me,
I won't hide the God who satisfies me,
And I'll always, publicly, boast in Him.

620. Good Morning, Lord

Good morning, Lord, my Father
Though I don't feel like, I praise;
Good morning, O God, Almighty,
Though I'm not in mood, I pray;
I love this rapport I share with You,
And nothing, nobody can change it.
Good morning, Adonai, my dearest,
Good day, El-Shaddai, my rarest.

621. Power House

This rustic, semi-dilapidated place,
Is the origin of most of my prayer experience.
Here, at Hillcrest (Zambia),
I prayed long hours,
Led Scripture Union Bible studies,
Agonized for the land and nations,
And laid a foundation for a long
And enduring intercessory tradition.
I will always be grateful to God for you,
O Hillcrest's Power House,
By the old, swimming pool.

622. Aroma of Rome

I don't need thousand whys to praise,
No accounting for my hands to raise;
For these, my limbs, for You, they are
Be it, not to use them for You, very far.
These brains of mine, will find rhymes
With all I own, I'll not spare any dimes.
For there will come a time, in old age,
When I may not function, on average,
Surely by then, O Lord, I'd only think
And I will sing, dance, without a blink.
Be to me, O God, like an only project,
Till life's end, my labor do not reject.
Oh, be to me, like a fresh rose flower,
Fill me with Thy aroma, hour by hour.

623. Be More in Me

You're my bright and fine flower
You feel my mind with great power
You surround me with a dear family
You do all this because You're holy.
Each day I live, is a blessing to me
I'm endeared daily, by beloveds I see.
What more can I ask of You, Lord?
Only for more, You, all You, O God.

624. Chief Judge

You're the lawgiver, Chief Judge
You're pure, You hold no grudge.
The sky, is above, flowers below
Angels sing, Nature says "hallo!"
You're gorgeous, beyond measure
Your name is great, true treasure.

625. Kwacha, Good Morning

O Zambia, the land so familiar
The place I knew God in earlier
Why would I forget you, and how?
It'd be an injustice, to do so now.
O Zambia, the land so fair,
The place with much clean air;
I would to God deck Thee with wealth,
Spare Thee dearth of economic health.
Awake, O Sun of Righteousness,
In blessing her, be no less,
Upon and for Thy Christian nation,
Do redeem her from vile invasion.

626. Waterfall of Blessings

You have hidden true beauty in Africa.
You spread four seasons in America.
Like curtains of gold, You awn Europe.
And greets Austrasia with good hope.
But, You will not relent to favor the earth;
The planets are far, they bring new birth.
The waters are good to drink, and to kill,
The falls portend danger, and bring thrill.
The eyes are not tired of seeing wonder,
The mind is old, it can't cease to wander.
But You're always good, always kind;
Even if I be lost, my soul You'll find.

627. Fairest Furthest

You give rivers and lakes to all nations
You cover every country with Your clouds
You provide the air to all humans on earth
And You saturate the sky with mysteries.
No-one can boast that they have more,
And no-one can complain that they've less;
For You have placed people where they are,
And You apportion them with Your grace.
Oh, Mighty One, how fair You are, O fairly,
You've loved all tribes and races, O dearly.

628. Holy Thy Holi

In India, You are celebrated, O love, at Holi;
For the whole world knows that You're holy.
To me, every day is, indeed, a festival of love.
For You shower blessings daily from above;
I will rejoice in Spring, in the festival of colors.
I'll be contented in Winter, in a glacier's parlor.
Your love blossoms daily in my heart's chamber,
Like a revelry resonating at end of December;
Every day, it's a time to forget old grievances,
It is time to hope, with musical contrivances.

629. Birds of Glory

God, who gives me reason to rejoice
God, who enjoys the reasons He gives.
God, who allows the blessing to flow.
God, who flows the blessings to me.
God, who glories in my dear successes.
God, whose successes glorifies Him.
God, who is just and justifies my words.
God, whose Word justifies my works.
God, who is eternal, everlasting, forever.
God, who never dies, till death is dead.

630. Bird of Beauty

You've created, Oh, Lord,
A mandarin duck,
A bird of beauty.
You've embellished it with colors,
And like no other,
It's gorgeous.
How lovely Your Tabernacles,
Oh, Lord, The Beautiful,
How befitting Your name,
Jesus. The Christ.

631. City of Kindness

God bless you, Oh, Toronto
In you, faithfulness brims sweetly,
For my little ones you took to care,
And when God implanted trials,
Oh, Toronto, you were ready,
You provided your wings,
And you opened ministry doors.
God bless you, Oh, Toronto,
And remember Lusaka,
Whence favor dies not but lives.

632. Maple Tower

Your justice I will never forget
And far be it from me to discriminate.
Your just demand, for law and for men,
I will not forsake and neglect the other.
You will be represented, Oh, Lord,
When I give an equal balance to all.
You will be satisfied, Oh, God,
When I regard the young and the old.
For Your righteousness is good,
Your decency builds nations.

633. Sun's Supreme

From the Far East in Japan
To the Far West in Nepal;
From the Far North in Canada
To the Far South in South Africa;
May Your praises rise like the sun,
May You be glorified,
Oh, Supreme God.

634. Valley of Visions

In Derwent Valley, Derbyshire,
The Industrial Revolution was born.
And I give You thanks, Oh, Lord,
For the ingenuity You give to mankind;
I acknowledge Your power
In generations of diverse eras.
You will never fail humanity,
You will always forgive its sins,
And You will always redeem its faults.

635. Awe of the Owl

The owl,
The magnificent of Your works
How precise,
How discerning, how concise?
You have put a campus in each of its veins,
You have given it eyes,
That see deep in darkness,
And when it calls,
Kings and princes shake.
Oh, God, how tender
You are to mankind,
That You have known the end of our days.
For no man dies before their time,
You will reward each one as deserved.

636. Worship at Wonderland

I love what You love, Oh, God,
I am in awe of Your brilliant works,
I sigh deeply at the wonders of life,
And I never stop asking, "How"?
For who has the brain as Yours?
Who can think through all at once?
Who can know the end from start?
Who can carry His people in His hands?
And who can bring them safe across seas?
Oh, Lord, be exhausted far above all,
Be lifted in praise, worship and homage,
And be given all glory, now and forever.

637. Elephant's Wit

They know everything, they remember
They do graze freely around December
They are large, and occupy the forest,
They map terrains, they know when to rest;
To them, family is everything, their purpose,
And they measure nature's depth and pulse;
Oh, Lord, You don't need man if You wish
But his young ones, You prudently shish
And when he is dry, You offer Your rains
For such is our God, in Heaven, He reigns!

638. Hippopotamus from Heaven

The hippopotamus conquers the waters,
And it swims across waves without fins
It dances strongly, it laughs loudly,
This beast is the king of inner lakes
And the queen of meandering rivers.
Oh, my God, even Leviathan knows his limits
For the gigantic ocean rejoices at Your voice
The created things in it adores Your power.
You are Lord of lords, and King of kings,
You are endeared by fauna and flora alike.

639. Grace Like Giraffe

They are tall, they glide in the breeze
But when You they sense, they do freeze
You can know through them, God's presence
For in their antennas, is God's essence,
How You have placed Your own spies,
And beautify luminaries in the skies.
There is no time when they cease to praise,
Each day, their voices in worship they raise;
Oh, Father of Grace, let me add a voice,
To life's anthem, let me make a joyful noise.

640. Gaze of a Gazelle

Beautiful, Lord, You're beautiful;
You enlarge our planet, You're fruitful.
The Great Hunter, You ring bountiful;
To love Your beings, You spring dutiful.

641. Happy Village

You're so different, happy and beautiful,
In Your presence, I feel all is best,
Even when I have nothing to do, for the rest,
I await Your Word, to obey and be dutiful.

642. Graceful Mountainside

Our eyes have beholden God' glory:
Go tell it to the mountains, let the valleys know
That He will come with His host of angels
And the redeemed will see Him and bow.
He has prepared faucets of ringing bells
And every then and now,
He has decked many displays to show;
Surely, God is in the midst of us
The Spirit of Christ Jesus is among us.
We will not be dismayed, not once
We will receive double, even thrice.
Our God is faithful, we shall be vindicated,
Our Fountain of Life is portent, we're insulated.
The dangers that lurk by daytime
The nagging that shakes our prime,
Oh, Lord, You will sustain us with food
And satisfy us with all that's good.

643. Sounds of Silence

Oh, Lord, our God, You created us
Through the Word, Your Son Jesus,
You also fill our hearts with faith
And compel us, Your will to do on earth,
Surely, You observe all our activities,
You take part in all our earthly festivities;
You cause us to do Your will, to obey,
Indeed, it's You who make us not go astray
So that we may please You and be blessed,
Then we will see good and obtain the best.
You have transcended the now and then,
You're immanent, innate, again and again.

644. Fairest Strides

Oh, Lord, what do You see
When You look down on this earth?
Don't You see Your creation in all diversity?
Don't You rejoice in the human rainbow,
The White, the Black, the Yellow, the Brown,
All amazingly elegant and precious
And there is none superior to another
But Your kindness reaches towards all.
Oh, Lord, my God, in this You're great
And for this reason, never will we fret.

645. Love the Church

I love You, Oh, Lord, my Father
Because You always fill my heart with joy.
I don't need anything, or another
Because in You, I have all I need to enjoy.
I love the Church of Jesus
And all those who call upon You in truth.
But I hate those who only please us,
The critical, and famous spiritual sleuth.

646. Saving Shelter

I will abide under Your holy shelter
I will seek comfort in Your shadows
Indeed, even a nightingale sings
And the lizard as a snail all rejoice
At the brightness of Your presence.
Be with my loved ones forever
And their destiny, let it be in green,
Their progeny, bless with long life
And in their low moments,
Be their essence,
For Jesus' sake, Halleluiah.

647. Whether the Weather

In the land of the coldest snow
Here in the flurries of the North
Oh, Lord, Your justice will shine.
In the present and the now,
As my thoughts rush via South,
In here, right here, Lord, I am fine.
May the polar bear and the seal
May penguins and, indeed, the eel
May they continue to be in
Your light and may they see You
Even in the night.

648. Whisper of Loves

I will never claim that I have not seen You
I will not doubt that daily I behold Your presence,
Oh, Lord, in the beauty of the flowers,
In the calmness of the evening,
And in the singing of the birds.
I will not say, "The Lord is far away from earth,"
Oh, God, You're here, in the whisper of loves,
And You speak beautiful melodies
In the blazing eyes of young doves.
Who can miss the blossoming of teenage daughters?
The strength of young men and the silence of waters,
Oh, Lord, beauty is who You are
Bright as the Morning Star.

649. Darling God

How lovely,
When the elements go to play
How beautiful on their feet,
When the saints bow to pray;
Oh, Nature and Creation dance,
They all stand ready, in dutiful stance
The soil, the oil and the spoil
All line up for man's cravings to foil.
Oh, my Love, my Darling God
You're great, O, Deity, O Lord.

650. Glorious Snow

It was all blue – deadlines inundating
I was buried in work, all forces falling.
I knew You would give me strength,
I was confident, You'd be my warmth.
I have completed all the things I started
And I have delivered all, all have parted.
You were with me in my hour of weakness
And You provided all I needed, no less.
I am no longer in blues, but there's light
And those who trust in You will be right.

651. Apple of My Eye

Oh, God, You told me long time ago,
That I would go only up, up and high
You have not failed to finish Your work
And You do not go back on Your word.
Oh, Lord, I am one who is on the move
I am an apple of the Lord God's eye
And Lord, I have all, I am ready to go.
Be merciful to me, in Your righteousness
And enlarge my tent in Your fondness.

652. Lovely These Places

Oh, lovely is the place where men dwell
Their creativity they will display and sell
They will always have memories to tell
And will indulge in goodness without fail.
Oh, Lord, it was not made for men, Hell,
You have given us Paradise, a divine well.

653. Last Day Bliss

I have heard Your Word, O God
I believe in the Father, who sent You,
I know that I have eternal life
And I will not be judged at the Last Day
I have crossed over from death to life.

654. Living Bread

You're the living bread
That came down from Heaven.
If anyone eats of this bread,
He will live forever.
And this bread, which You gave
Is for the life of the world;
That bread, was Your flesh.
Oh, dear Jesus, how merciful,
For You, let me be pursifull.

655. Begotten Son

Oh, God, You so loved the world,
Oh, Lord, that You gave
Your only begotten Son;
That whosoever believeth in Him,
Should not perish, but have everlasting life.
I see, how great the love, Father,
You have lavished upon me,
Oh, Father, that I am now called Your child,
Because, Lord, that's who I am.
The reason the world does not know God,
Is that it did not know You, Jesus.
We can no longer die, spiritually,
We have become like the angels.
I am a son of the resurrection,
I am a child of God.

656. Mighty Creator

I am Your handiwork, Oh, God
I aim, in Christ Jesus, created
To do good works, which You, O God
Did prepare for me to do before I was born.
For, in Your image, dear God,
You did create me, O, Mighty Creator,
So that I may to You, bring glory,
And for You, to let honor be my story.

657. Dearest Deer

"As the deer pants for streams of water,
So, my soul longs after You, O God.
My soul thirsts for God, the living God.
When shall I come,
And appear in God's presence?
Blessed be the LORD,
The God of the entire Creation,
From everlasting to everlasting.
How beautiful, too, on the mountains
Are the feet of those who bring good news,
Those who proclaim peace,
Those who bring good tidings,
Those who proclaim salvation,
Those who say to the nations, 'Your God reigns.'"

658. Genius Father

Surely, my Genius Father,
All the elements of nature, are sure
You created the networks unseen
You put in place sounds unknown
And You signposted Internet formula
All You require, is that men should know,
That they should search Your wisdom,
And apply on earth secrets of the Kingdom.

659. Creative Father

Surely, my Creative Father,
You craftly decked Leviathan,
You equipped the Python
And ornamented the peacock.
You decorated the dolphin
With unsurpassed intellect.
You did all this for Your glory,
So that men may magnify You, forever.

660. Soul Watcher

I love You, my God, my Father
You put blood in my bloodstream
You pump air in my airstrip
You augment voice in my vocal codes
And You keep watch over my soul.

661. Lion of Love

Oh, God of life, my Lord, God of light,
My all, God of love; life is only possible,
Because of You, light shines brightly
Because You care, and love flows widely
Because You are love, the lion of love.

662. Fairest in Justice

Your justice is steady, equal and bold
You govern men in utter righteousness;
You have equity, dispensing mercy of old;
Your law is light, altogether burdenless;
You have protected the weak, fed the rest,
Oh, God, when You judge, You're fair,
In all things, at all times, You're the best,
All glory is Yours, with no man, You share.

663. Invictus Victus

I am safe, so safe in Your providence,
Your hand rescued me from the bottomless,
I have pleasantries from Your divine province,
Your eternal space, hugs my soul in bellavance;
I am girded by Your supreme grace in excelsior,
Truly, Your divine goods make me healthier,
My blessing has fallen on solid path, I am invictus,
Oh, I am unconquerable, in Christ, I am victus.

664. Permanent Inheritance

You're our law-giver
Lord, surely, our Judge
My God, our Great King.
You governed us by Law
Then saved us by grace,
And have called us by mercy-love.
A life's constitution,
You have planted in hearts within,
And a divine institution,
You have established therein.
You conquer our selfishness,
Oh, Lord, and deliver us from elfishness.
You do protect our heritance,
By a sure and more permanent inheritance.

665. Beautiful Things

Without You, without Your presence
I am like one standing before a sand dune,
I feel like I am surrounded by misfeasance,
Overtly restricted, I feel stuck in a cocoon.
So, I prayed to You, and I heard Your voice
You showed me the promise of long time
My heart is alerted, my soul will rejoice,
In the beautiful things of Heaven, I'll mime,
For You, O Lord, You have answered me,
And Your good kindness, has set me free.

666. Ultimate Purpose

I will write a book for the secular
And then write two for my God
Each poem I write for politics,
Two I will instruct for the Lord.
I will teach law, and more law
And twice lecture in divinity.
In this world, this present life,
I will be active, be relevant,
But my ultimate goal, my purpose,
Is to please You, God, my Father.

667. Hallowed Be

Hallowed be the Lord God of Nations
Our Father, the Greatest, Most Powerful
The Most Glorious, the Most Victorious
The majestic, the Creator of heavens and earth
Hallowed be the Lord God of Nations;
To Whom dominion belongs, the exalted One.
O Lord, You are the head over all things,
And both riches and honor come from You,
You are the Greatest Ruler, the Mightiest
Hallowed be the Lord God of all nations.

668. Wonderful Works

May my Father, the Lord, be blessed
May His glory and name, also be blessed
For Your wonderful works, O Lord, be blessed
For Your matchless beauty, forever be blessed.

669. O, Adonai, O Elshaddai

Everywhere You are, praise the Lord
In the House of God, praise the Father
In your own home, praise the Lord God
In the office or workspace, praise Him
For He made the universe, praise God
He does mighty deeds, praise Elshaddai
For His excellent greatness, praise Adonai.

670. Praise Him

Praise the Lord, praise the Father.
Praise Him with pen and ink.
Praise Him with guitar and banjo.
Praise Him with songs and dancing.
Praise Him with drums and singing.
Praise Him on keyboard and piano.
Praise Him with loud shouts and cheer.
Praise Him with meditation and silence;
Praise Him with imagination and craft.
Praise Him, because of Him we laughed.

671. Depth of His Riches

Oh, the depth of the riches
Both of the wisdom and knowledge of God.
How unsearchable are His judgments.
How unfathomable His ways.
For who has known the mind of the Lord?
Who can become His counselor?
Who has first given to Him
That it might be paid back to him again?
For from Him and through Him
And also, to Him are all things.

672. Hosanna

Hosanna to God!
To Him be the glory in the church
And in Christ Jesus to all generations
Forever and ever. Amen.
He has become our God and Father,
Us, who once were not a people,
Us, who once were scorned and despised
Us, who once were traded for goods.
Us, who once owned others as property.
To us all, He has given grace
And delivered us from shame and ignorance.
Hosanna to the Son of God.

673. The Only Wise

God, who is able;
God, who is able to establish us;
God, who is able to establish us per His gospel;
God, who is able to establish us per Christ's preaching;
Oh, the mystery of His revelation;
For this mystery, He kept a secret in the past,
This mystery, He has now manifested in Scriptures;
Accordingly, He made an eternal commandment
So, through His Son, our Lord Jesus Christ,
All the nations will come to His knowledge,
To faith, obedience and eternal life;
To God, the only wise,
Through Jesus Christ, God's Only Potentate on earth,
Be all the glory forever.

674. Worthy Lamb

Oh, Lord,
Let praise always be my cloak
Let it be the balm that shields my heart,
So that as long as I have breath,
I should not fail to refrain,
Like the elders in Heaven,
"Worthy is the Lamb that was slain
To receive power and riches
And wisdom and might
And honor and glory and blessing."

675. Meadow of His Ville

Oh, shepherd of my life who has given me a soul,
A gift to the human body; I, and every created thing,
Whether that be in Heaven on earth, under the earth
The sea, all things in it, to You, who sits on the throne,
And to the Lamb, may there be blessing and honor
May there be glory and dominion, forever and ever.
Salvation and glory and power, belong to our God.
Blessings and wisdom, thanksgiving, honor and might,
All be to our God, forever and ever. Amen.

676. Majestic Silence

Whether it is in the silence
Of Your majesty,
Or in the presence
Of Your reality;
Whether it is in the splendor
Of Your royalty
Or in the surrender
To Your loyalty;
Holy, Holy, Holy,
Oh, Lord of hosts,
You're holy,
All creation in You boasts,
The earth is full of Your glory.

677. Praise in Every Genre

Singers, use your voice to praise Him
Dancers, make every move to praise Him
Poets, compose beauty in praise of Him
Musicians, string numbers in praise of Him
Writers, pen perfect prose to praise of Him
Choreographers, move bodies to praise Him
Ballerinas, step-up, gesture in praise of Him
Drummers, beat the skin to the praise of Him
Gamers, rave up those videos in praise of Him
And players, kill up the talent to praise Him!

678. Earth You've Colored

Each day you light up, is a treasure discovered;
And each night you dim, is a chance to sprawl.
Each flower that blooms, the earth You've colored;
And each ray that rises, Your love for me I recall.
Even when the wind blows, I know You're here;
And in the tiniest atom, there I find Your grace.
Your voice is heard clearly in the morning air;
And You reign as LORD in the furthest space.
My mind fails to fathom how You came to be;
And yet I am happy, Your infinite glory I see.

679. Dear My Rarest

I am in love with You, Oh, Jesus
Even as I loved You, as a fetus.
I loved You while in my mother's womb,
Surely, I will still love You in my tomb.
I'll forever love You, before my eyes close,
Before my finite farewell, before I bid adios.
You are always in my head, Sweet Savior
Yes, in my manners, thoughts and havior.
Of all I love, O Christ, You're the rarest
Since I found You, You're my dearest.

680. No Fear in Death

Oh, Lord, who has the chemistry of life,
The one He beats last on mortem's fife,
Who rewards our feeble being with faith,
And generates hope, a legacy of our baith;
To elect to live for You, O God, is wisdom,
And to ignore salvation's free gift, is dumb;
As for me and those whom You've given,
We'll hail, gratulate that You've forgiven,
For You only, we will strive to be pleasing,
And daily follow in Your steps, appeasing.

681. All Things to All

You watch our souls, Father God
You know each cell on our bod.
You see clear in sheer darkness
You oust those who would harm us.
Like a mom, You keep us warm
Like eagles, we scale a storm,
Like babes, comfort come from You
Like campus, You send a clue.
My God, be all things to all;
My Lord, answer when we call.

682. Everlasting

Give Him glory, He's unending
Tell His story, He's unbending;
O praise Him, for His matchless wit
O raise Him, as your breaths permit
Rave in Him, He is worthy,
Glow in Him, for His mercy
Lift Him up, with no regrets
Lift Him up, you He beget.
Make a loud noise, sing a hymn
Make Him big, trace His great limn.
Admire God, for He's adorable
Adore Jesus, for He's admirable.

683. A Wonderful God

Every day I wake up and look up,
I smell the dew of early morning,
I hear the birds make music and sing,
Then from within, a voice rings,
Those darling girls also begin chores,
Aroma of early morn coffee and tea,
And the enlarging bagels and bread.
I see the heavens are bluest today,
Even when the clouds are retreating,
There is hope brewing down my soul.
I shout, "What a wonderful God."
It is exhilaratingly frosty and pecking,
It's painstakingly gorgeous and giving.
In my mind, there are files to be done,
A cache of errands to be completed,
And love, from family and friends,
"I should be so fortunate," I pause.
All around me is potential laughter,
Smiles that ingratiate soul and heart.
Again, I twist, "I must be favored."
"Oh, what a wonderful God," I said.
Oh, Lord, how the entire world,
Even the universe in its radiance,
And the planets, luminaries and all,
They gladly dance at Your presence;
And men, women, boys and girls,
Do their daily routines, they're happy.
I sense there's good things trending,
And this is despite anything else,
I smirk, "What a wonderful God."
The waters remain calm till disturbed
The wind blows, and leaves show direction
There's plenty of air, though not seen
And spirits, good and bad, frolic the universe
What is the meaning of silence?

What is the significance of lightless?
What's food for one, is thrown by another
And calls are received by intended recipients
The body recognizes dance-worth sounds
And words achieve the aim they intended
Even in good times, there is regret
And in regretful moments, there's hope
The poor find peace where riches fail,
The rich worry of things poor people flout
Those with filled fridges and storehouses,
Don't always have hearts warned by love
Oh, God, my views You stun to the core;
And left in this wonderment, I wow,
"What a wonderful God."

684. How Excellent

I tried to see which of Your creation
I should attribute more credence to;
I contemplated on the highest,
And the lowest to the deepest pit;
Oh, Lord, all is excellent.
How excellent are Your mercies,
Excellent, too, Your lovingkindness.
How excellent are Your graces,
And excellent, still, Your justice.
Your incomprehensible power,
Your immeasurable glory
And Your indecipherable majesty.
Oh, Lord, my God, I worship You truly,
I bow prostrate before Your excellence
Oh, how excellent, how benevolent
Your never-ending goodness and truth.

685. Original Spirit

I lift up my hands to the Father of Grace
From whence comes both good and mace
To the Original Spirit, comforter of persons,
The perfecter, what's of the foe, He worsens.
The Fountain of Eternal Life, the Leader,
My advocate, my representative, my pleader.
Surely, He will be my hope and inheritance,
He confides duty, and retires me emeritus.
Oh, the total sum of this grant knowledge,
How gratifying it is, Oh, give Him homage;
This God is the Only God, the Only Truth,
He'll perform all, and His intention is sooth.

686. Multiplier Effect

I know that nothing happens for nothing
That, Lord, You have a man for everything.
I know, Oh, God, that seeds are a principle,
Which is given to us as a latent principal.
That when You show us one small thing,
You've, Oh, Lord, destined many to bring.
For there'll be plenty where there's little,
You'll perfect to the utmost what's brittle.
Your name is a formula for multiplying
Your hand is a buffer shield for supplying;
There's no-one whom You leave behind,
Those who seek growth in You they'll find.
You multiply, O Lord, what I already have,
For Your default posture to me, is love.

687. Masterful

Glorious works that Your hands hath made,
"How," my mind wows, did You all these make?
None with oldness or millennial breeze does fade,
And each in their uniqueness aren't' false or fake.
Oh, glorious in works and magnificent in power;
Oh, faithful for ages, our sweet-smelling flower.

688. Picturesque of Elegant Supernova

With one word, You made fauna and flora
Creation is a ring tone of Your divine aura.
You must've a sense of humor, O Jehovah;
In the twilight, I behold elegant Supernova,
Assuredly, those who take time to research,
Will find You in seven pillars of the Church;
They'll hear Your ardors voice in lullabies,
Even in cold Winter, You appear in the bise.
You're, Shimukuntwa petabwa, You're Lesa,
You're Shimwitwa pakakala, Creator Leza.

689. Rose of Rhapsody

Thy Kingdom is a dominion of power,
Built at the covering of divine fecundity,
Inspiring menfolk, shaping their flower.
Thy divine law is granted with profundity;
O Rose of Rhapsody, defender of gurus,
My limbs break in dance for Thy Utmost
I praise Thy Fairest as one on a cruise,
In Thee alone, my finest finds its boast.

690. Kingdom First

You litter the earth with goodies
You fill the kitchen with cookies
With needs, You satisfy my tummy
All my wants, You make yummy.
Ten minutes in Your deific presence,
Brings me infinite, terrific pleasance.
Your Kingdom I will seek early,
While I busk in Your dawn, pearly.

691. Love You, Bible

Oh, Lord, thank you for the Bible,
No god, not even their great Cybele,
No, none, not even their philosophies,
Nope, nil, nada, not even luminosities.
Not in science, art, and not even in law,
Oh, God, Your entire Word has no flaw.
And I love it more than my vital meal,
I read and study it with greatest zeal;
My soul longs for it, my spirit lives in it,
And, Oh, my God, to it, I gladly submit.
If I may live a hundred more years,
Your Word, shall always be Sear of sears.
It makes me wiser, feels my mind with wit.
In it, Jehovah, You sculpt the Divine Writ.
Oh, the Bible, how I love you, truly so,
I need you daily more than you know.

692. Condemned to Praise

To praise You
I am condemned;
To love You, my God,
I am chained;
If I fail to give You glory,
Let me be damned;
For You are a trophy,
A gem I have gained.

693. Honest Answer

You have given me an honest answer,
You're my true gain, chance enhancer;
I will forever be rescued from trouble,
Your godly rod has granted me double;
But the wicked aren't lucky all the time,
They won't escape from their own grime;
When You direct me to Your holy scripts,
O God, it falls as a gentle kiss on my lips.

694. Beautiful Thought

I have given thought to Your word
It was treasured first time it was heard;
In it, I have discovered nothing but good,
Oh, my Father, by it, I have daily my food;
You have also blessed my complete life,
And saved me whole from every strife;
All because I chose to trust in You,
For Your word is dear and true.

695. Pure Grace

When I shall be found in Heaven,
O Lord, let these gaping walls record,
Not on two or three or even seven,
But many times, Your grace did accord;
When I shall receive the royal diadem,
It won't be because I merited a crown,
But Your dear grace, did provide them,
The same grace'll place on me a gown;
May earth be witness to Heaven's golly,
And Hell's surrender, for God is holy.

696. All You Made I Love

My God, my Lord, my Father,
How I love all that You made,
I am awed by what You created
From nothing but Your words.
I see, hear, smell and even feel,
All these are from Your orders.
I'm speechless, I'm flabbergasted,
O this ingenuity, the engineering;
O how fantabulous You must be,
I hate wars, I hate this racism,
I'm not for abortions, infanticides,
For all bickering, I am a coward,
But I love those who love, laugh,
I'm for all who find joy and peace
O my Father, bring a new world,
Without any disease, nor death,
For You're our future, the life,
You're the present, our way,
And our hope, the real truth.

697. All of a Kind

You have made all of its kind,
Beautiful to behold;
You have placed soothing curiosity,
In the eye of the beholder;
Shame be to anyone and everything,
Which forfeits Your glory;
For You have architected all looks,
With everlasting glorific.

698. Only In-Christ

In Christ, I belong to the family of God
And I am a new person.
In Christ, passed has been my life of old
And to live for Him is my reason.
In Christ, there is for me no condemnation
And I can now come boldly into God's presence.
In Christ, to me has been granted the wealth of the nations
And His home in Heaven is also my residence.
In Christ, I have been rescued us from the darkness kingdom
And my sins have been forgiven.
In Christ, I am a person unto God holiness and wisdom
And I have been gracious chosen.
In Christ, I have received strength and blessing
And joy unspeakable and full of glory.
In Christ, I have inherited no more cursing
And peace is my constant and present story.
In Christ, I am more than an overcomer
And through Him I am loved.
In Christ, I am fearful, wonderful and a charmer
And as His partner, I am well beloved.
In Christ, I am called a God's child
And Jesus Christ is my Lord, Savior and Big Brother.
In Christ, I own the world every mile and wide
And God is my true and loving Father.
In Christ, I am commissioned to bear fruit
And whatever I the Father, I receive.
In Christ, I have received grace with a deep root
And at His throne more of it He does give.

699. All My Favorites

I have all my favorites in the knowledge of grace
For in here, I have found a good and lovely place.
Some days are testing but God sees me through it all
And when I stumble, His love lifts me from the fall.

I have witness deep down my grateful human heart
Which tells me that He can't from me at all part,
For the Spirit of Grace lives and works right in me
To will and desire the will of God for me to see.

He forgives all my sins when I ask Him to forgive
And when I lack strength He is generous to give.
God is closest to me when I am in great trouble
When enemies surround me, His grace He'll double.

I will live to see the Lord's goodness here on earth
And I will still be praising Him even in my death;
For I have loved the Father with an everlasting love
And I know that all good things come from above.

CHARLES MWEWA

700. The Doxology

The *Doxa*, the glory,
The nature and acts of God in all their self-manifestation;
And this is what God is and does,
Revealed in all of creation and
exaltation,
And which has been exhibited in ways
And means God desires to be
known
And particularly in the person of Christ Jesus,
God's Son of glorious
renown,
In whom essentially God's glory
Has been shone
Generations after generations
And made available to men by means of grace
And power to many nations.
To God our Father,
Maker and Sustainer
Be all the glory,
Now and forever.

For in the days of his flesh,
Jesus Christ manifested glory
By deeds and miracles
And released many from bondage,
Captivity, sickness and deadly shackles –
At Cana,
Where he turned water into pure wine
To feed many a thirsty soul;
At the tomb,
Where he raised Lazarus from the dead
And there many eyes saw;
At the Mount of His Glory,
There he taught many

Of the things to come
And at the Mountain of Transfiguration,
Eyes glittered and hearts were calm.
To God our Father,
Maker and Sustainer
Be all the glory,
Now and forever.

His attributes and power
Have been revealed
Through the entire creation,
The world falls short of His righteousness,
Character and manifested perfection,
For the might of His glory,
The praise of the glory of His everlasting grace
Has been revealed to the ends of the earth,
To many a nation and race;
The Father of Glory is He,
From whence
And to whom all things emanate,
The source of all good things
Spread wide for all
And to all they illuminate.
To God our Father,
Maker and Sustainer
Be all the glory,
Now and forever.

To date,
And through the lives of those
Who believe in His word and name,
And who wait with intent
For that blessedness
Filled with glory and fame,
The blessedness into which
Believers are to enter
Now and hereafter,

As they are brought
Into the likeliness of Christ,
And hence thereafter,
To be with Him
Through the body of His glory,
The brightness of His splendor,
And enchant them forever as their God,
Their light and their defender.
To God our Father,
Maker and Sustainer
Be all the glory,
Now and forever.

The Shekinah Glory,
In the pillar of cloud
Of the Tabernacle`s Holy of Holies,
Was only but an emblem
Of the glory
Of the Church of God`s own families,
And will be made manifest
In the appearing
Of the only and our great God,
The Savior Jesus Christ,
Whose throne is surrounded
By marble and gold,
As one who won His Father`s good reputation,
Praise and due honor
Who deserves all our worship,
And must to us all
Be our favor and banner.
To God our Father,
Maker and Sustainer
Be all the glory,
Now and forever.

How lovely is your Tabernacle,
God my Savior;
The wonder of your beauty
And power of your throne,
Compel me to bow —

Your glory fills the heavens
As frost cover the earth;
And when I look,
I behold the ramblings
And the rays of
Your shining glory.

When from afar off —
In dire inquisition and
Adventure I draw nearer;
To behold the duller of
The skins that covered
The inner courts and its
Beautiful embroidery;
I come in great humility
And contrite of heart
And at the Gate there I find you-

Son of God, in the blue:
The Savior of mankind
In scarlet red:
The King of all kings
In the purple:
And the Perfect Man,
In the fine linen.

Then I was drawn by my
Inadequacy and sin
For I had desired to come in
To view the beauty of
Your spacious courts.

At the Altar of Burnt Offering,
You were there as
My substitute,
You were the Lamb of God
That was slain
To take away my sins.
Oh, that pain you felt for me;
The anguish of shedding
Living blood;
And the deep agony
Of sacrificing for my salvation.

At the Brazen Laver, Oh, Lord,
I saw you in the shining glass,
You were the mirror of life
That reflected my visage,
Brightened my wrinkled face
And changed my life forever!
All my doubts finished
When you took my shame away
And washed my hands clean
That I might serve you in purity.
And washed my feet, too,
That I might walk in righteous.
At the basin of ancient waters
At which Aaron and
His Leviticus priesthood
Carefully washed,
There I saw myself the way I am.

And at the Door, you were the Truth,
The reality which make us free
So you can usher us into the
Inner chamber
To behold you at the Altar of Incense,
At which true intercession
And perfect praise

Pour gladly from redeemed
And grateful souls.
O, how beautiful are your altars;
O – how illuminating are
Your Candlelight, O, God;
O-how satisfying also is
Your tables of perfumed bread!

I would rather be a door keeper-
To smell the aroma of
Your sweet breads;
And to enjoy the warmth
Of your never-consumed
Candlesticks;
And to be filled with the fatness
That your anointing oils bring -
Than to dwell in the tents
Of the wicked.

Oh, rend and part,
Rend the skilled-woven veil,
Break it and part it
That I might behold
The seat of the only true
And Sovereign One.

You that sits on the throne,
You are holy and good.
Mighty and power
And all Blessings
Are yours forevermore!
You that is enthroned
In between the cherubim
On top of the Mercy Seat;
You that sits on the perfect
Law of liberty;
You that give life to the dead

And feed us with perfect manna,
The bread that comes from above,
The small, round,
Perfumed and white bread.
You that fills our months
With the pure Bread of Life,
How lovely
Is your Tabernacle!
O God, our Savior.
We will praise you
And worship you
Forever and ever,
Amen.

I have loved you, O Lord
With every breath within me
I have thought of you
In the concourses of the shadows
When my mind and heart have met trouble;
I have cried to you when all I cherish diminished
And I have desired your presence
More than my necessary meal.
O, my soul knows it needs the Lord,
My heart pants for His courts,
As David who danced before the Arc;
I attend to my every sob
Like one who knew not where to go;
I listen to the palpitations thereof
As one whose brain boils;
Yet, I have known no one
Whose countenance shines brightly,
Who trains my hands to hold truth
And my mouth to utter joy.
There is no one on earth, who listens,
No one among the children of men
Who ever hears my longings,
For at your feet, there my needs are met

At the altar of scented incense
There my soul finds solace;
Lord, you have been good to me;
In my human reasoning I have tested you,
In my fallen frailty I have stretched the limit of your grace,
In my unbridled reflections I have desired vain,
And in my manly ambitions I have looked at sin;
Yet when I come to your inner chamber,
My heart you fill with peace,
My soul you gown with righteousness.
I have loved your inner sanctuary,
And the place where your glory dwells;
I have treasured your Word,
More than my first meal after a fast.
I have walked by your side
And yet as thought a baby in its mother's bosom.
I have heard your whisper,
As if the waters where at attention;
I have dreamed of heaven,
In deed and in truth,
I have grown from my errors
And become better with every mistake,
All because you give second chances,
All because you are merciful,
All because you never give up on me.
O, the wonders of your love,
How deep the sum of it all,
How marvellous the thought of it!
Your love has compelled me,
Your mercies have drawn me,
Your compassion has captivated me,
To look at the children of the earth with pity,
To author politics and challenge minds,
To stand for them and demand for justice,
To speak for the weak and fend for the poor.
This, my Lord, is the portion you have afforded me,
This, my God, is the goodness of the land

That my life should remain a legacy,
For my struggles are testimony,
And my love for the African nation
And its people,
Be the reward that you have set for me,
The burden you have laid heavily
On my shoulders.
O, my God, blessed is a man
Who loves to pray,
A man who enjoys your presence,
A man who comes back to you
Even when he has erred,
For in and to you belong all good,
And from you comes all wisdom.
Amen.

ABOUT THE AUTHOR

Charles Mwewa (LLB. BA. Education. BA. Legal Studies. Cert. Law. DIBM. LLM Cand.) is a Dad, author, lawyer, educator, and moral and social influencer. Mwewa is the author of 30 books and counting in all genres – fiction (novels), non-fiction and poetry. Mwewa, his wife, and their three girls, reside in the Capital City of Ottawa, Canada.

AUTHOR'S CONTACT

Email address:

spynovel2016@gmail.com

Facebook:

www.facebook.com/charlesmwewa

Twitter:

https://twitter.com/BooksMwewa

Instagram:

instagram.com/mwewabooks/?hl=en

Author's website:

https://www.charlesmwewa.com

To order this book online:

https://www.amazon.ca/dp/1998788008

https://www.amazon.com/dp/1998788008

INDEX

4

417, 543

A

Aaron, 419
abandon, 433
Abraham, 419
Absence, 5, 79
accomplishments, 163, 655
accumulations, 163
acid, 365
acuity, 189
admission, 577
admonition, 433
Adolf, 558
adoration, 33, 645
Adunbalo, 453
adventure, 329
adversary, 44, 507
advocacy, 391
Advocates, 366, 625
Afghanistan, 369, 461
a-free-country, 336
Africa, 4, 59, 179, 194, 199, 237, 278, 279, 280, 282, 283, 289, 290, 291, 294, 315, 321, 336, 483, 493, 508, 548
African kraal, 565

Africanism, 590
Africans, 491, 493
agendas, 337, 359, 491
agony, 23, 100, 216, 428
agriculture, 355
AIDS, 194, 516
Air, 530
Akalela, 154
akimbo, 315
Akrotiri, 462
Albania, 467
Alberta, 367
Algeria, 462
Algonquin, 546
alien, 249, 340, 353, 354, 356, 357, 358, 359, 360, 361, 363, 364, 365, 366, 368, 370, 371, 381, 382
alienation, 382
aliens, 354, 382
alive, 29, 32, 79, 102, 192, 245, 382, 411, 491
allegations, 604
alligator, 589
Almighty, 386, 425, 636
altar, 106, 122, 409
Amalela, 154
Amanda, 541
amazing grace, 645, 661
ambitions, 397, 398
America, 4, 194, 228, 306, 369, 490, 491
anarchy, 237, 323

anathema, 596
Anathemia, 516
anatomy, 415, 615
ancestors, 278, 286, 295
ancestral corridors, 578
Ancient of Days, 429, 634, 652
Andorra, 465
anecdotes, 502
Angeles, 300, 488
Angelian, 37
angels, 3, 8, 20, 66, 69, 91, 108, 109, 110, 122, 152, 161, 171, 200, 256, 300, 488, 553, 581, 609, 633, 660, 682, 689
anger, 220, 397, 489
Angola, 465
Anguilla, 465
anguish, 100, 304, 428, 505, 631
Anishnaabeg, 546
Annette Goerner, 539
answers, 31, 74, 350, 412
Antarctica, 465
antenna, 32
antennas, 644
Anthony, 555
antibiotics, 507
Antigua and Barbuda, 469
Antilles, 484
Antioch, 585
antiquity, 349
ants, 437
anus, 280
Apartheid, 561
Aphrodite, 20, 352
Apostolic, 585

apples, 53, 333
April, 288
arbovirus, 516
Argentina, 466
Aristotle, 284
Armenia, 467
Armies, 325, 517
army, 351
Arnprior, 599
arrogance, 617, 624
art, 12, 31, 34, 37, 66, 89, 91, 101, 120, 124, 179, 228, 237, 283, 284, 285, 290, 300, 305, 339, 386, 406, 409, 487, 488
artists, 251
Aruba, 469
Ashen Pebbles, 229
ashes, 640
Ashmore, 475
Asia, 11, 194, 548
Asis, 452
assassination, 507
assignment, 437
Athena, 20
Atlantic, 317, 333
atom, 21
Augusta, 550
aura, 35, 55, 61, 91, 113, 261, 264, 555, 584, 653, 707
Aushi, 154, 155, 156
Australia, 467, 548
Austria, 467
authority, 489, 507, 606
Awanda, 72
Awesome, 224
Azerbaijan, 480
azure, 110, 111, 163, 631

B

Baba, 454
baby, 8, 93, 100, 303, 361
Babylon, 410
bad news, 499, 508, 514, 517
Bahamas, 470
Bahrain, 478
Balaam, 275
balance, 98
balcony, 532, 555
Ballerinas, 458
balm, 175, 423, 433, 645
bamboo, 92
Banda, 561
Banguanaland, 317, 318
Bangueulu, 154
Banks, 574
Baptist, 585
bards, 275
barracks, 619
Barrhaven, 533
Barrier Reef. *See* Belize
Batawa, 550, 563
Bay, 345
be praised, 436
beards, 64
beat, 2, 6, 14, 20, 54, 154, 164, 226, 253, 295
beatific, 387
beautiful, 6, 27, 37, 38, 49, 85, 91, 93, 94, 95, 96, 126, 146, 153, 182, 253, 297, 345, 352, 355, 357, 362
beauty, 10, 13, 19, 23, 25, 33, 65, 66, 88, 90, 97, 101, 104, 111, 119, 120, 124, 147, 152, 161, 162, 168, 171, 228, 280, 291, 297, 298, 315, 336, 408, 443
Beauty, 55, 91, 114, 119, 124, 147, 362
bed, 7, 13, 19, 91, 97, 98, 108, 122, 146, 275, 279, 338, 359, 378, 382, 393
bee, 31
bees, 125
beggar, 350
Beirut Road, 316
Bel Air, 300, 488
Belgian, 508
Belgrave, 583
beliefs, 575
Belize, 468
bellies, 397
belt, 140
belts, 23
Bemba, 177, 179, 182
benevolent, 622
Benguanaland, 290, 491
Benin, 468
Benz, 32
Bermuda, 469
Bernados, 331
betrayal, 637
Beverley Hills, 300, 488
Bhutan, 461
Bible, 142, 223, 372
biological combat, 507
Bishop, 287, 576
Bishops, 496
Bisrat, 455
Bites of Love, 27, 132
bitter, 148, 389, 408, 411

Black kids, 212
black lover, 6
Black Mamba, 452
Black man, 492
Black sweat, 490
Black thighs, 491
Blackfoot, 546
blastema, 560
bleed, 27, 34
Bleeds of Love, 34, 134
blessings, 280, 400, 403, 546, 561, 599, 614, 636, 646, 651, 675, 676
bliss, 72, 357
blissful, 91, 389, 504
blizzards, 540
blood, 34, 41, 85, 97, 154, 155, 168, 194, 199, 275, 279, 282, 294, 295, 301, 304, 313, 315, 317, 323, 334, 349, 375, 404, 415, 428, 430, 444, 447, 498, 506
bloom. *See* Air
blue, 68, 88, 107, 207, 248, 293, 336, 344, 381
Blue Oak, 549
boa constrictor, 138
body, 574
body language, 271
bondage, 275, 395, 420
bones, 109, 117, 163, 381, 428, 457
book, xxv, xxvi, 164, 315, 329, 393
books, 20, 219, 228, 275, 308, 340, 359, 363, 370, 396, 612
bookstores, 359
booster, 494, 519, 522
Bore-Bore, 452
boring, 40
Boro, 582
Bosnia-Herzegovina, 466
bosom, 7, 15, 18, 28, 33, 37, 67, 101, 127, 156, 171, 188, 278, 377
boss, 3, 244, 412
Bosses, 496
Botswana, 466
bottles, 577
bourbon, 533
Bouvet Island, 474
bow, 32, 218, 392, 402, 409, 434, 448, 449
boy, 263
bra, 116
brag, 615
brain, 33, 53, 63, 85, 275, 284, 395
brains, 190, 345, 380, 577, 578, 672
brave, 20, 29, 94, 163, 202, 304, 373, 408, 446
Brazil, 179, 480, 511
breakfast, 592, 597
breasts, 21, 77, 122, 246, 286, 368
bridge, 68, 378
briefcase, 576
Brighton Ontario, 568
British Indian Ocean Territory, 469
British Virgin Islands, 474
broadcast, 539
Brockville, 563
broken joys, 349

brother, 7, 163, 165, 168, 344, 507
Brunei, 469
Brutus, 332
Bulgaria, 462
bull constrictor, 267
bullets, 216, 313, 381
bum. *See* Air
Burkina Faso, 469
Burma, 470
burning hell, 397
burrito, 568
Burundi, 469
Bush, 332
Business, 209, 374, 501
businesses, 649
butter and bread, 195
buttocks, 85, 155, 295, 368
Buttocks, 85

C

caffeine, 227
Caicos Islands, 475
Cairo Road, 279
Calabasas, 300, 488
California, 592
Cambia, 472
Cambodia, 470
Cambodian fields, 338
Cameroon, 470
Cana, 420
Canada, 179, 207, 227, 293, 298, 303, 313, 331, 333, 471, 508
Canada Day, 580
canceled, 501
cancer, 154, 242, 337
cancers, 31
candle, 138

cannabis, 551
cannibus. *See* canabbis
Cantata, 450
Canuck, 190, 227
Can-Zam, 574
Cape, 317
Cape Verde, 471
Capital. *See* Ottawa
Capitol, 332
captivity, 420
caress, 3, 46
Caribbean, 227
cars, 74, 185, 190, 191, 220, 227, 250, 336, 340, 507
Cartier Islands, 475
cartoons, 558
Castle and Frank, 345
cathedrals, 418
Catholic, 418
Catholics, 585
caves, 28, 347
Cayman Islands, 475
celebration, 276, 339
cemetery, 396, *See* Williamsburg
Central African Republic, 477
central nervous system, 457
century, 302, 373
Cha-Cha, 592
Chad, 471
Chaimana, 452
Chaisa, 351
chalice, 43
chamba. *See* canabbis
chamber, 644
chambers, 15, 164, 320, 541, 575
chameleon, 125, 362

Champaign, 298
champion, 24, 201, 283
champions, 14, 60, 498, 616
Chandwe, 232
changing room, 353
char, 133
Chara, 12
Character, 321, 491
charcoal, 122, 155
Charity, 400
charm, 13, 20, 66, 71, 77, 80, 97, 113, 178, 225, 362
charms, 123, 557
Charsian, 134, 135, 136, 137, 138, 139
chastisement, 433
chauvinist, 373
chemical reaction, 373
Cherry Blossom. *See* Japan
Chief Mukuni, 209
Chikuzees, 297
children, 42, 47, 145, 146, 152, 161, 170, 206, 215, 227, 237, 278, 282, 291, 292, 313, 318, 331, 417, 431, 491, 499
Chilenga, 453
Chiluba, 561
China, 228, 466, 508
chipmunks, 661
Chishimba, 339
Chitambo, 315
Chiuta, 452
chocolate, 8, 21, 375
choir, 29
Choreographers, 458
chorus, 253

Christ, 399, 420, 421, 422, 423, 427, 430, 443, 445, 446, 448, 449
Christian, 223, 302, 445
Christian Brethren, 585
Christianity, 223, 451
Christmas, 252, 471, 580
Christmas Island, 471
chubby, 46
Chuku, 453
Chuma, 315
church, 372, 374, 431, 633, 697
Church, 142, 418, 422, 468, 479, 504
Cinderella, 315
cinnamon, 8
circles, 239
circus, 396
citizens, 227, 321, 356, 371
City Called Beautiful. *See* Valley of Roses
civil struggles, 334
civilization, 294, 301, 331
civilizations, 611
Clarice, 57, 58, 59, 60, 61, 62, 149, 153, 228, 594
Classics, 284
cleaner, 495
Cleopatra, 197
clergy, 372
clergyman, 372
clientele, 372
clients, 431
Clipperton Island, 471
clock, 164, 196
clothing, 584

coach, 40
Cobourg, 538
cocoon, 23
Cocos Islands, 471
coffee, 528
Coffee, 227
coffins, 515
coin, 94, 374
cold, 1, 4, 19, 22, 79, 85, 117, 154, 170, 177, 184, 287, 293, 333, 353, 367
college, 238, 495
Colombia, 472
colors, 83, 110, 169, 179, 187, 190, 209, 251, 380
comatose, 288
comfortable, 395
commands, 651
commoners, 357
common-flu, 520
community, 431
compassion, 321, 397, 455, 615
competitor, 45
complainant, 628
condemnation, 223, 504
confetti, 256
confidence, 204, 379, 424, 434
confluences, 612
congest airways. *See* Omicron
Congo, 59, 313, 315
Conqueror, 633
conscience, 363
conspiracy theorizations, 519
constitution, 372
constitutions, 335

consummation, 617
contemplation, 614
continent, 179, 290, 336, 493
continuum, 572
convictions, 366
Convoy, 558
cook, 353
Cook Islands, 474
Coptic, 585
Coral Sea Islands, 474
corn, 355
Corona, 487, 510
corporate, 385
Costa Rica, 465
Cote d'Ivoire, 477
cough, 519
counsel, 350, 370
Counsels, 625
countenance, 72, 114, 404
country, 179, 206, 302, 314, 354, 356, 361
countryside, 570
courage, 216, 312, 417, 498
Courts, 501
Covid-19, 298, 300, 488, 489, 498, 500, 503
COVID-19, 194
Covidic Serpent. *See* Omicron
Covidland, 516
coward, 29, 224, 373
crambo, 349
creation, 39, 90, 162, 386, 387, 420, 421, 443, 468, 645
Creator, 318, 447, 448, 464, 596
credit card, 269

Credit First Nation, 546
crime, 591
criminal, 505
Croatia, 481
Cross, 392, 427, 444
cruelty, 195, 491, 505
cry, 10, 27, 31, 43, 213, 232, 243, 321, 338, 428, 437, 444, 489, 500, 501
Cuba, 469
culture, 173, 294, 301, 381
Cumberland, 540, 597
curio, 251
currency, 30, 61, 119
curves, 90, 92, 101, 156, 362, 584
Cuteravive, 63, 153, 298
Cutie, 152, 161
Cyborg, 538
Czech Republic, 477

D

daddy, 74
Daddy, 47
dagger, 238, 282
daily foods, 215
Dallas Fort Worth Airport, 308
dance, 18, 26, 33, 47, 48, 78, 93, 118, 167, 174, 184, 232, 247, 249, 254, 279, 282, 298, 314
dancer, 156, 164
dancers, 377
Dancers, 458
dances, 261
Daniel, 648
Danseuse, 280
Darfur, 338
darkness, 648
darling, 20, 21, 51, 58, 67, 83, 127, 196, 294, 352, 429
Darling Daddy, 635, 669
Darling Savior, 632
Darwin, 365, 546
daughters, 20, 199, 211, 228, 250, 258, 395, 404, 405, 450
Daughters, 20, 47, 177
Day of Judgment, 414
De Rosa, 604
dead, 13, 30, 56, 101, 108, 197, 232, 275, 279, 291, 338, 364, 407, 414, 420, 501
deafness, 373
death, 16, 22, 35, 60, 64, 80, 85, 105, 164, 193, 204, 217, 218, 230, 245, 254, 339, 364, 389, 394, 396, 492, 497, 504, 506
debauchery, 575
debrief, 575
debtor. *See* Air
debts, 277, 444
decency, 238, 322, 584
declaration, 33, 302
deeds, 217, 218, 348, 414, 417, 420, 427
defences, 264
defender, 421, 435, 436
defenses, 366
degree, 5, 201, 492
dehydration. *See* Poorland
delicious meals, 33

Deliverer, 633
Delta, 519
democracy, 237, 335
democratic dictator, 518
demons, 200, 339, 553
Denmark, 477
Derek Chauvin, 492
Deseronto, 566
deserts, 102, 375
despair, 388
Despotes, 386
destiny, 48, 233, 238, 244, 405
destroyer, 391
destruction, 43, 432
detention. See Poorland
Deutschland, 330
Devil. See Satan
devils, 190, 581
Dhekelia, 467
diadem, 37
diamonds, 4, 92, 295
dignitaries, 578
dimple, 24
dirge, 232, 317
disappointment, 312, 388
disbelief, 575
disciplines, 625
discretion, 370
discrimination, 597
disease, 71, 332, 503, 507
Dish With One Spoon Wampum Belt Covenant, 546
Disney Hotel, 592
Disneyworld, 300, 488
disorder, 358
distress, 375, 403, 500

divine, 20, 26, 35, 90, 91, 92, 101, 114, 126, 134, 139, 140, 249, 280, 284, 295, 298, 345, 362, 378, 388, 391, 393, 401, 409, 414, 417, 456, 503
Divine, 612, 709
divinities, 261
divorce, 103, 373
Djibouti, 477, 665
DNA, 227, 296, 498
Doctors, 501
doe, 6, 29, 58, 138
dollar, 364
dollars, 596
Domini Angelus, 300, 488
Dominica, 465
Dominican Republic, 477
dominion, 611
Don't die young, 224
Don't fear anything, 224
Doomsday, 193
Doro, 582
Double Big Mac, 598
doubts, 394, 412
Dow Industrial, 501
dragon, 162, 247
Dragon Slayer, 452
Drakensburg, 7
dream, 9, 14, 31, 48, 71, 72, 78, 112, 143, 155, 174, 178, 197, 238, 251, 278, 279, 281, 309
dreams, 7, 69, 80, 94, 117, 168, 226, 243, 249, 280, 300, 303, 309, 329, 343, 346,

356, 357, 364, 376,
388, 488, 498, 626
drum, 644
Drummers, 458
drums, 14, 154, 177,
184, 295, 373
Dutch, 329
Dying While Black, 212

E

eaglets, 312
earth, 47, 70, 93, 94,
168, 193, 218, 226,
234, 246, 282, 318,
382, 396, 398, 404,
407, 412, 413, 421,
506, 508
East, 4, 170, 173, 181
Easter, 503, 504, 580
Eastern Orthodox, 585
East-Timor, 463
Eaton center, 336
economic, 74, 359, 369,
507
economics, 360
ecstasy, 268
Ecuador, 472
Ecumenical, 585
education, 276, 501
effigies, 185, 516
effulgence, 300, 488
Eglinton, 216
Egypt, 369, 477
elderberry, 549
elect, 247
elections, 335, 371
elegance, 28
elegies, 275, 516, 541
Elegy, 237

elements, 83, 102, 124,
147, 217, 339, 437
Eli, Eli lama sabachthani,
428
Elizabethan, 197
eloquent, 348, 424
El-Salvador, 472
Emmasdale, 569
Emmerance, 153, 298,
370, 567, 594
emotions, 7, 28, 411
endearments, 570
enemies, 85, 111, 408,
431, 433, 435, 617
enemy, 39, 79, 217, 340,
392, 411, 424, 440,
507, 631
energy, 33, 105, 112,
205, 224, 254, 606
engineer, 495
English, 333
enigma, 72, 365, 414
enrichments, 571
entertainers, 577
entrails, 10, 457
Environment, 537
environs, 24, 298, 578,
596
Ephesians, 223
epigram, 196
Epiloguia, 382
Epiphany, 13
equal, 116, 201, 284
equality, 285
equalizer. *See* Air
ergonomics, 349
Eric Garner, 489
Eritrea, 467
Esso, 191
estates, 250
Estonia, 467

eternal, 541
Eternal Spring, 527
Eternal Word, 637
eternity, 162, 423, 611
Et'hem Beu. *See* Albania
Ethiopia, 463
Ethiopian, 585
Eurasia, 517
Europa Island, 475
Europe, 548
Evangelical, 585
evidence, 101, 356, 630, 637
evil, 42, 75, 291, 319, 323, 338, 365, 408, 432, 436, 440, 441, 491, 619
Evolution Theory, 365
exaltation, 420
excellence, 21, 259, 521, 570, 608, 705
excellences, 626
executive, 349, 357
exegesis, 372
existence, 193, 396
export, 355
extremities, 44
eyes, 1, 6, 7, 8, 16, 18, 19, 28, 30, 38, 48, 51, 53, 56, 57, 67, 82, 121, 122, 124, 125, 127, 156, 162, 182, 212, 214, 236, 275, 293, 306, 348, 353, 359, 362, 370, 381, 402, 403, 420, 449, 492

F

Facie, 290
facular, 11
fair, 6, 16, 35, 54, 82, 83, 89, 101, 237, 301, 335, 398, 438
fairness, 424
faith, 168, 214, 223, 225, 275, 282, 302, 372, 388, 393, 395, 414, 418, 425, 427, 430, 431, 444, 446, 508
Falkland Islands, 475
Fall, 63, 172, 333, 368, 373
fall from purity, 368
fang, 22
Fanta, 252
fantasia, 11
fantasies, 122, 346, 352
fantasize, 357
fantasy. *See* ecstasy
farmer, 496
Faroe Islands, 475
fart. *See* Air
fashions, 362
fate, 31, 229, 247, 321, 414, 489
Father of Glory, 421
Father's Day, 211
fatherless, 639
Fauci, 514
favor, 299, 318, 345, 391, 403, 412, 417, 419, 422, 425, 435, 436, 564
feeble rights, 353
fellowship, 8
fellowships, 585
felon, 366
felons, 564
fertility, 156, 318

Filibusting, 198
fillaria, 315
Findley Creek, 598
finesse, 140
Finland, 475
fire, 17, 18, 29, 177, 376
firearm, 490
first dose, 522
First nations, 547
flesh, 3, 11, 26, 97, 164, 303, 388, 420, 428, 445, 446, 505
flights, 356
flirtation, 373
flora, 535
flour, 406
flower, 272
flowers, 47, 102, 184, 190, 225, 249, 252, 288, 357, 396, 437, 626, 656, 657, 664, 671, 673, 685
flutter, 272
foe, 29, 84, 277, 507
followers, 91, 369, 414, 418
Fondest, 4, 5, 6, 7, 8, 9, 10
foreign accent, 380
foreign land, 360, 374, 382
foreigners, 276, 356, 361
forget, 30, 62, 153, 218, 245, 250, 279, 282, 288, 304, 321, 344, 351, 374, 390, 392, 394, 396, 435, 436
forgive, 163, 165, 169, 404, 447
forgiven, 21, 391
forgiveness, 283, 296, 397, 430
formation, 413
fountain, 24, 52, 272, 417
foxes, 28, 284
fragile, 9, 215, 319, 349
frailties, 615
France, 306, 463, 508
frankincense, 406
fraternity, 423
fraud, 335
free, 267
freedom, 40, 193, 275, 282, 284, 304, 335, 370, 520, 523
Freeland, 589
freely breathe. *See* March 2024
Freetown, 317
French, 333
French avocat, 605
French Guiana, 466
friend, xxv, 1, 7, 39, 153, 240, 405
fruitful, 96, 214, 345, 535, 651, 681
Full Moon, 550
fundamentalists, 223
funniness, 572
fury, 573

G

Gabon, 478
Gambia, 472
Gamers, 458
Gananoque, 550
ganja. *See* canabbis
gargantuan, 621
Gatineau, 543, 589

Gaza Strip, 463
gazelle, 154
gems, 155, 199
generation, 373, 413, 494, 570, 610, 623
generosity, 630
Genesis, 403
genius, 63, 104, 113, 162, 196, 331, 345, 619, 621, 633, 643, 648, 658
Genius. *See* IndyGenius
Genocide, 321, 338
George Floyd, 489, 490
Georgia, 477
Germany, 468, 508
Ghaddafi, 490
Ghana, 466
ghettoes, 229, 276
giants, 377
Giffens, 390
gifts, 100, 252, 400, 401, 404
gigantic appetites, 348
Gilgamesh, 546
girl, 11, 66, 98, 99, 104, 154, 269, 346, 361
glitter, 113, 380
globe, 381, 535, 538, 612, 656
Glorioso Islands, 475
Glorious One, 649
glory, 18, 28, 47, 118, 119, 172, 243, 280, 302, 304, 334, 382, 393, 397, 398, 417, 420, 421, 422, 425, 426, 427, 431, 440, 441, 448, 504, 614
GM, 191
Gnostic, 585

God, 47, 61, 111, 142, 145, 152, 161, 168, 169, 179, 180, 199, 211, 218, 223, 224, 287, 291, 302, 308, 318, 325, 346, 361, 364, 367, 372, 373, 385, 386, 394, 395, 396, 397, 398, 400, 401, 402, 403, 404, 405, 406, 408, 410, 412, 413, 417, 419, 420, 421, 422, 423, 424, 425, 426, 428, 430, 431, 433, 435, 437, 439, 440, 441, 443, 445, 446, 447, 448, 451, 452, 453, 454, 457, 461, 463, 465, 466, 467, 468, 469, 474, 478, 481, 483, 499, 500, 503, 505, 506, 535, 541, 561, 564, 567, 569, 581, 585, 603, 604, 605, 606, 607, 609, 610, 611, 612, 613, 614, 619, 620, 621, 623, 624, 625, 626, 628, 631, 632, 633, 634, 636, 637, 639, 641, 642, 643, 644, 645, 647, 648, 649, 652, 653, 654, 655, 656, 657, 659, 660, 661, 663, 664, 665, 667, 668, 669, 671, 672, 673, 674, 676, 677, 678, 679, 680, 681, 682, 683, 685, 686, 687, 688, 689,

690, 691, 692, 693, 694, 695, 696, 697, 698, 699, 701, 702, 703, 704, 705, 706, 709, 710, 711, 712
God save the king, 541
goddess, 30, 35, 38, 49, 92, 101, 119, 255, 262, 567
gods, 8, 48, 85, 90, 109, 155, 339, 345, 404, 413
gold, 1, 4, 9, 18, 19, 25, 28, 47, 59, 70, 101, 107, 157, 211, 283, 295, 313, 333, 336, 354, 355, 408, 412, 417, 422
golf, 330
Golgotha, 315
Goma Lakes, 347
good name, 645
good pleasure, 439
good will, 382
Goodbye, 234, 235
goodness, 282, 408, 426, 434, 439, 447, 453, 595, 623, 650, 653, 687, 705
GOP, 512
gorgeous, 21, 30, 54, 67, 104, 111, 127, 200, 290, 340
gory, 172, 319, 490
Gospel, 427, 594
gossip, 113, 228, 378
governable masses, 371
Government, 625
grace, 3, 15, 49, 51, 83, 101, 104, 111, 114, 120, 171, 223, 290, 360, 390, 397, 398, 402, 417, 420, 421, 425, 428, 431, 434, 438, 441, 444, 463, 467, 480
Grace, 390, 402, 424
graces, 262
graffiti, 191, 279
Grand AM, 92
Grand Duchy. *See* Luxembourg
grandeur, 301, 336, 339
grasslands, 626
gratitude, 606
Gravorous, 516
Great Britain, 331
Great City, 584
Great Cup, 290
greed, 302, 319
Greek, 585
Greenland, 474
Grenada, 471
Grenadines, 480
grey matter, 363
groaning, 29
grocery, 495
groom, 656
grotesque wombs, 365
Guadeloupe, 484
guardian, 645
Guatemala, 244, 465
Guernsey, 480
guidance, 647
gullets. *See* March 2024
Gundos, 582
Guns, 237
gurus, 592
Guyana, 466
gyrations, 10

H

H1N1, 194
habitat, 606, 621
haciendas, 491
Hades, 321, 506
Hagos, 391, 435, 456, 654
Haiti, 477
Halifax, 331
Halleluiah, 607, 635, 665, 684
Halloween, 580
Hansard, 414
happiness, 120, 215, 284, 403
Harare, 244
harmony, 6, 23
Harry Walker, 206
hart, 6, 49, 54
hate, 31, 97, 143, 170, 219, 229, 243, 302, 316, 414, 415, 489, 490, 491, 495
Haudenosaunee, 546
haven, 261, 387
Hawaii, 297, 298, 299
heal, 21, 133, 204, 398, 429
healing charms, 347
health, 385, 409, 518
healthcare, 501
heart, 1, 2, 5, 6, 7, 8, 11, 12, 22, 23, 24, 29, 30, 31, 32, 37, 47, 48, 49, 54, 59, 60, 65, 66, 67, 68, 71, 75, 76, 77, 82, 84, 85, 101, 105, 106, 110, 112, 120, 121, 122, 126, 127, 133, 142, 146, 153, 156, 168, 171, 175, 178, 187, 218, 220, 226, 280, 282, 336, 343, 345, 347, 350, 351, 359, 362, 364, 390, 393, 394, 396, 405, 406, 407, 425, 431, 434, 437
heartaches, 364
heartbeat, 21, 24
hearts and souls, 537
heat, 2, 19, 52, 57, 170, 185, 220, 294
heaven, 16, 24, 63, 109, 180, 253, 261, 402, 405, 474, 567
Heaven, 111, 180, 226, 297, 387, 430, 433, 449, 478, 487
Heavenly Father, 290, 424
Hecatomb, 315
heirs, 404
Helen Britel, 209
Hell, 444, 506, 553, 564, 687, 711
Hell's Angels, 553
hernias, 358
heroes, 75, 97, 310, 377, 425
heroism, 304, 407
Hichilema, 561
Hidden Hills, 300, 488
High Commission, 554
High Priest, 443
hillbillies, 573
Hillsboro, 285
hips, 83, 253, 597
history, xxvi, 175, 198, 282, 294, 424
HIV, 561

Hobbes, 284
hockey, 227
Holland, 330
Hollywood, 300, 488
Holy Father, 632
Holy One, 604
holy scepter. *See* Jerusalem
Holy Spirit, 409, 604
homage, 326, 448, 494, 585, 620, 679, 706
homeless, 388
homicides, 323
homophobes, 489
Honey, 17, 507
honey gels, 256
honeycomb, 55
Hong Kong, 463
honor, 146, 162, 290, 408, 422, 429, 430, 439, 456, 464, 531, 559, 624, 625, 633, 646, 659, 689, 695, 698, 699
honorable titles, 371
hope, 35, 48, 69, 80, 133, 153, 167, 168, 199, 204, 225, 236, 276, 282, 295, 348, 359, 391, 395, 400, 414, 489, 499, 507, 625
Hope of Glory. *See* Jerusalem
Horgans, 579
horizon, 28, 203, 413
horses, 29
hosanna. *See* Jerusalem
hospitalization, 519
hot, 30, 254, 330
Hotel Taj, 32

Hotspring, 123
house, 74, 145, 250, 334, 353, 357, 360
hubby, 98
human dignity, 350
humanity, 156, 169, 322, 451
humiliation, 388, 393
humility, 504
Hungary, 462
Hunt Club Road, 555
Huron-Wendat, 546
hurricanes, 588
husbands, 170, 423
Hussein, 332
Hutus and Tutsis, 321
Hutu-Tutsi. *See* Burundi
hyperlocal outbreaks, 519
hypocrisy, 195, 354
hypocrites, 495

I

I am a proud African, 295, 296
I can't breathe, 489, 492
I die, 1, 49, 79, 105, 291, 414
I live, 24, 79, 106, 171, 250, 345, 414, 445
I'm black, 168, 169
ideas, 69, 361, 365, 379, 498
idyll, 114, 310, 314, 355
Idyllia, 153
idyllic terrains, 289
imagination, 162, 437
imaginations, 414
Imana, 454
Immanuel, 649

immigrants, 229
immorality, 364
imperfidious, 239
imperials, 379
impotent, 155, 318, 358, 378
impunity, 403
inaugural, 247
incomparable, 423
independence, xxv, 359
India, 11, 470, 511
Indiana, 314
Indonesia, 480, 508
industries, 626
Indy. *See* IndyGenius
IndyGenius, 257
infamy, 321, 411
infants, 620
infidels, 366, 641
infinitum, 572
infirmity, 506
Influenza A, 516
Infunkutu, 154
inhabitants, 413
inheritance, 419
injustice, 642
Inkosi, 453
inner court, 408
inquisitor, 589
insanity, 24, 43
institution, 634
instrument of love, 148
instruments, 638
intellect, 69, 85, 247
intercity, 577
Internet, 359, 496, 611, 690
interpretation, 372
intimidation, 581
intoxicating, 24, 403
intoxicating crisper, 256
intoxication, 404
intwilo, 286
investigators, 620
Iran, 480, 508
Iraq, 332, 369, 477
Ireland, 471
isolation. *See* Poorland
Israelites, 419
Italy, 481, 508
ivory, 9, 18, 53, 351

J

Jackie, 126
Jamaica, 483
Jamaican, 74
James Smith, 308
Jan Mayen, 480
Jane, 234, 345
janitor, 495
Japan, 478
jealousy, 31, 98, 221
Jenevive, 15
Jersey, 480
Jerusalem, 404, 531
Jesus, 142, 218, 300, 325, 392, 399, 409, 410, 414, 420, 422, 423, 430, 439, 443, 444, 448, 460, 462, 469, 472, 475, 476, 488, 499, 503, 569, 575, 603, 632, 634, 651, 667, 676, 682, 683, 684, 688, 689, 697, 698, 701, 702
Jew, 558
Jews, 466
jigsaw puzzle, 26
job, 33, 216, 276, 357, 381, 441

jobless, 357
Johannesburg, 336
John A., 563
John Quinn, 574
joke, 137
Jomo Kenyatta, 308
Jordan, 478
Joshua, 234
journey, 236, 244, 282, 286
joy, 26, 47, 54, 69, 81, 93, 106, 114, 163, 203, 215, 243, 246, 247, 252, 298, 299, 319, 332, 347, 353, 367, 379, 396, 407, 408, 426, 434, 450, 523
Juan de Nova Island, 476
Judah, 452
judges, 496
judgment, 322, 407
Juliana, 35
Julicia, 22
Julius Caesar, 197, 332
jury, 573
Just black, 35
Just Judge, 629
justice, 212, 288, 338, 340, 366, 379, 382, 505, 576, 605, 625, 629, 639, 641, 654, 677, 685, 692, 705

K

Kabumba, 452, 591
Kabwata, 292
Kalunga, 453
Kalungu, 452
Kanata, 130, 190, 564, *See* Canada
Kanuk, 290, 587
kapentas, 209
karma, 34, 334
Katanga, 313
Kazakhstan, 461
Keele, 4, 345
Kennedy, 216, 345
Kenya, 237, 480
Khartoum, 317
Khuzwane, 454
Kiibumba, 452
kindness, 163, 231, 282, 288, 390, 433, 434, 439, 505, 632
king, 247, 358, 378
King of Glory, 652
King of Salem, 404
kingdom, 115, 309, 358, 423
Kingston, 563
Kipling, 345
Kiribati. *See* Egypt
kiss, 72, 76, 120, 123, 246
kisses, 21, 105, 106
Kitchener, 298, 532, 549, 559
knowledge, 193, 350, 370, 394, 397, 448
Kolwe, 155
Kristin, 141
Kurios, 386
Kuwait, 481
Kyrgyzstan, 461
Kyumbi, 452

L

La Purísima. *See* Nicaragua
labia, 55
labor, 10, 162, 195, 237, 331, 353, 355
laborer, 250
lady, 16, 56, 67, 127, 197, 209
Lagos, 582
lamebration, 518
landlessness, 359
landmines, 317
Latin, 585
laughter, 3, 26, 47, 80, 100, 177, 193, 253, 572, 633, 646, 703
Law, 212, 429
law firm, 576
Law Society, 604
law-abiding, 356
lawlessness, 366
laws, 284, 318, 349, 356, 360, 366
lawyers, 496
layer, 29
Lazarus, 420
lazy, 16, 364, 415
LCBO, 595
Leader, 636
leaders, 276, 369, 502
league, 44
Lebanon, 470
lecture, 369
legacy, 275, 321, 331, 340, 396
legal system, 366
legs, 7, 9, 18, 21, 53, 77, 154, 170, 171, 188, 208, 214, 279
leopard, 182, 318
Lesa, 452
Leslie Roberts, 539
Lesotho, 369
lessons, 103, 380, 417
Leviathan, 284
Levites, 419
Leza, 452
libations, 451
liberties, 335, 337
liberty, 237, 275, 284, 304, 406
Libya, 480
Liechtenstein, 480
life, 7, 13, 16, 24, 30, 34, 40, 41, 47, 48, 50, 56, 60, 63, 64, 65, 67, 69, 79, 81, 97, 111, 124, 127, 140, 149, 153, 155, 156, 162, 164, 167, 176, 186, 200, 203, 205, 217, 218, 221, 222, 225, 226, 230, 233, 239, 243, 246, 249, 251, 253, 254, 275, 276, 284, 289, 299, 311, 312, 316, 319, 336, 337, 339, 345, 354, 363, 364, 373, 374, 377, 378, 381, 388, 393, 394, 395, 396, 397, 398, 404, 414, 415, 417, 423, 428, 432, 436, 438, 444, 445, 487, 497, 501, 504, 506, 508
like breath, 149
Lily of the Valley, 443
limbo, 315
limit, 139, 356

limp, 30, 348
Lindsay, 440
linguistic, 345
lion, 125, 152, 161, 606
lioness, 45
lips, 6, 8, 11, 37, 83, 101, 108, 139, 154, 246, 261, 343, 362, 381, 710
Lithuania, 481
little flock, 439
live. *See* Air
Liverpool, 331
Livingstone, 209, 210
Locke, 284
locusts, 318
Londres, 306
loneliness, 41, 572
Lord, 334, 372, 386, 390, 391, 393, 394, 398, 402, 405, 408, 417, 419, 425, 427, 430, 432, 433, 434, 436, 438, 439, 440, 441, 443, 444, 447, 448, 449, 499, 500, 503
Lord Supreme, 649
loss, 230, 232, 388, 412
loss of smell, 519
love theorem, 373
loveliness, 282, 651
lovers. *See* Parlaver
loves, 6, 28, 29, 33, 51, 57, 63, 66, 70, 74, 109, 110, 166, 223, 251, 401
Luapula, 154, 156, 286
lullaby, 2, 153, 344
Lullaby, 166, 344
lumberland, 597
luminaries, 643

lunacy, 8
Lungu, 561
Lusaka, 244, 249
lust, 319
Luther King, 334
Lutherans, 585
Luxembourg, 463
luxury, 74, 395

M

Macau, 480
Macdonald, 563
Macedonia, 481
Machiavelli, 284
machinations, 629
machine, 24
Madagascar, 465
madmen, 241
Maga, 515
magician, 32
magicians, 622
magnific, 387
magnificence, 613
Magnolia, 254
Mailaco, 140
majority, 515
Maker. *See* Creator
Maker of All, 652
malaria, 315
Malaysia, 480
Maldives, 481
Mali, 481
Malope, 290
mambo jumbo, 113
man. *See* boy
managers, 191, 496
Mandela, 290, 561
Mandingo, 156
manhood, 53
Manotick, 527, 596

Mansa, 154
Maple, 227
Marah, 464
Maramba, 209
March 2024, 523
Mariana Islands, 474
Marineland, 123
Maronite, 585
marriage, 64, 115, 146, 346, 373, 417
marrows, 295, 457
marry, 35, 50, 97, 115, 156, 239, 346, 373
Marshall Islands, 475
Marxism, 223
Masai, 339
masses, 285, 323, 371
master, 81, 386, 427
Master, 643
Masudur, 555
materialism, 397
matrimonial knot, 362
Mattamy, 533
mature, 200, 321, 354, 365
Mauritania, 481
Mauritius, 484
May, 75, 111, 148, 225, 288, 301, 369, 405, 406, 414
Mayotte, 481
McDonald Islands, 476
McDonald's, 329
meadow, 236
mechanics, 573
medicine, 189, 337
meekness, 606
Melchizedek, 404
mementoes, 229
memoranda, 11

Memories, 4, 5, 6, 7, 8, 9, 10
memory, 71, 239, 343, 345, 376, 407
men, 10, 20, 47, 55, 64, 74, 75, 85, 90, 91, 92, 116, 120, 125, 144, 156, 170, 200, 206, 209, 220, 227, 239, 241, 284, 286, 287, 293, 337, 351, 355, 362, 365, 366, 378, 379, 397, 401, 408, 420, 424, 427, 498, 505, 507
Mennonite, 585
Mercedes, 120
Mercedes Benz, 527
mercies, 396, 417, 434, 436, 440, 617
merciful, 628
Merciful Seat, 448
mercy, 232, 390, 391, 394, 397, 402, 411, 426, 435, 436, 438, 505
Meridian, 541
messengers, 194
Messiah, 443
Metcalf, 574, 595
Metcalfians, 574
Methusalem. *See* Jerusalem
Métis, 546
Mexico, 481
Mi'kma'ki, 546
Mi'kmaq, 546
Mibenge, 121, 286
microbes, 639
Micronesia, 480
migraine, 29

migrations, 597
military, 369, 507
million reasons, 100
mind, 2, 4, 10, 28, 33, 47, 65, 69, 103, 122, 153, 171, 175, 192, 196, 197, 202, 248, 280, 284, 306, 345, 353, 359, 361, 395, 398, 407, 417, 423, 436
Minneapolis, 489
Minnie-Mouse, 592
minority, 489, 515
Minto, 533
miracles, 64, 420, 455, 504, 650
misfits, 366
missile, 33, 45
Mission, 577
Mississaugas, 546
mistakes, 61, 142
mistletoe, 252
mitumba, 591
Mobility, 487
Moderna, 519
Modimo, 453
Moldova, 481
Monaco, 481
money, 63, 74, 115, 163, 193, 200, 206, 220, 238, 250, 350, 370, 374, 397, 406, 407, 496
Money, 193, 195, 360, 374, 507
Mongos, 582
monk, 574
monopoly, 371
monstrous machines, 353
Montgomery, 334
Montreal, 534, 583, 587
Montserrat, 481
Moon, 437
moral standards, 625
morality, 119, 332, 365
mores, 366
Morgues, 517
Morocco, 481
morphine, 227
Moses, 334, 508
Moss Kent. *See* Manotick
Most High, 623
mother, 22, 48, 70, 81, 121, 129, 168, 169, 182, 275, 290, 294, 409, 452, 460, 491
Mother Nature, 537
mother's love, 70
Motherland, 590
motif, 575
motives, 212, 323, 354
Mount Kilimanjaro, 339
Mount of His Glory, 420
Mount Pisgah, 334
mouth, 30, 34, 53, 122, 174, 182, 195, 264, 362
movements, 360, 633, 639
movie, 228, 496
Mr. Conductor, 316
Mudala, 130
Mukuru, 452
Mulock Drive, 206
Mulonga, 286
Mulungu, 451, 452
Mungu, 452
Munwa, 155
muppet, 542

murder, 247, 321, 338
murderers, 641
muscles, 415, 457
music, 6, 72, 78, 92, 177, 179, 184, 209, 226, 228, 253, 276, 279, 282, 291, 301
Musicians, 458
Musonda, 121, 276, 339
Musqueam, 546
mute, 102
mutual affection, 151
Mwalule, 561
mwana, 50
Mwanawasa, 561
Mwari, 453
Mwewa, 582
Mwewas, 579
My love, 1, 2, 33, 61, 76
myrrh, 162
mystery, 346, 362, 398, 413
myth, 393, 412
mythologies, 507

N

Naked boys and girls, 331
nakedness, 119, 122, 303, 404
Nakoda, 546
Namibia, 472
nanna, 129
Napanee, 566
nappiness, 120
narrative, 196
Narvos, 582
Nathan, 197
nation, 237, 259, 276, 302, 321, 333, 335, 356, 369, 421
national anthem, 276
nations, 20, 179, 229, 291, 318, 321, 335, 354, 356, 360, 369, 398, 418, 420, 448, 449, 507
native, 177, 278, 356, 360
Native Gem, 255
natural force, 270
nature, 72, 91, 104, 125, 152, 161, 162, 187, 225, 236, 243, 284, 291, 294, 295, 370, 378, 396, 413, 420, 504
Navassa Island, 474
Nazarene, 443
Nazarite, 405
nebula, 11
neck, 10, 18, 27, 188, 489
neighbor. *See* Air
Nepean, 597
nepotism, 324
nerves, 21, 28, 37, 189, 216, 346, 377, 415
Netherlands, 330, 474, 484, 508
network, 368
Never Again, 338
Never Left, 36, 140
New Caledonia, 481
New immigrants, 492
New York, 317
New Zealand, 474
newcomer', 574
Newfoundland, 599

Newmarket, 187, 206
Ngai, 454
Ngalula, 286, *See* Emmerance
Nicaragua, 463
Niger, 464
nightmare, 42
Niitsitapi, 546
nipples, 120, 122, 154, 155
Njinyi, 454
Nkosi, 453
Noah, 404
Norfolk Island, 474
normalcy, 487
North, 170, 181, 352
North and South Sudan, 478
Northern Cardinal, 527
Northumberland, 568
Norway, 463
nourishment, 637
Nova Lux, 574
Nshima, 278
nurse, 495
Nurses, 501
Nyambe, 452
Nyame, 452
Nyami-nyami, 209
Nzambi, 452

O

oath, 275
Oba, 454
Obama, 197, 334
observanda, 11
occupation, 305, 381
ocean, 199, 253, 298, 321, 368
oceans, 548
October, 352
ode, 28
offence, 102, 247, 264, 318
oil, 4, 185, 280, 282, 406, 407, 410, 437, 507
Ojo, 455
Olo, 452
Olugbega, 453
Oluwa, 453
Oman, 478
Omega, 451
Omicron, 520
Ommen, 519
omnific, 387
Omnipotent, 443
Omniscient, 451
Ondo, 452
Ontario, 179, 216, 298
opinion, 144, 427
opinions, 381
opportunities, 69, 173, 293, 354
Orange County, 300, 488
orations, 518
orchard, 52
orchestra, 6, 373
order, 92, 116, 171, 185, 247, 288, 356, 363, 366, 382, 504
Ori, 453
Oriental, 585
orison, 623
Osanobua, 453
Oshawa, 191, 582
Ottawa, 179, 191, 244, 528, 531, 532, 533, 536, 537, 539, 542, 543, 545, 548, 550,

551, 554, 555, 557,
559, 563, 565, 569,
570, 572, 577, 578,
579, 580, 581, 582,
583, 584, 585, 586,
587, 588, 592, 593,
594, 597, 599, 600,
725
overshadow, 262

P

Pacific Ocean, 298
pagoda, 546
pain, 1, 34, 40, 47, 100,
    115, 202, 203, 204,
    218, 225, 226, 232,
    243, 277, 304, 348,
    363, 382, 388, 425,
    491, 504, 506, 509
pains, 56, 106, 109
pajamas, 84, 170, 252
Pakistan, 461
palace, 20, 358
palm, 72, 298, 349, 423
Pamba, 452
Panama, 470
pandemic, 491, 499,
    500, 503
pandora, 573
panic, 573
Papua New Guinea, 467
parabola, 130
Paracel Islands, 475
paradise, 72, 297
Parafindia, 11
Paraguay, 484
pariah, 560
Paris, 306
Parlaver, 271
parliament, 372

Parliament, 280, 502
Parliament Hill, 543
partisanship, 372
partner, 373
passion, 29, 31, 47, 51,
    102
passports, 592
patience, 120, 146, 311,
    415
Patience, 59
patriarchs, 404
patriotism, 324, 371
Paul, 223
Payday, 376
payment, 417
peace, 18, 40, 69, 72,
    76, 94, 124, 173, 203,
    216, 217, 218, 231,
    236, 243, 247, 252,
    275, 282, 289, 304,
    320, 323, 332, 335,
    353, 375, 385, 393,
    397, 399, 408, 412,
    413, 423, 428, 434,
    456, 463, 465, 473,
    477, 545, 547, 561,
    563, 581, 605, 615,
    627, 631, 639, 659,
    660, 662, 666, 690,
    704, 712
Peace, 375
peacock, 59, 91, 125,
    152, 161, 291
peacocks, 101
pearls, 301, 348
pebbles, 74, 229
pedestals, 617
Peninsular, 122
Pentecost, 409
Pentecostal, 585
perdition, 449

perfect full stop, 616
Perfect full-stop, 311
Perfect imperfections, 39
perfect shape, 21
perfection, 259, 265, 396, 421, 590
Persian horse, 644
Petawawa, 191
Peter, 234, 391, 409
Pfizer, 519
Pharaoh, 197, 648
phathomation, 55, 90
Philippines, 480
phlegmatic, 6
Phonoriah, 314
pigeon, 103, 375
pilgrimage, 546
pillars, 544
pink paper, 368
Pitcairn Islands, 476
placate, 618
plan, 225, 242, 361, 503
Planes, 501
plateau, 32
platitude, 354
Plato, 284
players, 346, 458, 496
pleasures, 19, 347, 364, 411
plethora, 193
pocking noses, 377
poem, xxv, 22, 32, 48
poesy, 66, 189
poetics, 315
poetry, 48, 52, 171, 196, 333, 345, 359
Poets, 458
polar bears, 290
police, 94, 490, 501
politician, 372, 374
politicians, 371, 374, 502
Politicians, 372, 502
politics, 280, 284, 315, 369, 374
Politics, 371, 374
poll, 237
Polynesia, 480
poor, 40, 195, 220, 252, 275, 284, 291, 308, 351, 365, 407, 409, 414, 502
Poorland, 522
population, 418
Portugal, 483
Poshy, 74
posterity, 624
potentials, 229, 369
pothole, 279
poverty, 77, 117, 193, 277, 350, 356, 496
power, 6, 22, 30, 66, 105, 120, 128, 193, 202, 236, 237, 288, 317, 323, 335, 350, 351, 355, 359, 369, 378, 388, 394, 398, 420, 421, 423, 429, 437, 441, 453, 467, 489, 506, 534, 543, 582, 604, 619, 620, 641, 644, 648, 652, 654, 665, 667, 673, 678, 680, 698, 699, 705, 707, 708
Power, 371
powerful, 34, 39, 117, 224
praises, xxv, 172, 401
praising, 429

pray, 3, 18, 75, 94, 123, 133, 142, 392, 394, 398, 400, 406, 412, 425, 430, 433, 446, 449
prayer, 29, 100, 275, 287, 318, 397, 398, 412, 428, 476, 505, 581, 585, 607, 611, 626, 631, 652, 672
prayers, 146, 346, 438
preacher, 233
precepts, 651
premium, 572
Presbyterian, 585
presence, 3, 10, 35, 36, 63, 64, 78, 79, 105, 106, 113, 143, 240, 252, 260, 269, 281, 392, 429, 434, 468, 531, 603, 612, 618, 623, 635, 646, 648, 649, 657, 659, 661, 681, 682, 684, 685, 690, 694, 699, 703, 708
president, 247, 329, 490
pretty, 23, 35, 49, 101, 362, 411
prevention. *See* Poorland
prey, 75
pride, 15, 78, 125, 221, 275, 280, 288, 290, 305, 327, 377, 414, 457, 507, 518
priest, 407, 408
prime minister, 329
Prince, 443
prison, 169, 174, 241

prisoner, 255, 425, 427, 639
prize, 53, 155, 379
problems, 115, 224, 279, 369, 502
procreativity, 162, 378
proctor, 529
profession, 495
professionalism, 366
professor, 365
professors, 496
profits, 431, 576
progress, 354, 636
prolific, 387
promiscuity, 373
promises, 16, 371, 399
propaganda, 366
prophet, 407
Prophet, 405
prostitutes, 209
Protestant Church, 585
Protocol, 371
providence, 193, 388, 408, 434
province, 179, 364, 434
prudence, 370, 443
psychotic, 8
pubic hair, 154
pubics, 123
public, 355, 401
publicity, 401
publishers, 432
Puerto Rico, 481
Pulsing perfidiously, 378
punishment, 85, 433
purpose, 69, 164, 205, 378, 401, 441
purses, 379

Q

Quakers, 585
Quebec, 331, 534, 536
queen, 35, 109, 171, 333
Queen Elizabeth II, 541
Queens, 534
Quinte, 566

R

Racism, 491
racists, 489
rainbow, 169, 385
Rands, 336
RBC, 595
realism, 332
reason, 7, 10, 16, 28, 49, 50, 55, 98, 153, 174, 204, 232, 237, 284, 294, 345, 350, 357, 359, 393, 407
rebel, 630
recession, 191
Recover, 89, 100
recrimination, 237
Red Sea, 648
redemption, 430, 444, 447
refreshing station, 353
Refugee camps, 318
regalia, 615
regimes, 237, 335
regrets, 28, 103, 168, 225
relativity, 361
religion, 103, 413
relocation, 58, 356, 357
remember, 65, 150, 245, 278, 282, 286, 290, 292, 297, 374, 427, 499
remorse, 233
repent, 604
rescue, 637
researchers, 370
reservoirs, 24
restaurants, 208, 360
Reunion, 484
Rhumba, 291
rhyme, 137, 196, 315, 329, 531, 590, 623
rhythm, 30, 106, 154, 177, 184, 226, 290, 332, 339, 572, 590
rhythms, 6, 46, 54, 63, 83, 92, 152, 161, 166, 232, 254, 278, 282, 291, 292, 295, 373
ricardian, 514
rice, 355
rice and beans. *See* Poorland
Rich people, 360
Richard Thairu, 308
Richard the Third, 197
riches, 117, 163, 309, 350, 360
Richmond, 197
riddles, 413
Rideau River, 527
riffraffs, 14
righteous, 407, 499, 500
righteousness, 391, 421, 430, 446, 505
Rila Cross. *See* Bulgaria
risk, 192
rock, 17, 46, 93, 440
Romania, 483
romantic, 32, 34
romanticism, 332

Rome, 369
Romeo, 197
room, 532
rosaries, 261
Rose of Sharon, 443
roses, 7, 11, 13, 29, 48, 122, 251, 357
Rosey Eden, 539
Rossetti, 256
rough-necked ore, 265
roundabouts, 549
Rousseau, 284
rubbish, 496, 504
rubies, 361
Rugaga, 453
Ruhanga, 453
Rules of the Game, 366
rumba, 591
Rundlehorn Drive, 367
Russel, 597
Russia, 511
Ruth, 124
Ruwa, 453
Ruxtovia, 91
Rwanda, 321, 322, 338, 483

S

sacrilegious, 319, 321
Saddam, 332, 490
Sail without Ship, xxv
Saint Helena, 466
Saint Kitts-Nevis, 464
Saint Lucia, 484
Saint Pierre, 484
Saint Vincent, 480
salary, 364
saliva, 24, 267
saloons, 55, 501
samba, 591

Sambo, 315
Sameland, 252
Samoa, 464
San Marino, 464
Santa, 252
Santonica, 11
Sao Tome and Principe, 484
Sara, 234, 235
SARS, 194, 516
Sasha, 197
Satan, 506
satisfaction, 363, 432
Saudi Arabia, 472
Savior, 422, 426, 447, 449
Scarborough, 529, 541
Schipol, 329, 330
schizophrenic, 358
school, 238, 364
schools, 250
science, 64
scientists, 365
Scientists, 365
Script, 393
Scripture, 648, 672
season, 13, 22, 37, 49, 174, 204, 210, 252, 367, 379, 479
seasons, 225, 249, 312, 333, 340, 656
secret, 51, 400, 401, 431
secrets, 1, 115, 315, 347, 393
secure, 240, 275, 412
Security Council, 332
self-denial, 170
Selma, 334
Senegal, 483
sensation, 16, 123

senses, 2, 28, 73, 189, 196, 300, 309, 367, 405, 488
Serbia-Montenegro, 483
serenity, 321, 367
serpent, 125
serpents, 330
Seventh-day Adventist, 585
sex, 102, 120, 415, 416
Seychelles, 484
shadow, 84, 106, 171, 236, 240, 247, 277, 360, 388, 487
shadows, 7, 123, 177, 199, 254, 275, 330, 333, 376, 640
Shae, 260
Shaka, 290
Shakespeare, 197
Shakira, 290
shallow minds, 395
shepherd, 439
showers, 588
shrunken tables, 229
sickness, 100, 399, 420, 506
Siddim, 404
Sierra Leone, 484
signals, 271
silence, 26, 28, 73, 122, 164, 205, 220, 436, 622
silent, 33, 45, 121, 321, 332, 347, 487, 508, 541, 569, 612, 647
sin, 218, 364, 399, 402, 409, 428, 444, 445, 446, 449, *See* Poorland
Sinatra, 197
sinews, 171, 189, 415, 457
singers, 29, 115, 458
sins, 404, 430, 439, 447, 505, 506
sirens, 578
Sisess, 73
sister, 51, 65, 165, 344
skin, 26, 81, 83, 121, 200, 318, 410
skinny, 360
skirt, 35, 83, 92
sky, 2, 7, 24, 68, 123, 180, 248, 253, 339, 344
skydom, 73
skyscrapers, 355
slave labor, 353, 490
slavery, 349
Slovakia, 483
Slovenia, 481
smells of after rains, 367
smile, 38, 92, 100, 108, 124, 213, 215, 297
Smokes with Thunder, 209
snow, 102, 110, 138, 433
Snow and Mirage, 352
soccer, 290, 346, 496
social rules, 366
socio-economic unequalness. *See* Poorland
soils, 117, 253, 289
soldiers, 73, 304, 317, 490
Solomon, 476
Sonate, 385
song, 16, 22, 52, 63, 90, 152, 161, 171, 172,

282, 285, 323, 343, 373, 382, 405, 441
Song, 69, 90, 134, 135, 136, 137, 138, 139
Song of an Alien, xxv
sophistication, 104, 394
sore throat, 519
sorrows, 232, 275
soul, 1, 2, 4, 6, 14, 22, 71, 75, 76, 77, 79, 84, 100, 101, 102, 106, 109, 112, 124, 133, 137, 146, 163, 171, 174, 189, 200, 218, 220, 232, 242, 253, 277, 282, 300, 303, 345, 347, 367, 375, 385, 390, 393, 394, 395, 397, 411, 414, 420, 426, 429, 433, 435, 439, 440, 441, 450, 457, 473, 488, 574, 575, 599, 607, 614, 623, 627, 635, 637, 644, 648, 655, 657, 661, 662, 666, 674, 690, 691, 693, 694, 699, 703, 709
South, 170, 173, 179, 181, 290, 336, 352, 360, 369
South Africa, 179, 290, 336, 369
South Georgia, 476
South Sandwich Islands, 476
Sovereign City, 593
Sovereign Lord, 650
Sovereignty, 369
Spain, 478, 508
spear, 197, 248

specialization, 373
speeches, 99, 280, 348, 502
Spica, 278
spices, 11, 314, 406
spirit, 97, 165, 184, 405, 499, 544, 546, 574, 627, 632, 709, *See* Air Spirit, 462
spirits, 10, 236, 339, 398
spirituals, 507
splendor, 25, 51, 97, 301, 362
splendous bastions, 259
Spratly Islands, 476
spring, 33, 63, 353, 357, 368
Spring, 63, 190
Sri-Lanka, 483
St. Augustine, 284
St. George, 345
St. John's, 599
St. Lawrence, 534
staccatos, 345
Stagnet, 77
stamina, 29
stanzas, 73, 251
stars, 22, 25, 225, 249, 340, 495, 496
starvation, 507
state of affairs, 355
statement, 113, 249, 312
staycation, 574
steak, 62
Stehouwer, 456
Stewart Street, 543
stories, 48, 73, 103, 125, 172, 178, 229, 346, 347, 348
storms, 588

stranger, 64, 361, 362, 364, 365, 373, 374, 377, 382
Strasberg, 549
stratagems, 42, 629
strategy, 622
strength, 34, 50, 59, 77, 97, 105, 107, 109, 143, 163, 288, 335, 348, 350, 364, 398, 500
struggle, 50, 277, 348, 431
struts, 15, 35, 91, 147
student, xxv, 363, 529
sublime. See Air
submissions, 654
subway, 345
Subways, 293
success, 359, 389, 417
sufferings, 400
suffocation. See March 2024
Suitors, 156
Suku, 453
summer, 574
Summer, 63, 176
summerian, 37
sun, 2, 7, 14, 37, 49, 61, 94, 163, 180, 184, 190, 198, 199, 209, 213, 219, 225, 306, 352, 437, 505, 508
Sun, 209, 348, 437
sunshine, 63, 133
superiors, 349
superpowers, 369
supplications, 606, 636
Supreme, 386, 448
Supreme Deity, 448
Supreme Jury, 448
Suriname, 464
SUVs, 538
Suzy, 73
Svalbard, 471
Swaziland, 369, 483
Sweden, 478
sweet, 6, 11, 22, 24, 27, 35, 37, 61, 63, 66, 67, 71, 72, 73, 94, 101, 104, 122, 123, 127, 150, 153, 155, 179, 230, 253, 279, 345, 357, 367, 405, 408, 438, 507
Sweet Savior, 460
sweetness, 26, 32, 53, 125, 377
Switzerland, 483
sword, 23, 237, 304, 332, 433
symbol of blessings, 403
symphony, 113, 225, 253, 339, 373
symptoms, 500
synovia, 11
Syria, 467
Syriac, 585

T

Tabernacle, 419, 422
Tabernacles, 438
Taiwan, 478
Tajikistan, 461
talents, 275, 359
Tam'ra Lich, 558
Tanzania, 483
Tashany, 69, 153, 298, 594
Tata, 452
tattoo, 25, 254

Taverns, 501
teacher, 40, 81, 233
technician, 495, 496
technologies, 395
temple, 24, 35, 500
Temple, 419
tender, 3, 9, 37, 46, 65, 69, 76, 109, 114, 126, 151, 153, 154, 178, 278, 309, 390, 429, 435
tenderness, 23, 66
tendons, 280, 457
Tent of Meeting, 404
terebra, 585
terra firma, 313
terrific, 387
territories, 546, 570, 571
terrorists, 305, 323
text, 141
Thank you, 48, 69, 144, 345, 436
The Leader, 443
theme, 266
theory, 369
Theos, 386
thorns, 66, 393
thousand, 66, 215, 385, 418, 508
thousand islands, 566
threats, 356, 380, 435, 436
throne, 38, 109, 180, 229, 394, 422, 423, 424, 446
tic tac, 598
tiger, 557
Tilo, 453
Timbuktu, 154
Tina, 262
tissues, 457

To lock or not to lock, 517
today, 32, 48, 102, 164, 168, 225, 245, 294, 316, 496, 508
toffee, 227
Togo, 483
Tokyo, 244
tombs, 323, 374
tomorrow, 32, 239, 340, 394, 397, 407, 408
Tonga, 480
tongue, 8, 22, 30, 66, 123, 162, 174, 229, 234, 344
tonight, 32, 40, 102, 379
tornado, 612
Toronto, 18, 170, 208, 244, 380, 566, 567, 588, 593, 677
touch, 7, 16, 29, 32, 105, 107, 140, 188, 224, 227, 232, 415
traffic, 539
tragedy, 140, 195, 322
train station, 269
Trans-Canada-Highway, 599
Transcendent, 386
Transfiguration, 420
Transit, 207
Transpo, 580
treasure, 591
treasures, 19, 288, 311
tree, 8, 92, 162, 252, 505, 596, 597
trekkersland, 354
Trent, 579
triangle, 52
tribalists, 489
tribe, 173, 179, 180

Trinidad and Tobago, 483
triumph, 332, 438
Triumvirate, 332
Tromelin Island, 476
trophies, 97, 250, 311, 395, 417
True Sir, 386
Trump, 490
trumpets, 348
trust, 1, 145, 151, 237, 284, 302, 350, 365, 388, 412, 424, 425, 427, 431, 433, 435, 436
truth, 17, 103, 111, 115, 124, 149, 308, 361, 365, 402, 413, 414, 415, 433, 437, 445, 502
Truth, 101, 361
truthful, 96, 361
Tsleil-Waututh, 546
Tsuut'ina, 546
TTC, 207
Turkey, 463
Turkmenistan, 461
Turks, 475
Tuvalu, 480
TV, 495, 496, 528, 548
Twatotela Crescent, 367
Twendenanga, 594

U

UAE, 483
Uber Eats, 598
Uganda, 483
UK, 483, 508
Ukraine, 478
Ukulunkulu, 452
ulcers, 241
ulnar tunnel, 527
Ultimate Trapper, 663
umbilical cord, 359
unapproachable glory, 606
unbiased, 641
Unfaithfulness, 242
ungratefulness, 630
unions, 288
Unitarian Universalist, 585
United Churches, 585
United Nations, 332
universal, 169
universe, 352, 437, 606
Unkulunkulu, 452
unscientific, 365
Urezwha, 453
Uruguay, 484
USA, 508
UVs, 538
Uzbekistan, 461

V

vacation, 574, *See* March 2024
vacations, 367
vaccine, 513, 517
vaccine boosting. *See* Vaccine Inequalities
vaccine effect. *See* Vaccine Inequalities
vaccine equality. *See* Vaccine Inequalities
vaccine futility. *See* Vaccine Inequalities
Vaccine Inequalities, 521
Valentine, 82, 149

Valley of Roses, xxvi, 603
vanilla, 579
vanity, 125, 332, 358, 398, 429
Vanuatu, 484
vapor, 508
vegetables, 548
vegetables and fruits, 145
Venezuela, 465
venom, 123, 125, 216
venomous charm. *See* bull constrictor
veronica, 11
Veronice, 11
vessels, 457
vetoes, 229
Viagra, 378
Victoria, 75, 209, 599
Victoria Falls, 209
victories, 614
Victorious One, 652
victory, 172, 290, 388, 419, 435, 438, 441, 444, 454, 518, 604, 635, 644, 647, 655, 660, 662
villains, 538
vineyard, 404, 407
violence, 406, 490
violin, 381
VIP, 329
virginities, 347
virtue, 119, 284, 338, 370
virtuosos, 275
visage, 55, 91, 239, 282, 289, 319
visages, 248

visions, 243, 280, 352, 357, 498, 596
visitors, 540
vocal cords, 272
voice, 2, 11, 28, 48, 63, 71, 72, 77, 88, 171, 229, 231, 233, 253, 290, 332, 335, 362, 374, 379, 390, 394, 418, 419, 436, 449, 500, 505, 618
vomitus, 170
V-power, 21
vultures, 56

W

Waka Waka, 290
Wake Island, 476
wallets, 185, 379
Wallis-Futuna, 466
walls. *See* Jerusalem
Wandos, 582
war, 41, 70, 120, 202, 279, 315, 319, 321, 323, 338, 489, 507
Wari, 453
warmth, 6, 52, 133, 331
warrigals, 507
warrior, 45
warriors, 617
waste, 577
waterfall, 280, 394
waterfalls, 162
watermelons, 53
waters, 20, 24, 29, 33, 101, 162, 209, 317, 333, 347, 362, 396
wealth, 74, 193, 327, 350, 371, 385, 395,

406, 408, 409, 490, 518
weapon, 43, 46, 223, 374, 391
Wesleyan, 585
West, 170, 173, 181, 360
West Bank, 464
West Oak, 549
Western, 425
Western Sahara, 464
Western Virus, 516
wheat, 355
whispers of love, 352
Whites, 489
wife, 7, 39, 42, 43, 44, 45, 46, 58, 60, 98, 149, 153, 197, 228, 298, 313, 404, 412, 423, 431, 441, 491, 504
Williamsburg, 549
win, 120, 144, 202, 203, 371, 388, 432
winds, 102, 110, 124, 185, 220, 233, 351
wine, 403, 404, 405, 406, 407, 408, 409, 410, 420
wineskin, 405, 409
wings, 69, 109, 110, 121, 156, 162, 171, 187, 214, 288, 311, 344, 360, 388, 411
winner, 90, 155, 201, 395
winter, 166, 174, 357, 368, 513, 580, 675, 707
wisdom, 129, 140, 154, 228, 264, 295, 352, 370, 396, 398, 439, 443, 448, 570, 604, 606, 609, 612, 625, 657, 659, 690, 697, 698, 699, 701
witchcraft, 470
witness, 260
wives, 355, 408
woman, 3, 18, 33, 35, 39, 40, 42, 43, 45, 46, 50, 85, 120, 152, 154, 161, 171, 200, 316, 373, 377, 393, 440
womb, 15, 246, 313, 335
wonderland, 551
Word, 218, 372, 433, 434, 505
work, 33, 96, 99, 109, 143, 191, 192, 196, 198, 239, 312, 331, 360, 363, 364, 376, 379, 396, 432, 441, 499
worker, 363
world, 179, 507, 508
worries, 81, 393, 394, 395
worry not, 439
worship, 402, 422, 625
wrath, 323, 395, 436
writer, 574, 458

X

Xavier, 640
xenophobia, 489
Xhosas, 290

Y

Yala, 452
Yatta, 452
Year of Faith, 430
Yemen, 484

Z

Zabros, 582
Zambesia, 290
Zambezi, 289
Zambia, 59, 179, 184, 209, 210, 244, 275, 276, 289, 313, 367, 472, 562, 565, 586, 672, 674
Zand, 435
zebra, 152, 161, 183
Zebra, 585
Zeus, 57
Zimba, 104
Zimbabwe, 463
Zudu, 582
Zulu, 582
Zulus, 290
Zumu, 582
Zungu, 582